James J. Flynn

JUSTICES OF THE SUPREME COURT

OF ACHIEVEMENT IN MODERN AMERICA

NEGROES OF ACH

IN MODERN AME

Books

FAMO

NEGR

NEGROES
OF ACHIEVEMENT
IN MODERN
AMERICA

By James J. Flynn

Introduction by Roy E. Wilkins

Illustrated with Photographs

DODD, MEAD & COMPANY

NEW YORK

We wish to express appreciation to International Library of Negro Life and History for the use of the following photographs: Roy E. Wilkins, General Benjamin Oliver Davis, Junior, General Benjamin Oliver Davis, Senior, Justice Constance Baker Motley, Dr. Ralph Johnson Bunche, Percy Lavon Julian, Reverend Martin Luther King, Jr., John Hope Franklin, Louis "Satchmo" Armstrong, Mary McLeod Bethune, John B. King, Edward W. Brooke, Shirley Anita Chisholm, Medgar Wiley Evers, Asa Philip Randolph, Marian Anderson, and Asa T. Spaulding.

These credits are also due:

Wide World Photos: Justice Thurgood Marshall

Blackstone, Shelburne, N. Y.: Augusta Baker

United Press International: James Howard Meredith

Library of Congress Catalog Card Number: 70-111911

Printed in the United States of America
by The Cornwall Press, Inc., Cornwall, N. Y.

For Kathleen and Denise, who will live,
I believe, in a world that will know
no prejudice or discrimination

ACKNOWLEDGMENT

To Dorothy M. Bryan I owe the greatest debt. Her patience, valuable advice, and continued encouragement kept me strong in the determination to complete this volume.

Introduction

One of the immediate responses of the last ten years of civil rights activity has been a demand for factual information on all levels about the Negro citizen. There is a particular need to make available accurate source material for today's students whose current studies will provide the base for their future development.

Negroes of Achievement in Modern America makes a useful contribution toward this end. Professor Flynn has put together a collection of biographies of contemporary individuals who have made and are making notable contributions in a variety of fields such as education, business, science, the arts, labor, sports, politics and civil rights. This text is written primarily for the teen-ager, but I suspect that it will also be a handy reference for many who have long since attained adulthood.

It is my hope that those who read these sketches will be stimulated to delve more deeply into this too-long neglected area of American life. The judgments and relationships all of us make will be fruitful precisely to the extent that they rest upon a secure foundation of knowledge.

—Roy E. Wilkins
Executive Secretary NAACP

Foreword

When an author attempts to choose a definite number of people to be included in his book, he fully realizes that there will be outstanding representatives of his theme omitted. These omissions are necessitated by the limitation of space.

In order to be as all-inclusive as possible in covering the fields of achievement, it has been decided to add shorter biographies of certain Negro men and women, who, because of the limitation mentioned above, could not be more fully covered. These vignettes do not in any way indicate that the people discussed more briefly here are any less significant than those who have been more fully presented. The assignment of space has been determined primarily in relation to the crucial subject matter of this book and the desire to attain a comprehensive, balanced outlook on the field, as represented by these good Americans who have contributed so much to the advancement of a most important cause.

—JAMES J. FLYNN

Contents

Contents

Ralph Johnson Bunche

[1904-   ]

STATESMAN

Bunche is today Under Secretary of the United Nations and is regarded by many militant activists as a conservative ally of the political establishment. But during the thirties, when he was chairman of the Department of Political Science at Howard University, Bunche functioned as a militant young intellectual who criticized both the American social system and the established Negro leadership organization.

—Francis L. Broderick and August Meier,
Negro Protest Thought in the 20th Century

Detroit, Michigan, in 1904, was not yet the Motor City of the United States. In fact, Detroit was not listed within the twenty-five largest cities in the United States in the census of 1900. It was in this small urban community, on August 7, 1904, that Olive Johnson Bunche presented to her husband, Fred, their son, whom they named Ralph.

Fred Bunche had married Olive Johnson after a long engagement. An amateur musician, she played the piano for her two brothers and sisters, who made up what was called the Johnson Quartette. They sang for church suppers, picnics, and local dances. It was at a club picnic that Fred first met Olive. For several years he attempted to convince her to become Mrs. Bunche, but without success.

Olive wanted to marry Fred Bunche but she worried about his ability to support a family. She also feared the hardship that would be faced by her own family when she married and her small contribution to their support stopped. However, love finally won out, and the two young people were married in early 1903.

Fred Bunche was a barber in a shop where only whites were served. Early in his life, young Ralph understood what it meant to be black. At no time while his dad worked in that barber shop was he permitted to enter it.

Although the family was never in complete want, their strained financial situation did not permit much beyond the absolute necessities of life. Their lot was not improved when Ralph's sister, Grace, was born, in 1908. Added to the family troubles was the need for Fred to get his wife to a dry climate as a means of improving her health.

Before the Bunche family moved to Albuquerque, New Mexico, Ralph had already begun his schooling. He entered the Barstow School, on the East Side of Detroit. It was here that he began his adventure with books.

Ralph Bunche discovered early that he would have to earn money to supplement the small family income. His first job was as a newsboy. This forced him, for the first time, to mingle with boys who were white. He sold papers in downtown Detroit, and managed to make friends with his fellow newsboys and customers.

As a growing boy, he knew the happiness of a loving family, and the delights of games and adventures with his friends. At home, the Johnson Quartette would liven up a Sunday night with the singing of the latest popular numbers. Shortly after Olive and Fred married, they brought Grandma Johnson to live with them. She was the real head of the household and was called Nana by the entire family.

Ralph sought his fun by hiking to Belle Island, an amusement park, or by saving five cents and going to the movies.

When the circus came to town, he would follow the parade. Sometimes he induced his friends to take the ferry ride between Detroit and Windsor, Canada—a "foreign country." His love of music attracted him to the German bands that played on the Detroit street corners.

The move to Albuquerque, New Mexico, came when Ralph was ten. His dad obtained a job as a barber in the black section of the growing community. The family was most hopeful that the dry climate would improve the mother's health.

Like the Indians in New Mexico, the Bunches lived in an adobe house, that is, one constructed of mud. Ralph was fascinated with the Indians and spent much of his time in visiting them and asking them questions. There are those who suggest that the great love of history that Ralph Bunche developed probably began here in the Indian adobe homes.

Albuquerque also proved to be a place of sad remembrances for Ralph and his sister, however. Mrs. Bunche's health did not seem to improve following the move from Detroit. Two years after the family arrived in the Southwest, Olive Bunche died. Three months later, a brokenhearted Fred Bunche followed his wife in death. Ralph, now twelve years of age, and a student in an elementary school that was not noted for its high standing, found himself under his grandmother's wing. He would have to be the man of the house for Grace and Nana.

Grandma Johnson understood only too well that there was little or no future in Albuquerque for her small brood. Her decision to move to Los Angeles, California, did not help them to any great extent, though. They soon discovered that making a living in Los Angeles was even more difficult than any struggle they had ever known before.

Young Bunche did not have time to sit around and worry about the family's economic plight, however. He sought all types of jobs—delivering newspapers, working in the composing room of a newspaper, and serving as a houseboy in the home of a well-known movie star. The real reason why Grace and Ralph managed to succeed against such tremendous odds as they grew up was their grandmother. Bunche has summed it all up with this description of her, "The strongest woman I ever knew, even though she stood less than five feet high."

When Nana settled in Los Angeles with her two grandchildren, she placed Ralph in a junior high school close to their home. In June, 1918, he was graduated with honors. September found him enrolled in Jefferson High School in Los Angeles.

High school was indeed an experience for Ralph. Here he mixed with boys and girls his own age, of all races and coming from a variety of backgrounds. The seeds of prejudice had not yet touched this large city school. Bunche had classmates who were Japanese, Chinese, Filipinos, Mexicans, whites, and fellow blacks. His color made no difference to these youngsters—to them he was a likable boy, interested in sports and his studies.

Frequently, it is the student who must do after-hour work to remain in school who finds time to participate in extracurricular activities, while keeping up his studies. Bunche was one of the few blacks in his junior high school class to go on to high school, and he was determined to make good.

Ralph went out for football, basketball, and track. He was not great in any one of these sports and was dissuaded from continuing in them when his Nana declared, "Ball playing's fine, boy, but I want to see your marks." It was as a member of the debate team that he really made his mark.

During Bunche's years at Jefferson, the debate team to which he belonged was the best in the state. The same topics that were engaging John Hope Franklin (see John Hope Franklin elsewhere in this book), were the focal point of the efforts of Ralph and his teammates. The platform experience that the young debater received stood him in good stead in the years to come. The effort of preparing the arguments for presentation gave him the ability to work out his findings in a strong logical manner.

Graduation for Ralph Bunche came in June, 1922. Nana Johnson proudly listened to her grandson give the valedictory address for his class. He also was awarded medals for outstanding work in civics, English composition, and debating.

Several of the teachers at Jefferson were determined to get Ralph a scholarship to the University of Los Angeles. Athletics were not his strong capability, but he had won his letter in basketball at Jefferson. On the strength of that, and some pressure from alumni, a four-year scholarship to UCLA was granted to Ralph Bunche. In order to be able to continue in college, it was necessary for him to find a job—or several jobs. He worked as a janitor, part-time carpet layer, a waiter in a Navy officers' club, and as a faculty assistant in the political science department. The neighbors contributed money to help him get through his freshman year.

When the university gave him that scholarship for athletics, no one believed Ralph would actually earn it. Undaunted, he went out for football, baseball, and basketball. He improved so much in basketball that he played guard on three championship varsity teams. Later, his son was to be a championship tennis player.

Not content with holding down a job, playing ball, and keeping up with his studies, Bunche found time to be sports editor of the yearbook, write a column for the college daily newspaper, and preside as president of the debate society. He was also active in the Cosmopolitan Club, where he was given the opportunity to talk with students from all over the world.

Bunche decided to become a major in international relations. He explains that, "After reading Parker T. Moon's *Imperialism and World Politics* I knew I just had to go on in international relations." There is no doubt that UCLA was the training ground for Ralph's future as an American statesman.

June, 1926, was a time of rejoicing for Nana Johnson as she saw her grandson receive his B.A. degree, *summa cum laude,* and an election to Phi Beta Kappa, the national honor fraternity. His sister Grace stood by his Nana's side, proud of her big brother. She had married during the previous year, and was looking forward to seeing her husband follow in her brother's footsteps at UCLA.

Ralph went back to his grandmother's home and began to file applications for graduate school. In 1927, he was awarded a scholarship to work toward a doctor of philosophy degree in international relations at Harvard. Money was still Bunche's major problem. Harvard would have been an impossibility except for the $1,000 that was given him by the Negro Women's Club in Los Angeles.

Arriving in Cambridge, Massachusetts, he was, nevertheless, forced to seek employment, for the $1,000 would not last long, and a growing young man has to eat. He worked in a book store where the owner was nearsighted and thought he had hired a white student. Later, when he discovered that Ralph was black, he was pleased to keep him on.

During the academic year 1927–1928, Ralph Bunche worked toward his M.A. degree. It was awarded him in the spring of 1928. No different than many young graduate students, he now sought a teaching position that would give him the necessary money to continue on at Harvard, working for his Ph.D. degree.

Howard University, in Washington, D.C., offered him a teaching position as an instructor of political science. When he arrived at Howard, he discovered there was not any political science department. He immediately went about setting up one. Before the academic year ended, he was promoted to the rank of assistant professor. This was unique, for the usual waiting period for promotion from instructor is four years.

The eager young man had no qualms about teaching summer school at Howard. In his class in American Government, in the summer of 1929, was a lovely young co-ed named Ruth Harris. Ruth had come up from Montgomery, Alabama, to earn a B.A. degree. One of the courses that she had to take was government, but she was not happy with the prospect. The enthusiasm, dedication, and learning of the young instructor soon had her looking forward to his classes, however. Apparently, Ralph was also taken with Ruth's interest in his teaching, for, before long, they were seeing each other after class. Before summer school met again the next year, Ralph and Ruth were married.

On June 23, 1930, in the chapel on the grounds of Howard University, the young couple exchanged their marriage vows. The honeymoon was a short trip to enable Ruth to show off her new husband to her many cousins. Ralph had to be back at Howard in early July for the opening of summer school.

The newlyweds moved into a small apartment just off the campus of the university. Ruth continued her studies, but took no further courses in political science. She was forced to drop out during the next year when their daughter Joan was born.

In 1931, Bunche was offered the position of assistant to the president of the university. He assumed this position as an administrator, but continued to teach one course. He always knew that, if he was to reach to the heights of his profession, he would have to complete his work for the Ph.D. degree.

Ralph returned to Harvard in September, 1932, to study for the doctorate. This was possible because he had been awarded an Ozios Goodwin Fellowship. He moved Ruth and little Joan to a house in Somerville, a town close to Cambridge, where Harvard is located. His second daughter, Jane, was born while his family was living in Massachusetts.

The work that Bunche engaged in to earn his Ph.D. required him to travel to Africa. In order to carry on this necessary research, he received a Rosenwald Field Fellowship. This was granted through the efforts of one of his professors, who was interested in Bunche's work.

A candidate for a Ph.D. degree must write a thesis. This is a manuscript on some subject that will permit the writer to present material never before used. Ralph decided that his thesis would compare the rule of a mandated area, French Togoland, with that of a colony, Dahomey, in French West Africa.

For three months, Ralph traveled alone in Africa while his family remained in Massachusetts. He was not overburdened with money, so he was forced to use a native truck to travel into the interior of these countries for his research. His accommodations were never of the best, and the food did not help his digestion. His investigations took him through West and North Africa, where he complained about the methods of political science inquiry that placed all their emphasis on government reports.

Back in Cambridge, Bunche worked hard to complete his thesis. He presented the finished product to the faculty at Harvard University in 1934, and was awarded his Ph.D. degree. The thesis was considered so well written and researched that it received the Tappan Prize, which was awarded annually for the best written thesis in the social sciences.

The Bunche family returned to Howard where Ralph took up his administrative and teaching positions once again. In 1936, he received a post-doctoral grant from the Social Science Research Council to study for two years in anthropology and colonial policy. He did this studying at Northwestern University, the London School of Economics, and the Union of South Africa's Capetown University.

The admission of a black man to South Africa for the purpose of study was not a usual happening. However, Ralph Bunche fully convinced the government that he was not coming to incite a black revolt. One wonders what his chances would be there today if he were a research scholar.

For his second trip to Africa, Bunche bought himself a second-hand Ford. He traveled to the Kenya highlands, where he lived for three months among the Kikuyus and was named an honorary tribal citizen. He learned much about their tribal customs and manners.

The generous grant he had received made it possible, when he finished his African research, for him to take a trip around the world. He would have loved to have brought Ruth and the children with him, but there was not enough money for all. The family had grown by one more since the Bunches' return to Howard. There was now Ralph junior to keep the two girls company. Ralph senior was able to visit Malaya, China, Japan, and Hawaii on his trip.

Before leaving on his world tour, Ralph published a small brochure titled *A World View of Race,* which had the support of the Progressive Education Association. He was now beginning to be sought out for various lectures and positions.

In 1938, Bunche became a staff member of the Carnegie Corporation of New York. He was given a leave by Howard University, so he was able to remain in New York until 1940. While with the Carnegie Corporation, he served as chief aid to Gunnar Myrdal, the Swedish sociologist. Myrdal was making a survey of the black man in America for the corporation. In 1944, Myrdal published his findings in his *An America Dilemma.* The work of Ralph Bunche in gathering the material for this definitive book can be seen in chapter twenty-two, where the author states: "The data on Southern politics presented in this chapter are for the most part taken from Ralph Bunche's seven-volume study, 'The Political Status of the Negro,' unpublished manuscript prepared for this study (1940)."

The summer of 1940 found the Bunche family preparing to take a motor trip to California. Young Ralph was quite taken with the possibility of getting out of the heat of New York City and seeing the country about which his father had told him so much. The two girls were more receptive to the idea when their mother assured them they would visit a movie set while they were in Hollywood.

The trip was a tremendous success. Ruth was pleased to have her family together for some six weeks, and to have them enjoying themselves. Ralph senior, as was to be expected, managed to do some research, but, at the same time, he relaxed. When it was all over, everyone was more than ready to return to Washington, and Howard University.

By now, Dr. Ralph Bunche had been promoted to full professor. He returned, greatly refreshed, to the classroom and his administrative work at the university, where he remained until the outbreak of World War II.

The Japanese attack on Pearl Harbor was the cause of Ralph Bunche's attempt to join the Army. On Monday morning, the day after the attack, he appeared at the recruiting station. A thorough physical examination indicated that, while he was eager to serve, the service could not accept him for reasons of health.

Greatly disappointed, Bunche was impelled to get into some type of work that would convince him he was doing his part to defeat the dictators. Continuing to teach and administrate at Howard was not what Ralph Bunche wanted to do for the duration of the war.

The opportunity he sought came when Secretary of State Cordell Hull asked him to serve in the Office of Strategic Services. This organization had as part of its responsibility the keeping of the Joint Chiefs of Staff up-to-date on all the vital information concerning colonial peoples, and on colonial areas in which American armed forces were located—that is, in those areas which were controlled by other countries.

Africa was made up of many colonies. It was Ralph Bunche's job to gather all the material that would aid the military in understanding Africa. He was also expected to keep abreast of matters concerning colonies in the Far East.

The most significant work contributed by Bunche was to have the United States military personnel properly briefed when the Allied American forces staged their invasion of North Africa. It was the effective landing in North Africa that made the Normandy invasion, which took place in 1944, a real possibility.

Ralph continued to work with the OSS until January, 1944. During those years when he kept the military of the United States briefed on colonial peoples, his reputation was growing. The Department of State was very familiar with his careful, well-studied research and, before long, he was invited to join this branch of the Government.

Late in January, 1944, Ralph Bunche was given the position of divisional assistant for colonial problems in the Division of Political Studies. As time progressed, he moved steadily up the State Department ladder. In February, 1945, be became acting associate chief in the Office of Special Political Affairs. Here he was responsible for matters involving trusteeships. (A trusteeship is a territory that is being watched over by another country in anticipation of eventually giving it independence.) *The Christian Science Monitor*, one of America's finest newspapers, commented on the Bunche appointment with these words: "He knows about all there is to know on this subject" (trusteeship). Incidentally, he was the first black man to hold the post of acting chief in the State Department.

Bunche had been in his new position for only two months when President Roosevelt died in Warm Springs, Georgia.

For months before this sad event, the State Department had been preparing for the first meeting of the United Nations Organization. It was planned to draw up the charter at this meeting, which was to take place on April 25, in San Francisco, California.

Ralph Bunche was sitting down to dinner with his wife in a small restaurant in Georgetown, just outside of Washington, on April 12, 1945. The Bunche children were away in boarding schools. It was good to relax, for the pressure on him had been great since moving up in the State Department. The couple had just placed their order when the restaurant manager announced to the diners that President Roosevelt had died. Ralph Bunche hurriedly called his office and was told to return there immediately. His wife ate alone that night.

Many wondered what the new president, Harry S. Truman, would do about the United Nations. On his first morning as President of the United States, Harry Truman told the world that the San Francisco meeting would go on as scheduled. This meant that Ralph Bunche would soon be on his way to the West Coast.

He decided to take Ruth to the UN meeting with him. They boarded a special train in Washington on the morning of April 18, and arrived in San Francisco some four days later.

At the conference, Bunche played an important behind-the-scenes role as a technical expert on trusteeship for the United States delegations. It was this that brought him the acclaim, not only of the delegates from his own country, but also of those from all the other countries with whom he made contact.

The work that he had been doing on the UN Charter since 1944 paid off in San Francisco. His major contribution was in drawing up the non-self-governing territories and trusteeship sections of the Charter. He also worked on plans for the disposal of the Italian colonies.

Ralph and Ruth Bunche returned to Washington exhausted. What Ruth wanted her husband to do was to take her and the children to Cape Cod for a long rest. As Ralph expresses it, "When Ruth wants something she usually gets her way." So the Bunche family played and rested for almost six weeks, until he was called back to Washington by the then Secretary of State, James Byrnes. For the remainder of 1945, and most of 1946, he attended international conferences in Europe and the United States.

It was inevitable that it would not be long before the people at the United Nations would call for the services of Ralph Bunche. In May, 1946, the General Secretary of the UN, Trygve Lie, requested that Dr. Bunche be assigned to his organization. He was to be "on loan" to the world organization for a short period of time. His position was Director of the Trusteeship Division. The New York *Herald Tribune* commented on Bunche's appointment with the statement: "... he is as well qualified as is humanly possible for the post. Americans must regard (him) with pride and humility."

Bunche came up to New York to take over his new post— and to find a place for his family to live. He managed to locate a pleasant apartment in Queens, a borough of New York City. The children were most happy to learn that they would be in the hub of the entertainment area of the United States. Ralph was also pleased because now he could hope to be able to watch his favorite ballplayer, Jackie Robinson, play for the Brooklyn Dodgers.

The most important assignment in Dr. Bunche's career came when he was in Palestine as special assistant to the representative of the Secretary-General, United Nations Special Committee on Palestine. From June to September, 1947, the committee studied the Palestinian situation and recommended partition of the country into Jewish and Arab states.

It was Ralph Bunche who received the credit for drafting the final report of the committee. It was indeed an historic report. From this stemmed the appointment of Dr. Bunche

as secretary of the United Nations Palestine Commission.
This new assignment came on December 3, 1947. *The New
York Times* stated, in part: "His experience, understanding,
and character should be of inestimable value to the new commission as it takes up its complicated and critical task."

This new responsibility was not especially to Bunche's liking. His strength, as he saw it, was in the area of trusteeships.
However, he had never shirked a job and he did not intend
to do so now.

Dr. Bunche was to be the commission's "trouble shooter
in carrying out the partition decision of the General Assembly." In that position he convinced the members of the commission that they should request the UN Security Council to
put together an international armed force to effect the partition of the Holy Land. Ever since the decision had been made
to partition Palestine, there had been fierce fighting between
Jews and Arabs.

As a result of the commission's request, the UN appointed
Count Folke Bernadotte, of Sweden, to act as a mediator in
this Jewish-Arab impasse. Dr. Bunche accompanied Count
Bernadotte to Palestine.

While Count Bernadotte was riding in a car in Palestine
with a UN observer, he and his passenger were shot and
killed. This sad event took place on September 17, 1948.
Bunche became Bernadotte's successor as the acting mediator.

Dr. Bunche, with his years of experience behind him, was
able to work carefully and intelligently to bring about a
settlement of this sticky question. He managed to have long
conferences with both the Arabs and the Jews. The serious
talks began in January, 1949, and ended in July of the same
year. The results were four armistice agreements between
Israeli and the Arab States. The importance of Bunche's
work is to be found in the tremendous prestige that the
United Nations acquired for having successfully settled this
problem. In 1949, the UN needed every positive action it

could get, for many people had yet to be convinced that the world organization was necessary. Ralph Bunche must also be given credit for keeping the peace in the Middle East for almost a generation.

The return from the Middle East was, for Dr. Bunche, a triumphal tour. Upon arrival in New York, he was awarded a ticker tape parade up Broadway. New York City saw this man of courage, surrounded by his family, received one of the big ovations accorded a returning hero. A trip to his home town, Los Angeles, gave him another parade, with the Mayor declaring it "Ralph Bunche Day." Like many other national heroes, he received some thirty-seven honorary degrees between 1947 and 1952.

As was expected, the Springarn Medal was awarded to Ralph Bunche after his return from Palestine. (Arthur B. Springarn was a leading mover in the founding of the National Association for the Advancement of Colored People—the NAACP.) However, the surprise that really thrilled the Bunche family came in 1950.

Dr. Bunche was preparing in that year to assume a two-year teaching assignment as professor of political science at Harvard University. He had managed to get in some fishing and to see some of the new shows and movies he had missed while he was in the Middle East. Just before he was to fly to Boston, a reporter from *The New York Times* called the Bunche apartment. Ralph answered the telephone to learn that he had been chosen as the 1950 recipient of the Nobel Prize for Peace. As he describes his reactions: "It took me at least a minute to fully realize what I had been told. I then asked the reporter was he sure. When it was apparent that his information was correct, all I could say was, 'I can't believe it.'"

The entire Bunche family went to Sweden for the ceremonies. It was a joyful occasion for this tall, portly man of international fame. His work in Palestine had put a dangerous situation at rest—at least for the time being—and he certainly deserved a prize for his magnificent accomplishment.

Following his two years at Harvard, Ralph Bunche was again restless to get back to where the action was—the United Nations. Offers had been made for him to assume responsible positions, such as the presidency of City College of New York City, or the post of Assistant Secretary of State. He preferred to move back to the UN as its Under Secretary-General.

War broke out in the Congo in 1960. The Secretary-General, Dag Hammarskjold, sent Ralph Bunche there as his special representative. The latter's work was to direct the United Nations operations in this unsettled part of the world. As a result of Dr. Bunche's efforts, peace has been maintained in the Congo area ever since that time.

Ralph Bunche has been given many important tasks in the UN. With the untimely death of Secretary-General Hammarskjold and the election of U-Thant to that top position, Bunche has been asked to oversee the United Nations peace-keeping force in Cyprus. Since 1954, he has also had responsibility for matters relating to the peaceful use of atomic energy.

With all the pressure and activity that have kept Ralph Bunche involved in international affairs, he has never failed to interest himself in the issues facing the black American. He sees the conflict that exists between the black and white populations in America as inevitable. He has expressed it as well as it can be said: "Many are the non-scientific solutions for the problems of black-white race relations that have been offered. Racial equality and tolerance have been pleaded for far and wide. But these solutions ignore the seemingly basic fact that whenever two groups of peoples in daily contact with each other, and having readily identifiable cultural or racial differentiations, are likewise forced into economic competition, group antagonisms must inevitably prevail."

Dr. and Mrs. Bunche live in a beautiful apartment on the East Side of New York City, from which he walks to his office in the United Nations building each morning. He has taken on some weight since he moved around the basketball courts in California. However, his six-foot frame carries the additional weight well. His hair has turned gray, and glasses now are an essential part of his impressive appearance. His children have married, and he and Ruth are always joyful when the grandchildren come to visit. With all his serious responsibilities, he still likes to watch a baseball game, only now he travels to Shea Stadium to see the Mets play. His interest in the movies and the legitimate stage leads him to many opening nights on Broadway. When the rare opportunity comes, he takes his car and drives up to the mountains to do some fishing.

A man who finds no difficulty in enjoying himself, and who lives for his family, is bound to offer substantial contributions to his fellow men. Ralph Bunche has contributed a great deal toward making this world a better place in which to live. He will continue to offer further contributions, not only in the area of international affairs, but also in solving the problems of his people.

> Your color has nothing to do with your worth. You are potentially as good as anyone. How good you may prove to be will have no relation to your color, but with what is in your heart and your head. That is something which each individual by his own effort can control. The right to be treated as an equal by all other men is man's birthright. Never permit anyone to treat you otherwise. For nothing is as important as maintaining your dignity and self-respect.
>
> —Nana Johnson's talk to Ralph Bunche when he was a youngster.

Brigadier General Benjamin Oliver Davis, Sr.

[1877-   ]

Lieutenant General Benjamin Oliver Davis, Jr.

[1912-   ]

MILITARY LEADERS

> General Davis has always shown a determination to place his career above all else. A dedicated soldier since the Spanish-American war, his promotion is well deserved.
>
> —*The New York Times,* October 25, 1940

It is seldom that a father and son reach the high military rank of general while both are living. It is more unusual when the father and son are black men, yet this is true of Benjamin O. Davis, senior and junior. It has indeed been a hero-tale type of story for both the father and the son as they have moved up through the military ranks, proudly wearing the uniform of their country.

Louis Davis had what was considered an excellent position for a black man in the last quarter of the nineteenth century. He was a messenger for the United States Department of the Interior. President Rutherford B. Hayes had just won a disputed election and had settled down for four uneventful years in the White House when Benjamin O. Davis was born.

Henriette Stewart Davis, his mother, had considered herself fortunate to have married Louis Davis. They had known each other for a long time. Louis and Henriette attended the same school and lived on the same street in the nation's capital. However, the Davis family had a social standing much higher than that of the Stewarts. Louis could brag that his father had been a slave who had bought his freedom in 1800, moved to Washington, D.C., and opened a successful business in the retail field.

It was on June 1, 1877, that little Benjamin was born in a small house on "K" Street, not far from the present Lincoln Memorial. The birth was not recorded as a great event, for Benjamin tells us, "Pop had to go to work the next day, or so he constantly told me."

Benjamin certainly was not brought up in an impoverished home. He tells of the outings, parties, and pleasant places that he enjoyed as a child. His parents maintained a well-kept home and managed to take a vacation in the North each summer. His mother was active in the Baptist Church and, on several occasions, made trips to church conventions that were held as far south as Alabama and Florida.

The Davis home was a beehive of intellectual activity. Louis was an avid reader, and he transferred his love of books to his family. Benjamin learned to read long before he ever entered a Washington public school.

Elementary school was not a challenge for Benjamin Davis. His fellow students were not as bright as he was, so that he soon became a problem child. In those days, there were no child psychologists to explain that a bright student will soon become bored unless challenged.

Mr. and Mrs. Davis could not understand why their normally quiet and studious son suddenly became a problem in the classroom. It was only when he entered high school that the situation changed. In high school he was challenged, because few youngsters ever continued their education beyond the elementary level. Those who went on to high school were usually those who were academically orientated and economically well-off.

High school opened up a whole new life for Benjamin. He was introduced to science, higher mathematics, and, above all, an in-depth course in United States history. He read everything he could find on the American Revolution, the Mexican War, and the military exploits of the Civil War heroes.

Benjamin Davis would gather a few friends at his house on a Saturday morning, and they would march across the one bridge separating Washington, D.C. from Virginia. Once on the Virginia side, they would act out a game as soldiers on the ground that is now Arlington National Cemetery. Benjamin would inform his friends of the historic events that had taken place on the same location. He would point out the Lee Mansion and explain the role played by General Robert E. Lee in fighting for the Confederacy during the War Between the States. His admiration for the Union leaders centered around the military exploits of General Ulysses S. Grant.

While in his second year of high school, Benjamin discovered that it was not too far from Arlington to Fort Myer. Here he managed to make friends with several soldiers who stood guard at the gates of the fort. Before long, he was to be seen frequently standing with the visitors who were present for dress parades and other special events. The officers and men of Fort Myer liked Benjamin for his honest and forthright enthusiasm for all things military. They were the army contingent that served as the honor guard for the President and other high officials in the capital. The soldiers of Fort Myer still perform this service, as they were observed by many on TV when President Kennedy was buried and when President Nixon was sworn into office.

Louis Davis was proud of his son's interest in the military. However, not unlike many parents, he and his wife were hoping for their boy a type of career such as that of a doctor, dentist, or lawyer. When Benjamin was graduated from high school in June, 1897, they breathed easier knowing he was enrolled in Howard University for the fall semester.

The United States, in the fall of 1897, was being exposed to all the propaganda that William Randolph Hearst and Joseph Pulitzer could pack into their newspapers. Hearst, of the *New York Journal,* and Pulitzer, of the *New York World,* were printing lurid stories of the mistreatment of Cubans by the Spaniards. Lehigh University students held daily drills and paraded under the banner, "To Hell with Spain."

Benjamin Davis was restless when he attended classes at Howard University. The tempo was picking up as the U.S.S. *Maine* was sunk in Havana Harbor. College students in those days were most anxious to get into uniform. They were impatiently awaiting the call of their country. Benjamin, among many other young men, was sure of what he would do if his country declared war on Spain.

On April 11, 1898, President McKinley sent a message to Congress requesting war with Spain. Benjamin waited only long enough to finish his exams at Howard, then, on July 13, 1898, he went into active service. During his freshman year he had joined the Reserve Officer Training Corps (ROTC) so that, when he reported on active duty, he did so as a first lieutenant in the Eighth United States Infantry.

The Spanish American War has been called by one author "our splendid little war." It was all over in seven months. Davis was sent with a black battalion to Key West, Florida. Before his outfit made the war zone, the Spanish had asked for a peace conference.

Lieutenant Davis was mustered out of the service in March, 1899. The following June, he enlisted as a private in Troop I, Ninth Cavalry of the Regular Army. The outfit that Davis joined was a black contingent led by General John Pershing. This earned Pershing the nickname "Black Jack." He, of course, went on to lead the Allied Armies in Europe during World War I.

The war with Spain had made the United States a world power. For the first time, it was necessary to send troops outside continental United States. Benjamin Davis was shipped to the Island of Samar, in the Philippines. Many contingents of American forces had been assigned to the Philippines to put down the troubles in that section of the world.

The two years on Samar were not easy for the American troops stationed there. The weather was horrible, and the natives were restless. Benjamin, characteristically, worked hard and was determined to make good. Within a few months he was promoted to corporal; by the end of the first year he was made squadron sergeant major.

In February, 1901, after returning to the United States, Benjamin Davis was commissioned a second lieutenant of Cavalry in the Regular Army. Today, with a large standing army, this might not appear as a great step forward. However, in 1901, it was most difficult to move from the enlisted ranks to officer status. Again, Benjamin Davis was commissioned in the Regular Army, not the Reserves. If promotion was to come, it was easier to get a Reserve commission than it was to get a Regular Army commission, which proves the outstanding ability of the man who was promoted.

His first assignment as a commissioned officer was to the Second Squadron of the Tenth Cavalry. He served later as adjutant at Fort Washakie, Wyoming.

It was quite a thrill for the young lieutenant to come home to Washington, D.C. and show off the new gold bars on his shoulders. During one of his leaves, late in 1901, Benjamin met Elnora Dickerson. Elnora was working in the War Department as a clerk when Benjamin first saw her. Through a friend in the office, he managed an introduction.

There was not much time during that leave for these two young people to become better acquainted. When Benjamin returned to his post in Wyoming, he wrote to Elnora, and she was quick to reply. This mutual attraction, carried on with the aid of the United States Postal Service, blossomed into love.

Benjamin's return to Washington in the spring of 1902 brought with it his engagement to Elnora. The wedding was planned for September. When September came, Benjamin could not get his expected leave because his outfit was alerted to go to Cuba. That troubled country had broken out in a civil war, and President Theodore Roosevelt was planning to intervene. Fortunately, the crisis passed and Lieutenant Davis was able to come home in late October.

Mr. and Mrs. Dickerson were proud to have their daughter marry the fine young soldier. The small church in downtown Washington was crowded that October 23, 1902, when Elnora came down the aisle to be given in marriage by her father. The *Washington Post,* in a small article, noted the lovely traditional costume of the bride.

Lieutenant and Mrs. Benjamin Davis had no time for a honeymoon. They left immediately for Fort Washakie. The couple were able to set up light housekeeping in a two-room apartment on the post, provided by the Army.

The Davises remained in Wyoming until he was promoted to first lieutenant. That happy event took place on March 30, 1905. Within a week, Elnora gave birth to their first child, Olive Elnora. The little girl was called Olive for her dad's middle name, Oliver. During the summer of 1905, word was received that Lieutenant Davis was to report to Wilberforce University, in Ohio, where he would serve as a professor of military science and tactics in the ROTC program.

It had been the decision of the War Department that the college campus was the place to train potential officer material. Reserve Officer Training Corps were established on many college campuses, where young men could attend classes in military science while studying for their bachelor

degree. They would go to military posts for summer training, and upon graduation from college, would receive a
Reserve commission in the Army.

Wilberforce College had a rather large ROTC unit. The
new young professor of military science and tactics reported
there in the summer of 1905. The calm, quiet life of a mid-
western college campus was quite a change for the lieutenant.

Wilberforce was an all-black college, and Davis found the
challenge of training young men of his own race for military
leadership most rewarding. The classroom atmosphere was
to his liking, and he felt thoroughly at home instructing in
military science, his first love.

The Davis family had a cozy house on the rim of the Wilberforce campus. Elnora would place little Olive in her carriage and set it out on the broad lawn in front of their home.
Benjamin would draw up a chair near the carriage and
leisurely mark papers or prepare his lectures. Those four
years at Wilberforce were a most happy time for the couple.

In 1909, Lieutenant Davis' tour of duty at the college was
over, and he was ready for reassignment. His orders called
for him to report to Fort Ethan Allen. This was a normal
assignment for a first lieutenant. Benjamin moved his family
to New England, only to discover that he was to report as
military attaché at the consulate in Monrovia, Liberia. Davis
promptly packed and moved Elnora and the baby to distant
Africa.

When the War Department assigned Lieutenant Davis to
the United States Ministry in Liberia, he was given a tremendous opportunity to round out his military education and
experience. This type of duty is considered highly desirable,
for it not only shows the officer the attitude that his superiors
hold toward him, it also gives the military man an opening
into the mystic area of diplomacy.

Benjamin Davis arrived in Monrovia just a few years after
James Spurgeon left the country. (See *James Spurgeon*.) The

life there, so very far from family and friends, was at first not appreciated by Elnora. However, as time passed, she began to understand the deprivations, the trials, and the handicaps of this young country, and the tremendous effort being put forth to overcome them. By the time her husband was reassigned, in early 1912, Mrs. Davis was a strong advocate of the government of Liberia, and aid from the United States was being extended.

The trek back to the United States was made all the more difficult because Elnora was expecting her second child. Olive was by now becoming a regular "Army brat," as she moved with her father every few years. The term "Army brat" is given to a child of a Regular Army man who travels with him on his various assignments.

The new assignment for Lieutenant Davis was Wyoming once more—this time to Fort D. A. Russell. He was back in the Cavalry—in the Ninth Division. The work was pleasant and his associates were most friendly. He was given work in the commanding officer's area, and found little time to move among the men. Davis was too valuable as a liaison with Washington to be out commanding a unit of troops. It was a preview of what was to come for him.

On December 18, 1912, Elnora gave birth to a sturdy baby boy. The father could hardly wait to have him baptized Benjamin O. Davis, Jr. The son he had so much wanted was his pride and joy. This youngster was indeed entitled to the name "Army brat," for his entire boyhood years were spent with the Army—continuing on into manhood.

The Ninth Cavalry was moved to Fort Douglas in 1913, as trouble with Mexico began to erupt. Davis was reluctant to have his family, and especially the baby, live in the hot, flat, desert country of Arizona, so Elnora moved, with the two children, back to Washington and her family. Benjamin remained on border duty until 1915. During that time he saw his family only on short leaves, and always left them with dragging feet.

When the time came for his reassignment to ROTC duty, in 1915, Benjamin Davis was sent back to Wilberforce University, where he assumed again the position of professor of military science and tactics. The one advantage was the fact that Elnora and the children were to be with him. It was with this assignment that Davis was promoted to the rank of captain.

Mrs. Davis, who was expecting another child in 1916, had lost a great deal of her vitality and vim. She discovered that looking after the two lively children grew to be too much for her in her frail condition, so her husband brought in help to relieve the pressure. When the baby came, it was strong and well-formed, but the strain was too great for the mother and she did not survive. The little girl was named Elnora for her mother.

Unhappy Captain Davis had to break up his family. Little Benjamin was only three when he and his two sisters were sent on to Washington to live with their grandmother. He remained there until he was six years old. At that time, 1919, his father married Sadie E. Overton.

Following Elnora's death, in 1917, Benjamin Davis was given a temporary promotion to major. A temporary promotion meant that he could wear the insignia of a major, but he could be dropped back to his permanent rank of captain at any time. The reason for this was that the Army budget did not permit permanent promotion.

World War I had begun in Europe in 1914. By 1917, America's entrance into the conflict was almost a certainty. Davis was sent back to the Philippines, this time as supply officer of the Ninth Cavalry, at Camp Slotsenburg. The next year, Major Davis was given the temporary rank of lieutenant-colonel.

On returning to the United States in 1920, Davis took his

three children and his new wife to Tuskegee Institute in Alabama, where he had been assigned. It was here that Benjamin, Jr., now eight years old, continued his schooling that had begun in Washington, D.C.

In 1924, the Davis family was again on the move. Before Benjamin Davis transferred to Cleveland, Ohio, to assume the position of instructor of the 372nd Infantry of the Ohio National Guard, he was given the permanent rank of lieutenant colonel.

Benjamin, Jr., was ready for high school when the transfer to Cleveland came. He attended Central High School. During this period it was apparent that the boy was an excellent student. He took his studies very seriously. His work was always done to perfection, yet ready for submission long before the due date. In his senior year, he won six leatherbound volumes of Shakespeare for ranking highest in his class. That year he was also class president. Ben Richardson wrote, in *Great American Negroes,* "Benjamin Davis graduated with one of the highest scholastic averages of the entire student body of the city."

When he graduated from high school, Benjamin went to Western Reserve University for a year. He then transferred to the University of Chicago, where he majored in mathematics, planning to teach that subject. He remained at the University of Chicago for the academic years of 1930 through 1932.

During the time that Benjamin, Jr., spent at Western Reserve and the University of Chicago, his father was traveling to Europe and serving again at Wilberforce University, where the War Department moved him in 1929. He was no sooner settled at Wilberforce than he was ordered to accompany six parties of war mothers and widows on their pilgrimage to the cemeteries of Europe. The Secretary of War, as well as the Quartermaster General, highly recommended him for the outstanding work he did in connection with this assignment. During this tour of duty he was promoted to the rank of colonel.

After several transfers from Wilberforce University to Tuskegee Institute and back again, Davis, Sr., in 1938, became instructor and commanding officer of the 369th Infantry of the New York National Guard. Colonel Davis was extremely popular with the men of the 369th Harlem Regiment. Made up entirely of blacks, the regiment was quartered in Harlem, a black area of New York City.

Benjamin, Jr., who had spent almost all his earlier life on Army installations, was restless while attending the University of Chicago. During the years since graduation from high school his two sisters had married, and his father was now in constant motion. He truly had no home to which he could return, and, with the coming of the depression, there was little possibility for a job.

In 1931, Benjamin Davis, Jr., sought and received an appointment to the United States Military Academy at West Point. His interest in things military was never a problem, but he had some strong reservations about the strictly segregated policy practiced at that time in the United States Army. His father's great success was unique. Davis, Jr., knew that blacks had little chance for advancement in the armed services. Practically all the high-ranking officers in the army were graduates of West Point. It was almost half a century since a Negro had graduated from the Military Academy. More important to Benjamin was the fact that few blacks were accepted at West Point, and when they were, they either did not finish or were dismissed before graduation.

The man responsible for Benjamin Davis, Jr's. appointment to West Point was Chicago's first Negro Congressman, Oscar DePriest. He nominated Benjamin for an appointment. The first hurdle was the written test that Davis was obliged to take, which proved difficult in spite of his fine scholastic record. He was not prepared for a written test, which was sprung on him after he took his physical examination. He failed on his first attempt. His failure to pass the written test the first time did not stop young Davis. He was convinced that his failure was not based on the fact that he was black. He sought and received a second chance.

For two months, in 1932, Benjamin worked night and day on the subjects which would be covered in the examinations. He was determined to make the passing grade this time. On July 20, 1932, he was admitted to West Point.

That first year at the Military Academy was most difficult. His classmates carried out a form of hazing known as "the silent treatment." Throughout his first year, none of Davis' fellow cadets ever spoke to him, or answered when he addressed them—except in the line of duty. If he tried to join in a conversation, all the cadets stopped talking. He was left entirely alone. This complete silence lasted for his entire initial year at the Academy.

With the end of that first year, the Academy officials called a meeting of all the cadets. At that meeting the curtain of silence was lifted. All cadets, Benjamin was not the only one, who had successfully stood up under the silent treatment were cheered and welcomed into the company of their fellow students. When Davis went to this meeting, he was not sure as to what would happen to him, for he was black. That first year proved to him—and to his classmates—that he was composed of the stuff from which heroes are made.

The author of We Have Tomorrow, Arna Bontemps, summed up that first year at West Point with this comment: "Ben Davis, Jr., had stood the most severe test any boy had stood at West Point in at least fifty years, and he had passed it to the satisfaction of the whole class of his fellows." The wall of silence fell down like the walls of Jericho, and was never raised again.

June 12, 1936, was a beautiful day at West Point. The sun was shining on the extensive campus, high on the cliffs overlooking the Hudson River. The class of 1936 sat proudly erect as General John J. Pershing, the hero of World War I, gave the commencement address. On the platform behind the speaker sat army brass from all over the United States. Among this group was a colonel who was beaming with pride for his son, who was to be commissioned in a few minutes. This man was Colonel Benjamin O. Davis, Sr. In the audience were Benjamin, Jr.'s stepmother and his two sisters, who were equally proud of his success. A cheer arose from his fellow classmates as General Pershing shook young Davis' hand and presented his diploma to him.

Many graduates of the Academy carry out a tradition as old as the military school itself—getting married immediately after graduation. Benjamin had met Ethel Scott when he was in his second year at West Point. She had come up to the Academy for the Christmas Dance. This young lady from New Haven, Connecticut, saw as much of Benjamin as was possible during his remaining two and a half years at the Academy. They decided to marry on graduation day.

In the Protestant Chapel on the grounds of West Point, in the presence of both their families, this young, happy couple were married. Like his father before him, Benjamin's honeymoon consisted of taking his bride to his first duty station.

As a lowly second lieutenant, Benjamin was sent to Fort Benning, Georgia. There he served as a company officer of the Twenty-fourth Infantry. During his stay at Fort Benning, he attended the Infantry School, and was graduated in 1938.

Upon graduation, Benjamin was assigned as an instructor in military science and tactics at Tuskegee Institute. This was the assignment that his father had had many times during his career. Benjamin, Jr., had lived at the Institute as a boy, and felt as if he were coming home. It is interesting to note that, shortly after being commissioned, Benjamin was sent to an ROTC assignment. This was because the Army did not have sufficient numbers of Negro officers to fill these billets. It was not the black soldier's fault as much as it was the Army's attitude toward the black soldier that made for the problem.

Benjamin and Ethel found a delightful vine-covered cottage about a mile from the Tuskegee campus. She spent her days shopping for curtains, rugs, and furniture. This was their first real home, for they had lived until now in a furnished apartment on the base at Fort Benning.

The stay at Tuskegee was a happy one. In June, 1939, Benjamin Davis, Jr., was promoted to first lieutenant, and fifteen months later he was raised to the rank of captain. The war in Europe, that was to touch the United States with the attack on Pearl Harbor, would bring a change for Benjamin and Ethel.

A month after his son was promoted to captain, Benjamin Davis, Sr., was raised to the temporary rank of brigadier general. He was transferred to Fort Riley, Kansas, for duty as commander of the Second Cavalry Division. Permitted to assemble his own staff, General Davis requested his son's transfer to Fort Riley. From February, 1941, until May of that year Benjamin, Jr., was aide-de-camp to his father. They were both known as strict disciplinarians, but very fair, so they were liked as well as respected by the men under them.

Benjamin, Sr., was at retirement age in June, 1941. The Army, unlike most organizations, goes through the process of retiring its personnel—and then calls them back to active duty. The same month that General Davis was retired, he was called back to active duty and assigned to Washington, D.C., as assistant to the Inspector General.

For a number of years since being commissioned, young Davis had wanted to go into flight training. His father's transfer to Washington made that possible. Benjamin, Jr., had been forced to wait because the Army Air Force would not admit blacks to pilot training. In 1940 it changed its policy to a limited training program for Negroes.

The tests required to prove an aptitude for flying were

passed by Benjamin Davis, Jr., with ease. When the results were posted, he discovered he had scored the second highest mark. For the blacks who had passed the examination, a flying school was set up at Tuskegee Institute. Captain Davis won his wings in March, 1942. He was proud that he was in the first class of Negro fliers in the United States armed forces. He was transferred to the Air Corps, and was immediately placed in command of the Ninety-ninth Fighter Squadron at Tuskegee. During the time that Benjamin was earning his wings, his country had entered World War II.

The tempo of war makes for many unusual incidents. Young Davis was promoted to major, and then to lieutenant colonel in March, 1942. He worked hard and long with the Ninety-ninth Fighter Squadron, and in early 1943, moved with them to North Africa. He was the first Negro officer to command an Army Air Force combat unit. The Ninety-ninth, with its 250-man ground crew and twenty-seven pilots, did heroic work in North Africa, Sicily, and Italy.

Benjamin Davis, Sr., was transferred to England in October, 1942. His work was to make an inspection of all the black units on the British Isles. He was to learn as much as possible about the morale of the large contingent of black troops in England, and report his findings to Lieutenant General Dwight D. Eisenhower, then commanding general of the European Front. He was also to inform Major General John C. H. Lee, chief of the Service Supply, under whose command most of these troops would serve.

The friction that had been reported between white and black soldiers in England was, according to General Davis, "due partly to resentment on the part of the white troops against the way the British people entertained the black troops." He was most concerned that the actions of a few would be charged against the entire group, and warned against this. The official instructions of the Army declared that there was no distinction between white and black troops, but General Davis had his own thoughts. He expressed it in this way: "I fear overmuch emphasis *is* being placed on color in our Army."

The Davises, father and son, were able to meet in London just before General Davis was to return to Washington. It was a joyful reunion for both. Colonel Davis had his dad take some small presents back to his wife and the rest of his family. Ethel was living in New Haven with her people and doing volunteer work for the Red Cross.

It was not too long, however, before Colonel Davis was back home himself. The need for more pilots, and the realization by the high command of what fine pilots the Negro men made, brought Colonel Davis home on October 5, 1943. He had proved himself an excellent leader. Now his job would be to direct the training of the all-black 332nd Fighter Group. They were stationed at Selfridge Field, Michigan. Davis trained this group for active duty. In January, 1944, the 332nd was sent overseas with its commanding officer, Colonel Benjamin Davis. Upon arrival, the unit was attached to the Twelfth Fighter Command of the Mediterranean Allied Air Force, under General Ira C. Eaker.

The work of the 332nd was magnificent. Equipped with the P-39 and the P-37, the unit strafed enemy shipping and did low-level skip-bombing at Monte Cassino, Anzio, and other strategic points in Italy. Their achievements included the sinking of a German destroyer, and the protecting of Allied bombers in their attack on the vital Romanian oil fields. The 332nd also destroyed more than 250 enemy airplanes.

On May 29, 1944, Lieutenant Colonel Benjamin O. Davis, Jr., was promoted to the rank of full colonel. General Davis was flown to Italy to pin the Distinguished Flying Cross on his son's breast. As one author concisely, yet completely, expressed the occasion, "It was a happy moment for both father and son. . . ."

Late in 1944, the 332nd was transferred to the Fifteenth Air Force. By February, 1945, while the Allies were invading southern Germany, Colonel Davis' unit was given a great responsibility. The flyers were instructed to destroy the German radar stations on the Mediterranean coast so that the American troops could land safely. Those landings were successful because of the effective advance safety work of the 332nd. The escort assignment of the 332nd was carried out without the loss of a single Allied bomber to enemy fighters.

The New York newspaper *PM* reported on April 27, 1945, that Colonel Davis, "led a strafing attack on railway targets in Austria, remaining in the danger area for an hour to destroy locomotives and rolling stock. The action won him the Silver Star for gallantry in action, the first time it has been awarded to a Negro fighter pilot in the Army."

When the war ended in Europe, Colonel Davis was placed by General Eaker in command of the 477th Composite Group at Goodman Field, Kentucky. In July, 1945, Davis became field commander. From 1946 to 1949 the colonel was in command of the Lockbowne Army Air Force Base. Here he was joined by his wife Ethel. They both were happy to settle down together to the routine life of a military base.

In order for a high-ranking military officer to continue to move up the ladder of promotion he must have graduated from a staff school. Therefore, in 1949, Colonel Davis entered the Air War College at Maxwell Air Force Base, Alabama. One year later, he was graduated with honors. This brought a transfer to Air Force Headquarters in Washington, D.C., where he served as Deputy Chief of Staff for Operations.

Washington was pleasant in the postwar period. General Davis and his wife Sadie maintained a beautiful apartment near Georgetown, a suburb of Washington, and they often entertained Ethel and Benjamin there. The Colonel and his lady spent a great deal of their leisure time on the golf courses around the Capital. Ethel had taken up the sport while Benjamin was in Europe. She managed to convince her husband that the exercise would help reduce the weight that his desk jobs had helped to accumulate, as well as build him up. The six-foot-two-inch Colonel was quite a sight as he trudged alongside his five-foot-three wife on the local fairways.

The first few years of the fifties found Colonel Davis moving to various schools for further training and study. In November, 1953, he joined the Fifty-first Fighter-Interceptor Wing of the Fifth Air Force as commander. The Fifty-first was stationed in Korea.

In February, 1954, the *United States News and World Report* stated: "Benjamin O. Davis, Jr., now is being looked over by a Pentagon selection board for promotion that will make him the first Negro general in the U.S. Air Force. Colonel Davis has already headed the fighter operations branch of the Air Force, moved from that job last (year) into the kind of post often held by a brigadier general—command of the 51st Fighter-Interceptor Wing in Korea." On October 27, 1954, Colonel Benjamin O. Davis, Jr., became a brigadier general when President Eisenhower sent his name to the Senate for confirmation.

A ceremony took place in the Pentagon like none that had ever been held there before. A black retired brigadier general pinned the stars on the shoulders of another black brigadier general. It was a father and son performance. Following the ceremony, General Davis, Jr., returned to his Korean post in the Far East.

In 1955, Davis was assigned to the Chinese Nationalist Island of Taiwan. His job was to maintain a strong air defense on the island. Ethel, who traveled with her husband, told something of their experiences in Hong Kong as they headed for Taiwan in a letter to a friend. She said in part: "To see sunshine, breathe clean, sweet, fresh air, see smiling animated faces, and brisk steps was invigorating on the one hand. To see thousands of jobless, hungry refugees, many of them living in cardboard houses with a board for a bed put together on the sidewalks in front of shops was depressing. . . ."

The years in the Far East came to an end in 1957, when the General was assigned to Ramstein, Germany. Here he was Chief of Staff of the Twelfth Air Force. This group was an important segment of NATO. Later in the same year, Davis took on the new duty of Deputy Chief of Staff for Operations in Wiesbaden, Germany.

Brigadier General Davis returned to Washington, D.C., in August, 1961, when he served as the Director of Manpower and Organization Operations USAF Headquarters. In 1964, he became a major general. In 1966, he was promoted to lieutenant general.

General Davis became a permanent member of the Air Staff Command in the Pentagon. His work was to research problems affecting manpower, for the regular and reserve units of the United States Air Force. It was inevitable that General Davis would some day leave the Air Force. When the Mayor of Cleveland asked him to accept the post of Commissioner of Public Safety, he resigned from the service to accept the offer. Now, as a civilian, he will continue to serve the public.

The black men who served under these two officers and gentlemen were proud to be Americans. They served in the uniform of their country, not only to free the world from dictators, but also for their own freedom. As Negroes who had the basic rights of all Americans, they had every reason to believe that those rights would be recognized. Their confidence was bolstered by the attitude and the accomplishments of this black father and son, both bearing the well-deserved and freely bestowed rank of General in the Armed Forces of the United States. However, there is still much to be accomplished before all of the one million Negroes who served in World War II will realize the full equality that they have as a right.

As long as men like the Davises devote their lives and their talents in the services of their country, and so long as, like them, other black men may assuredly reach for the stars, America is their land of opportunity.

It is officers like the Davises who have done much to break down prejudice within the Army Officers' Corps.

—*The New York Times,* June 21, 1945

Constance Baker Motley

[1921-   ]

FEDERAL DISTRICT JUDGE

> Level headed, lucid and sharp witted, and persistent as a
> questioner. Usually logical and simple in her summations.
>
> —*The New York Times,* February 6, 1964

Foley Square, in lower Manhattan, is the legal compound
that houses the court complex for the federal, state, and local
governments. It is to this section of New York City that the
Honorable Constance Baker Motley travels each day, to sit as
a federal district judge—the first and only black woman to
hold this important post. Constance Motley patiently and
faithfully waited, worked, and hoped for the day when she
would receive the word that President Johnson had sent her
name to the Senate for confirmation as a judge in a federal
court of the United States. She could think back with quiet
satisfaction on a life devoted to helping all humanity, regardless of race, creed, or color. This attractive, scholarly woman
greets you with a warm kindly manner. She answers questions quietly and frankly.

World War I was beginning to fade from people's minds
in 1921, but the postwar recession was playing havoc with
the American economy. It was into this atmosphere that
Constance Baker was born on September the fourteenth.
Rachel Huggins had married Willoughby Alva Baker some

eleven years before and they had settled down in New Haven, Connecticut.

It was warm for September when Will Baker left for his work as chef at Yale University's student club, Skull and Bones. He was tired even before he began because his wife Rachel was expecting her ninth child, and most of the household chores had fallen on his shoulders. Those of the children who could were giving some help, but the bulk of the effort had been his. Will Baker had only been on the job for a few minutes when his eldest child came to tell him he had another daughter.

Will and Rachel called their ninth child Constance. There were three more children after her, so this little girl was never lonely—or idle.

Constance Baker lived in a home filled with love and contentment. Her brothers and sisters all helped one another. The older children washed and dressed their younger kin. The older girls were also expected to help their mother with the housecleaning, cooking, and dishes. Like most men who work as chefs, the father of the family would not have dreamed of cooking at home! He left that task to his womenfolk. The boys had paper routes, or performed odd jobs around the neighborhood to help supplement their dad's salary.

When Constance was ready for school, she accompanied her older brothers and sisters to the local public schools of New Haven. From the start, she took a great interest in her studies. She was either first or second in her class from the beginning. However, she also had time to enjoy play. Exposed as she was to many brothers, it was not unusual for them to use her to fill out their need for a linesman in football, a guard in basketball, or a left fielder in baseball. Her main interest was in basketball, and while in high school she was on the girls' team.

At New Haven High School this keen young student

showed a marked ability in debate. One of the few girls to make the debating team, she was always overwhelming in answering her opponents' arguments. She was considered by the coach—and her fellow debaters—to be the strongest member of the team.

It was when Constance Baker was in high school that she first felt racial discriminations. While she was a child, her large family and her father's position had shielded her from the traumatic experiences of race prejudice. However, when she was fifteen she was turned away from a public beach in New Haven because she was black.

This experience committed the young girl to an active interest in matters connected with civil rights. Constance haunted the school and public library for material on black history. There was not a great deal to be found. She joined the youth council of the New Haven branch of the National Association for the Advancement of Colored People (NAACP). Her experiences with this group roused in her the desire to become a lawyer. Her parents wanted all their children to go to college, but the salary of one man spread over a dozen children did not make this feasible.

Following her graduation from high school, Constance tried in vain to get more permanent employment than an occasional job as a domestic. However, this was the time of the great depression, when even experienced help went unemployed. It looked as if this ambitious girl could never get the money to continue her education.

In 1939 the world stood on the brink of a second world war. Although Constance had been out of high school for over a year and a half, she had not given up her favorite avocation—speaking. She addressed a group at the Dixwell Community House, a local black social center. In her talk she stressed the fact that blacks must be given greater responsibilities. In the audience was Clarence W. Blakeslee, a white businessman and philanthropist and a sponsor of the center.

Blakeslee was so impressed with this young eighteen-year-old girl's presentation that he offered to finance her higher education.

Constance Baker had studied much concerning her people's problems in the South. Since she had never visited this part of the country, she decided to attend Fisk University, a black institution in Nashville, Tennessee. She enjoyed the opportunity presented to study at a school a distance from home. She was also impressed with the quality of the education she received at Fisk. This young girl had ambitious plans that included entering a law school of standing. In fact, she had set her heart on Columbia University in New York City. She knew that, while she could probably enter Columbia from Fisk without too much difficulty, it would be better to be on the scene when the time came to start her law studies. So, after one and one half years at Fisk, she transferred to New York University.

Miss Baker was in a hurry to get to law school, so she stepped up her schedule to include summer classes. In June, 1943, she received her B.A. degree, and the following fall she entered Columbia University Law School. The years that were spent working toward her undergraduate degree were not at all easy. Tuition and books are only two of the expenses that a college student must face. Clothes, food, and transportation costs must also be met. Constance held a number of odd jobs while she struggled toward her degree. She realized that, if her hopes were to be achieved, she would have to work very hard.

Law school was a completely new experience for the young college graduate. There she found herself more on her own. She was expected to do most of the work by herself, while her professors merely guided. To Miss Baker there was only one true interest, and that was the law. Soon after entering Columbia, she joined the legal staff of the NAACP Legal and Educational Defense Fund as a clerk. The Defense Fund was headed by Thurgood Marshall, now a Justice of the Supreme Court,* who did much to direct and help the young law student.

Constance Baker could concentrate her attention on the law, but she could not forget she was a girl. Always interested in the nicer things in life, and always ready to enjoy a good show or party, she could not turn down Joel Motley when he asked her to go to a New York play with him. He had met Constance in the office of the NAACP, where he had gone to do some research. Joel Motley had come from Decatur, Illinois, to study law at New York University. Like Constance, he was more or less alone in the big city. Their common interest in the law, plus their love of life, soon made them inseparable. Days found them meeting each other for lunch and strolling in a nearby park more and more frequently. After classes, they dined together in small, reasonable restaurants in downtown New York. When Joel could spare the expense, they would go to the opera. When funds were low, they visited one of the many museums scattered around the city where admission was free or priced very low.

On August 18, 1946, Constance Baker and Joel Wilson Motley were married. It was during the same year that Columbia awarded her the LL.B. degree. This was a good year for the young legal couple. They established a study in their small apartment that Constance took great pride in making attractive. While she kept house, she prepared to take the bar examinations. A law degree does not give the holder the right to practice law. It is necessary to take an examination administered by the courts of the state where the candidate wishes to practice. This is called the bar examination. Constance, busy being a housewife, finally got around to taking the test in 1948, and passed it with flying colors. She was now a full-fledged attorney-at-law. Joel went

* See *Famous Justices of the Supreme Court,* by James J. Flynn, and page 66 in this book.

into a staid law firm, satisfied with the day-to-day chores of a young lawyer.

Constance Baker Motley was drawn, from the very beginning, to cases involved with civil rights. Her work with the NAACP, and its leading civil rights lawyer, Thurgood Marshall, had made her all the more determined to practice in this area. She was given her first opportunity to make a courtroom appearance when she joined with Charles Houston (a pioneer in the struggle for racial equality), in handling a famous case in Maryland.

The NAACP's postwar assault on segregation was turned on higher education with a special purpose. It was the belief of the black leaders that their chances were better here because the number of their people seeking higher education was small. They felt that the southerners would not be upset by this small number. Most of them felt that the inclusion of only a few blacks could not hurt. The blacks were attacking their problem with a subtle, practical approach. However, it was a sad commentary on a nation that had just fought a bloody war in the cause of world freedom, yet failed to protect the basic rights of many of its own people.

Mrs. Motley went into her first case with a strong conviction that victory was the only answer. The University of Maryland was chosen for this initial court struggle because it involved a graduate school. This was the type of case the NAACP believed would be easier to win. Charles Houston said, following the conclusion of the suit, "Constance Baker Motley worked tirelessly on this case and deserves much of the credit for its success." As a result, this suit made certain that the doors of the University of Maryland would be open to black students without limitation. This was one of the forerunners of many such cases that have slowly but surely changed admission policies in our state universities.

In 1949, Constance Motley was appointed an assistant counsel by the NAACP. From that time forward she played an active part in almost every major civil rights legal action that reached the courts. It was in her handling of the case of Autherine Lucy that Lawyer Motley first received national prominence. Miss Lucy, a young black woman, sought entry into the University of Alabama. The university refused and the NAACP took up the student's cause. Mrs. Motley prepared the briefs that were used in the federal courts to declare Miss Lucy's rights—and those of all minorities. The courts ruled that the University of Alabama must accept Miss Lucy. While she had success in establishing her rights in the federal courts, the aftermath of the decision did not prove too encouraging. Miss Lucy entered the university on February 3, 1956. She was suspended on February 7, after a riot by whites at the university. She was expelled on February 20. One can imagine the frustration, heartache, and discontent felt by Mrs. Motley when, after all her hard work and dedicated interest, the final result was negative. However, it only led her to be all the more determined that she would fight another day—and win conclusively.

Constance Baker Motley went on to fight and win seven major civil rights cases before the United States Supreme Court. Thurgood Marshall worked very closely with Mrs. Motley in many legal battles between 1946 and 1963. He declared, "A more dedicated, determined and qualified colleague I have never had the pleasure of working with than Constance Motley. She is a brilliant, capable attorney." Other victories included the admission of black students to the universities of Florida, Georgia, Mississippi and Clemson.

Mrs. Motley must also be given the credit for making it possible for Charlyne Hunter and Hamilton Holmes to enter the University of Georgia. She aided Thurgood Marshall in preparing the brilliant arguments that opened the doors of the University of Mississippi to James Meredith. It took her sixteen months of hard work at a cost of $24,000 for the NAACP before Meredith was admitted to the University of Mississippi. When it was all over, she commented on those long, hard months: "We worked sixteen months on the Meredith case before his name was seen in the papers." Meredith did not arrive on campus without an escort. The federal courts had spoken, yet, for his personal safety, this young man was constantly guarded by United States marshals. The governor of Mississippi declared that James Meredith would never set foot on the university campus. However, in June, 1963, this gallant and determined youth stood proudly by, with head held high, while his diploma was handed to him. Mrs. Motley considered that moment the most thrilling in her life. She is convinced that the victory in the Meredith case overcame one of the greatest obstacles to school segregation. It is true that since James Meredith entered the University of Mississippi, blacks have had no difficulty in being admitted to institutions of higher learning in all the states of the Union.

The spring of 1963 was a busy period for Constance Baker Motley. Her legal talents were being sought to defend her people's rights on the elementary school level. It meant traveling to Georgia, Florida, Alabama, New Jersey, Ohio—and back to New York in between—as more and more school cases demanded her time. However, it was in Alabama that the real test came. Birmingham was a city of tension when a group of black elementary students carried on a demonstration outside their school. As the result of their action, the school board expelled some 1,100 students. Mrs. Motley rushed to Birmingham to take to the courts the case of these children, who were being deprived of their rights to an education. The work at hand was to put these youngsters back in their classrooms before they lost too much school time. It was a difficult task, and Mrs. Motley explains it well when she states, "We had to bring to bear all our years of experience, all our legal resources, all our money." When it was over and the victory had been won—the children were returned to their classrooms—she felt that this was her moment of greatest professional satisfaction.

Mrs. Motley was back in Birmingham, Alabama, a few months after her success in the Meredith case. Her assignment was to prepare the legal moves that would make possible the enforcement of court orders calling for the desegregation of schools in four Alabama counties. The public schools in the state were undergoing a period of turmoil. Some schools were closed, others had state troopers at their doors to prevent black children from entering. The troopers were working directly under orders from Governor George C. Wallace of Alabama. The problem was finally settled by court enforcement of the integration orders, and by the federalizing of the state National Guard by President John F. Kennedy. The issue was no longer a local one; the power of the Federal Government had entered the scene. Governor Wallace was forced to see that his position could not be maintained and he must accede to integration. Immediately, some twenty black children entered formerly all-white schools in three localities. *The New York Times* explained this correctly as "A legal battle directed by Mrs. Constance Baker Motley . . . who was largely responsible for the Governor's (Wallace) predicament."

With the coming of the sit-in type of protest, many black people were arrested, and Mrs. Motley was called on frequently to defend them. She found the sit-in a most decisive type of reaction to a sense of injustice suffered by Negroes, and had great admiration for those who used it as a means of protest. Among the many that she was called upon to defend was Dr. Martin Luther King, Jr. These cases kept her constantly on the move throughout 1962 and 1963.

Constance was a capable lawyer, but she was also a woman. She recalls that in the midst of most of her important cases she would walk out of meetings to have her hair done, or to shop for a new dress. She laughs when she recalls that Thurgood Marshall was quite perturbed to discover that he had to wait almost one hour for a session to discuss trial strategy, as she was fitted for a new dress.

Always most concerned for her family, she spent much time on the telephone, while she was out of town, talking to her husband and son. She constantly advised them on such crucial matters as what they should be eating and how they should get plenty of rest, and admonished them about "messing up the house." Her interest in her home sent her on shopping sprees in the various cities where she was handling cases, for new dishes, paintings, etc.

During this same period, the term "freedom rider" was being heard of in all sections of the South. The "freedom riders" were those who rode integrated buses into southern states. On May 24, 1961, twenty-seven of this new group were arrested in Jackson, Mississippi. By June 12, the city officials announced that their jail was overcrowded. More than one hundred "freedom riders" had been arrested. Mrs. Motley moved into these cases with a strong determination to have the issue of segregated transportation facilities settled once and for all. The work was long and tedious, but the reward was fulfilling. On February 26, 1962, the Supreme Court of the United States ruled against segregated transportation in the case presented to them. This was not implemented until February 17, 1964, when the Court ruled for complete desegregation in transportation for the entire state of Mississippi. Mrs. Motley could indeed be proud of her work in this field of civil rights. It was a long road to success, and she was indeed tired. She had traveled, in 1963, over 70,000 air miles, handling civil rights cases all over the country.

Following the Alabama work, Constance Motley returned to her home in New York City. She was delighted to come back to her husband and their son Joel, Jr. By 1963, the boy was enrolled at the Dalton School in New York City. He was growing tall and strong, but his interest in baseball, football, tennis, and track did not overshadow his excellent work in the classroom. In spite of Mrs. Motley's many and varied trips away from home, she always managed to keep a close watch on her son's progress. Her husband and son have always been uppermost in her thoughts. Their home is her first love, and she is in her glory in the kitchen. Among her friends, she is known as an excellent cook. The apartment is furnished delightfully, for Constance is an avid interior decorator.

Constance Baker Motley was not able to spend much time with her family in 1964, however. The entire civil rights movement was on the march. In Americus, Georgia, a group of black demonstrators were arrested and denied bail. The charge was insurrection, and the penalty, if convicted, could be death. This was a most serious case, and when Mrs. Motley was asked to head up the defense she left immediately for Georgia. The preparation for the trial demanded that a federal court rule on the constitutionality of the insurrection and unlawful assembly charges. When the case was finally heard before the three-man federal court, Mrs. Motley won her point. The court voted two to one that the charges were unconstitutional.

As the years moved on, the black population began to make their rightful claims in the area of housing. Mrs. Motley moved into the fray, handling trials in Michigan, Missouri, Ohio, and New York.

The work of a courtroom lawyer is far different from that of the research attorney. The courtroom lawyer must be capable of presenting a case personally, in addition to being shrewd and sharp in questioning and cross-examination. The typical TV lawyer is rarely similar to the real-life attorney. Very few lawyers ever get the opportunity to plead a case before the Supreme Court of the United States. It is the attorney who has given special time and effort to constitutional questions that moves in this elite legal company.

Constance Baker Motley argued before the Supreme Court on six occasions, and won each time. One other case that she worked on was settled before it was heard by the highest Court.

Mrs. Motley presented before the Supreme Court cases covering the most important segments of the civil rights issue. One of the most significant was *Hamilton v. Alabama,* in which the basic issue was the right to be defended by counsel in capital suits. This right is guaranteed in the Bill of Rights of the Constitution of the United States. After Constance Motley had made her well-studied plea, the Court agreed that Alabama was wrong in depriving Hamilton of his right to an attorney. By this action, Hamilton was saved from a death sentence.

All the time that Mrs. Motley spent in putting her best efforts into the civil rights struggle did not stop her from being active in her own home state—New York. From 1958 to 1964 she was the public member of the New York State Advisory Council on Employment and Unemployment Insurance. She had been appointed by Governor Harriman, and gave much attention to the economic and social responsibility that the work demanded. One of her fellow workers on the council remembers her as "a member who always knew what the latest figures were and made sure we understood their importance."

In February, 1964, a special election was held to fill a vacant seat in the New York State Senate. The Twenty-first Senate District, on Manhattan's upper West Side, had a vacancy, and Constance Baker Motley was chosen by the Democratic leadership to be their standard bearer. Her Republican opponent was Thomas G. Weaver. When the returns were counted on Election Day, Constance Baker Motley found that she had won by a vote of 3,555 against 2,261 for her opponent. It was her first elected office. While in the Senate, this active, capable, and intense woman worked constantly on the problems of housing, education, and employment. These were the problems that were most important in her district. They are still with the district, but not to the same degree, thanks to the legislation—especially in the area of discrimination—sponsored and put through by Senator Motley during her stay at the state capitol.

A woman with the impressive background of a Constance Baker Motley was bound to move forward in the field of politics. When, in 1965, the Democratic leadership was looking for a replacement for their Borough President in Manhattan, they turned to Senator Motley. A Borough President in New York City is the chief officer of the county. She was the first woman ever to hold this position. Her work was basically administrative. She had now run the gamut from legislator to administrator. There was but one other area yet to be explored by her—that of the jurist. Like all lawyers, she yearned for the day when she would sit on the bench as a justice.

President Lyndon Johnson sent the name of Constance Baker Motley to the United States Senate just before Christmas, 1965. He asked the Senate to confirm her as a federal district judge for the Southern District of New York. What a marvelous Christmas present that was for the Motley family! Constance celebrated by preparing a super Christmas dinner for members of her immediate family. Her husband and Joel, Jr., home from Harvard, accompanied her to Riverside Church to give thanks. Shortly after the start of the New Year, the Senate acted favorably on the nomination, and Mrs. Motley became the first Negro woman ever to serve as a federal judge.

What does this extraordinary woman think of the civil rights movement of her people? She sees the movement and its goal as being summed up in one word—"dignity." This was one way in which Mrs. Motley expressed her thoughts.

ROY E. WILKINS
National Secretary, National Association for the Advancement of Colored People

CREDITS TO THE ORGANIZATIONS THROUGH WHOSE COURTESY THESE PHOTOGRAPHS
APPEAR HERE ARE LISTED ON THE COPYRIGHT PAGE.

GENERAL
BENJAMIN OLIVER DAVIS,
JUNIOR
Military Leader

GENERAL
BENJAMIN OLIVER DAVIS,
SENIOR
Military Leader

JUSTICE
CONSTANCE BAKER MOTLEY
Federal Judge

JUSTICE THURGOOD MARSHALL
Justice of the Supreme Court

DR. RALPH JOHNSON BUNCHE
Statesman

AUGUSTA BAKER
Librarian

PERCY LAVON JULIAN
Scientist

REVEREND MARTIN LUTHER KING, JR.
Clergyman

JOHN HOPE FRANKLIN
Educator and Historian of the Black Race

JAMES HOWARD MEREDITH ACCEPTS HIS B.A. DEGREE IN POLITICAL SCIENCE
FROM CHANCELLOR J. D. WILLIAMS OF THE UNIVERSITY OF MISSISSIPPI
Civil Rights Leader

LOUIS "SATCHMO" ARMSTRONG
Musician and "Ambassador of Good Will"

ROBERT TEAGUE
News Correspondent and Broadcaster

MARY MCLEOD BETHUNE
Educator

JOHN B. KING
Educator

EDWARD W. BROOKE
United States Senator

SHIRLEY ANITA CHISHOLM
Congresswoman

MEDGAR WILEY EVERS
Civil Rights Leader

ASA PHILIP RANDOLPH
Labor Leader

MARIAN ANDERSON
Concert Singer

ASA T. SPAULDING
Businessman

JOHN (JACKIE) ROOSEVELT ROBINSON
Athlete, Businessman, and Civic Worker

"You can have twenty-seven degrees from twenty-seven different universities, but if your skin is different, you're still forced to use the door marked colored. We want an end to that—and every thing like it." Writing in *Ebony* magazine some years ago, she declared: "The year 1963 is, in fact, the year in which the Negroes secured their freedom from all state-imposed racial segregation. There is now no question but that the courts will strike down any racial segregation or discrimination which the states may impose." She was indeed completely correct.

A woman of many interests and enthusiasms, Constance Baker Motley has received over twenty-five honorary degrees. She holds membership in the Association of the Bar of the City of New York, the Advisory Council of Riverside Church, the International Federation of Women Lawyers, and many other worthwhile groups and national associations. And she does not just lend her name to these groups; she is an active participant.

Since 1961, the Motleys have lived in a modern apartment house on the West Side of New York City. Each Sunday, weather permitting, she can be seen riding her bicycle in Riverside Park. By her side is her husband and, when possible, her son. In the quiet of the evening, she sits with an open briefcase full of legal work beside her, in her lovely living room, listening to classical music from her large collection of records.

Weekday mornings, she leaves her home to travel to Foley Square, usually by subway, below the streets of Manhattan. In the sedate Federal Building she patiently and impartially and skillfully guides the lawyers for both plaintiff and defendant in cases involving civil and criminal law. Her years on the other side of the bench have made her one of the most just, fair and thoughtful members of the judiciary.

Constance Baker Motley is a young woman who has seen much of life. Her dedication to the uplifting of her people has made her indeed their savior. She has served the community well. As a federal judge, she has the opportunity to devote her God-given talents to a continued service for the cause to which she has dedicated her life.

> A tall, striking woman with piercing dark brown eyes. She speaks with a low and lilting—but persuasive—voice.

—*The New York Times*, September 11, 1963

Percy Lavon Julian

[1899-   ]

SCIENTIST

> An inspiring teacher from the beginning of his career—
> even after leaving the classroom he has continued to
> guide the thoughts of his fellow scientists and to lead
> young men in the ways of true scholarship . . .
>
> —Part of Citation of Honorary Degree to Percy Lavon
> Julian, Doctor of Science, Northwestern University

To be a first child in a family of six does not always make
for an easy life. Percy Lavon Julian grew up in that position
and learned to make the best of it.

The Julian family lived in Alabama when Grandpa was a
slave. After James Julian was freed, at the end of the Civil
War, he took his family to Montgomery, where they are still
remembered.

One of James's children was named Percy. He was fortunate in having the opportunity to be educated in an
Episcopal Mission School in Montgomery. The education
offered was sufficient to enable a bright child to learn how to
read, write, and do some elementary arithmetic. Young Julian
was different from most black children in America during
this period when very few had the chance to get any type of
book learning.

Percy Julian was hard-working as a young man. One of his
first positions, when he was sixteen, was that of a rural school

teacher in Alabama. He was hired by a group of Negroes, aided by a Baptist Mission, to teach their young. He had a leaky, cold, one-room shack in which to impart his knowledge.

The pupils, some of them as old as their teacher, sat on hard wooden boards, and, during the winter months, shivered in their thin clothes. Julian was "paid in kind." Parents would bring him potatoes, cotton, etc., which he exchanged in payment for his food and board. When he had taught a student all he knew, that youngster was considered finished with formal education.

It was at a gathering of teachers that worked for the various missions that Percy Julian met Margaret Walker, who had gone much further with a formal education than he had. She was able to quote poetry and to recite long sections of Shakespeare's plays. She fascinated young Julian.

After their first meeting, Percy had to wait six months before he again saw Margaret. This time he made sure that she promised to write to him when she arrived back home. She lived and taught in a town about twenty-five miles from Montgomery. Travel being what it was in those days, it could have been twenty-five hundred miles!

A correspondence was begun that finally ended in marriage. Margaret saw in Percy the type of man she wanted for a life partner. He was sincere, dynamic, and eager. She knew that, if they had children, Percy would see that they advanced in life. The two were married at the Episcopal Mission School, where Percy had studied, on February 2, 1898.

Margaret gave birth to her first child on April 11, 1899. He was named for his father, Percy Lavon Julian. Lavon was his grandmother's maiden name. The father was not at home the day his first child was born. He had given up teaching for the same reason that thousands of teachers are leaving the profession today—not enough money. In 1899, Percy Julian was working as a railroad mail clerk. He was traveling

on a train headed for Virginia at the time of the birth of
his son, so he was not aware that he was a father until almost
a week later.

The Julian children came along rather regularly after
that. When they numbered six, their father took a position
as a letter carrier so he could be home more often. He believed that it was the father's job to help the mother as much
as possible. Although he worked long hours in order that
his family might live comfortably, he always found time to
be with his children. He stimulated them by giving them
regular assignments to advance their knowledge and understanding. They would have to read a book and report on it
to the family. If one asked a question which the others could
not answer, they would all have to do research on the topic
and report their findings. It was a most productive way of
doing things. The children learned how to do research, write,
and speak, all in one operation.

Percy Julian, Senior, taught his children a fundamental
philosophy that benefited them throughout their entire lives.
He emphasized, "Never pretend to be something you aren't.
Make yourself something to be proud of, and then you don't
have to pretend." This standard of conduct was a help to
Percy, Junior, as he moved up the ladder of success.

Percy Lavon Julian would have been something less than
capable if, after growing up in his father's house, he had not
become a successful man. His childhood was happy and con-
structive. There is little or no evidence that his color im-
peded him in any unusual way. He did face the same problems that confronted all black students who were forced to
study in segregated schools. He received an inferior education.

Young Julian discovered early that, while it was possible
to sneak away for a swim occasionally or for some fishing, as
the oldest child, he had many responsibilities at home. It was

only when he had finished looking after his younger sisters and brothers that he could play with his friends.

The elementary school that accepted Percy as a pupil was anything but an academic oasis! The one thing that helped him was the fact that he had already learned to read and write in his own home. His teacher was the product of a mission school and barely knew more than his best student.

Upon graduation from the elementary grades, Percy was not able to continue his formal education at a high school, because there was no high school, in the sense that we use that expression now, available to the young black boy or girl who lived in Alabama in those days. There was only a state-supported teacher-training school that accepted Negro students and served as a sort of high school. Percy Julian attended classes there.

Obviously, what the state supported as a teacher-training school could not have provided much better than a seventh grade education today. The subjects were elementary and the quality of education was poor. The teachers, who had never been given the opportunity to get a first-rate education themselves, could only impart the limited knowledge they had acquired.

When Percy finished at the state teachers' school he wanted to go on to college. Somewhere along the education highway he had encountered the mysteries of chemistry. The story is told that, while walking past a white school in Montgomery one day, he saw some boys working in the chemistry laboratory. He climbed the fence to get a better look at what they were doing. He was so engrossed in what he saw he did not feel a policeman tugging at his coat to remove him because he was trespassing.

On his way home from that experience he decided, "I am going to be a chemist." He ran into the house, and told the story to his mother, who agreed that if he wanted to be a chemist, he had her permission. Whether this tale is true or not, its existence points up the early desire of Percy Julian for a career in science.

Percy's father was alert to the academic needs of his son. If he was to major in science, he would have to attend an accredited college. Only in a first-class institution were to be found the faculty and equipment that could develop a well-trained scientific scholar. It was for this reason that young Percy matriculated at DePauw University, in Greencastle, Indiana. The year 1916 was a trying one for the United States. The nation was facing a presidential election as well as the possibility of participation in World War I, which had been raging since 1914. That year was certainly trying for Percy Lavon Julian.

The trip to Indiana was the first venture out of the South for Percy. He was seventeen years old—and wide-eyed—as his train moved northward into a problematical world. His goal was just one thing—he wanted to major in chemistry.

His first academic experience at DePauw was his meeting with the Dean, Dr. William Blanchard. When Dr. Blanchard heard that Percy wanted to major in chemistry, he worked to change the boy's mind. His ambition was to use his knowledge of chemistry to become a researcher in the field. The Dean hoped to have the young student seek another field, for he firmly believed that research chemistry openings for a Negro were practically nonexistent. Percy Julian was not to be dissuaded, even though he came to DePauw ill-prepared for college.

The one obvious handicap that appears repeatedly in most of the biographical data in this book stems from the fact that when Negroes sought entrance into white colleges, they were not academically prepared. They might have come from black high schools, rated at the top of the class, but, by and large, their education was inferior to that received by white students. Percy was classified as a sub-freshman during his first two years at college. He was forced to take a number of courses he never had the chance to study in high school. Those first two years were hectic, since Julian was obliged to assume a double schedule of courses. He was following a full load of high-school subjects and his regular college work as well.

If Percy Julian could have concentrated only on his school work, that would have been a monumental task in itself. But it was also necessary for him to earn enough money to pay his living expenses. During this period he tended furnaces, waited on tables, and played the piano in a little jazz band.

There have been many students who have carried heavy course loads, worked after class, and majored in a difficult area, but there are few of these who have finished in the top ten per cent of the class, as Julian did. He performed so well that he was chosen as the valedictorian of his class on graduation.

With the fine record that Percy Julian made at DePauw, he should have received a graduate scholarship in chemistry. However, his professors went out of their way to make sure he would not receive one. It was not that they did not have great respect for his ability, but they feared that if he went on, he would be disappointed. Realizing that since he was black, his chances for success were practically nil, they honestly believed they were doing him a favor.

Percy Julian was a disappointed young man. He had received an offer to teach chemistry at Fisk University. He took it unhappily. It is difficult to dampen the enthusiasm of a young college graduate though, and Julian was no exception. He firmly believed that if he waited and planned, his day would come.

His work at Fisk was most rewarding. His students were interested and awakened a new determination. He wrote a new set of lecture notes because of the ability of his students. When he sent these notes to Dean Blanchard, the latter wrote in response: "Your lectures are so clear that I am going to tear up many of my own and use yours instead."

While checking a chemistry magazine one day, after he had been at Fisk for two years, Percy Julian read about a graduate fellowship in chemistry that was being offered at Harvard University. He applied—although he was convinced that he never would receive it. To his surprise, Harvard granted him the fellowship.

The trip to Cambridge was like swinging on a star! Everything that Percy had ever dreamed of accomplishing was coming true. Harvard had one of the best-equipped chemistry laboratories in the United States. Here he was to study under the leading research chemists. For the entire academic year of 1922–1923 Percy Julian worked toward his master's degree. When the year ended, he had completed all of his courses with a straight A record.

The Harvard master's degree did not open the door to a career as a research chemist, however. Percy had to go back to teaching. This time he took a position at West Virginia State College. It was a great comedown from Harvard. The laboratory had very little equipment, and Julian was the only chemistry teacher. In spite of the inadequacy of his working tools, the president of the college told Percy that he must go on with his research.

Percy Julian resolutely began the job of gathering all types of chemical apparatus. He wrote to the leading chemical companies requesting, without cost, any materials and apparatus they could spare. Eventually, he began to repeat the delicate experiments of the famous Viennese chemist, Ernst Spath.

In 1925, Percy Julian received an offer from Howard University to become chairman of their chemistry department. This was a type of offer he could not afford to turn down. Howard, the most important of the Negro universities, had the funds to equip a fine laboratory. After Percy Julian arrived at Howard, he planned and built a million-dollar laboratory.

For more years than he could remember, Percy Julian had been interested in the way carbon atoms group themselves to make up many of the substances of which all living things are made. Even with the wealth of equipment at Howard, he could not satisfy his exploratory interest in this subject. He needed a fellowship so he could study under the greatest living authority in the field, Dr. Ernst Spath.

Julian had long been saving his money for the opportunity to meet Spath, who lectured at the University of Vienna. He left New York on the North German Lloyd liner the S.S. *Bremen* in July, 1929. The trip was uneventful for the young man, who cared only about getting started on his life's ambition.

From the very beginning, Spath and Julian became fast friends. Dr. Spath said later, "Percy Julian knew as much as I did about my experiments when he came to Vienna." In 1931, the University of Vienna awarded Julian a doctor's degree in organic chemistry.

Dr. Percy Julian returned to the United States to again assume a teaching position at Howard University. However, his teaching load was made light so that he might begin a new scientific project. He really never got this project off the ground before he was invited by his old mentor, Dr. Blanchard, to return to DePauw to work in his chemistry research department. The Dean went out personally to raise the money needed to aid Dr. Julian's project.

Percy Julian had been engaged in attempting to make a drug (physostigmine) that could be used in the treatment of an eye disease. It was possible that the drug could also be used for correcting intestinal troubles. The exact chemical structure of the drug was known by scientists, but, as yet, no scientist had been able to produce it in a laboratory.

Often, when a scientist knows the chemical structure of a

substance found in nature, he is able to gather together its elements and thereby produce the same substance. When a product is produced in this manner, it is artificial. The process used by the scientist in producing it is called synthesis, and the product is said to be synthetic. This is what scientists did during World War II when they produced synthetic rubber.

Scientists may synthesize substances for various reasons. One good reason could be because the natural substance is rare. When this is the reason, the work is very costly. However, if the scientist can make the desired product synthetically, it readily becomes plentiful, and therefore can be sold at a lower price.

Dr. Julian soon discovered that he was not the only scientist attempting to synthesize physostigmine. At Oxford University in England, Sir Robert Robinson, a world-renowned chemist, had been working on this project for years. When Robinson published his findings as to what he believed the structure of the drug was, he was challenged by Dr. Julian. The latter was sure that Sir Robinson was incorrect and asserted that he was going to prove his point. Friends warned Percy Julian that to question a man of Robinson's reputation could wreck his own career, but he was determined to go ahead, nevertheless.

This proved to be one of the most important decisions of Dr. Julian's life. His final work on the drug proved without question that he was correct in his contention that Robinson's findings were in error. He received letters, telegrams, and cables from the top-name chemists all over the world, praising his work. Dr. Percy Julian knew that at last he was what he had always hoped to be—a leading research chemist.

When Dr. Julian returned to DePauw, he had come back to work in the chemistry research department. He was not to be involved in the teaching area of the college in any way. However, when the experiment with physostigmine had been completed so successfully, Dr. Blanchard offered Percy Julian the chairmanship of DePauw's chemistry department. Dr. Julian would have liked the appointment because he had discovered that he missed his work in the classroom. However, many of Blanchard's colleagues did not believe that the college was ready to install a black man in such an important post. Dr. Julian was disappointed, not only with his fellow scientists at DePauw, but over the fact that his color should have been *mentioned*. He was ready for any offer that would get him away from that academic community.

Fortunately, before long, he received a telephone call from William J. O'Brien, vice-president of the Glidden Company, which is one of the best-known chemical research corporations in the United States. This massive organization operates thirty-four plants. It is involved with such diverse products as food, paint, and metals. Mr. O'Brien explained to Dr. Julian that his company was most anxious to employ a research chemist who would devote his time exclusively to examining the soybean for all its potential uses.

The Glidden interest in the soybean was particularly directed toward its possibilities for improving the paint industry. In the soybean there is casein. Japanese chemists had taken this milk-like substance from the soybean. However, in the United States this process was unknown, so casein was very expensive.

Casein has many other uses besides improving paint. One is in perfecting the surface of paper. If the paper used in this book did not have casein in it, the printing ink would have been absorbed and the pages would appear smudged. You will note that, if you take your pen and write on a newspaper, the ink spreads. This kind of paper does not contain casein. Another use for this substance is in waterproofing paper cartons.

Percy Julian grasped the opportunity to work for Glidden. It got him away from the hurtful academic atmosphere and, at the same time, increased his yearly income by almost one hundred per cent.

It was the hope of the Glidden people that he could devise a way to develop a synthesized casein that could be produced more cheaply for mixing with paints. When applied, this would make a surface more watertight.

Dr. Julian was not able to synthesize casein. To date no one has been able to accomplish this feat. However, Percy Julian was able to take the soybean and remove from it the protein, which is similar to casein. They built a separate plant for the purpose of carrying out that process. With this chemical breakthrough, Glidden now had an inexpensive substitute for casein.

In chemistry, as in science generally, a breakthrough that brings one find usually gives way for other discoveries. With the removal of the protein from the soybean, another product emerged—soybean oil. Dr. Julian worked on this oil and was able to take from it, at very little cost, large quantities of white crystals called sterols.

Arthritis is a most painful disease. It affects the joints of the body so that, eventually, people suffering from it may become completely crippled. For many years the medical profession could offer nothing as a relief. It was then discovered that a hormone called cortisone was helpful. Cortisone was not available in large quantities and was, therefore, very expensive. From the soybean sterols, Dr. Julian was able to produce a substance called Compound S. This made possible the manufacture of large quantities of cortisone at a very low cost.

Probably the most important derivative from Percy Julian's work on the soybean protein was what the Navy called "bean soup." One of the most dreaded calls aboard a ship at sea is "fire." In most instances, the fire originates in the paint locker or in the fuel bin. Water is not a sufficient deterrent for this type of fire. What is needed is something that will cut off the oxygen supply to the flames. Dr. Julian was able to work with the soybean protein in such a way that it provided the base for a thick foam. When this foam is sprayed on an oil or gasoline fire it cuts off the oxygen and douses the flames almost immediately. You have probably seen this discovery in action on TV. When a plane that is in trouble is about to make an emergency landing, the runway is sprayed with the foam. It cuts the possibility of fire when the aircraft touches down. You may also have seen it used to extinguish a fire in a truck carrying highly explosive propane gas after an accident.

Dr. Julian proved to be a true "find" for Glidden. This company had been doing well enough before he came with them; but by 1940, he had been responsible for the building of a protein plant costing nearly one million dollars, and the firm had more than quadrupled its sales of soybean protein.

In 1953, Dr. Julian decided to leave the Glidden Company. By a strange quirk, it was the same sterols that had tied him so closely to Glidden that pulled him away from the organization. An American chemist, Dr. Russell Marker, had discovered that it was possible to obtain the sterols for Compound S from a Mexican plant. Not only could you get the sterols from the plant but they could be extracted in greater quantities than from soybeans.

This was a challenge for Percy Julian. He decided to open his own laboratories. In 1954, the Julian Laboratories, Inc., were established in Franklin Park, Illinois. The following year, he founded Laboratorios Julian de Mexico, in Mexico City. These two plants manufactured not only cortisone but also many other types of drugs. In 1961, Dr. Julian merged his two companies with the E.I. Lilly Corporation, one of the largest drug manufacturing concerns in the United States.

The work of this scientific scholar, who has published more than one hundred scientific articles in addition to his valuable discoveries, seems to have placed his color firmly in the background—with that one unhappy exception at De-Pauw. His is one of the unique biographies in this book, in that it was not necessary to indicate his color as a threatening deterrent to his eventual success once he had overcome the deficiencies of his early segregated schooling.

Percy Julian is a prime example of the fact that a black man is not inferior mentally to a white one. As a research chemist this scientific humanitarian has proved himself equal, and in many instances superior, to any other man in his field.

> I was taught by my parents to take the little that came my way and make the most of it.
>
> —Dr. Percy Julian

Thurgood Marshall

[1908-   ]

SUPREME COURT JUSTICE

> A man can make what he wants of himself if he truly
> believes that he must be ready for hard work and many
> heartbreaks along the way.
>
> —Thurgood Marshall,
> *The New York Times,* January 3, 1967

The year when the Negroes of America began to feel intensively that they must do something to attain that status for
which a civil war had been fought was 1908. In the very city
where Abraham Lincoln lived before he went to Washington
to become President of the United States and an active advocate of equal rights for all, Negroes found themselves the
victims of anti-black riots. Whites ran wild in Springfield,
Illinois, and, before the conflict was over, one black man lay
dead and seventy others were injured. The Negroes could
hardly help feeling that all hope for their race was on the
wane.

In Baltimore, Maryland, on July 2nd of that same year,
1908, Norma Marshall gave birth to a son who was named
Thoroughgood, after his grandfather. As the boy began to
grow up, his name was shortened to Thurgood. This boy,
born in 1908, when his people believed all was lost, devoted
his life to making their discouraged dreams come true.

The roots of the Marshall family went far back in the

history of the United States. The story is told that Thurgood's great-great-grandfather was brought from the Congo as a slave by a Maryland planter. After being in the New World for some time, he was given his freedom. All of this happened before the North-South conflict.

Thurgood's grandfather on his father's side was a merchant sailor. This strong, rugged, old man of the sea had two first names—Thornygood and Thoroughgood. He used them both because he was not sure which was correct. It was also a help in collecting pensions, for he could collect under both names!

The father of Thurgood's mother was also a man of the sea. He was known as Isaiah (Olive Branch) Williams. His interests were directed toward the opera and the reading of William Shakespeare. When he tired of the sea, he put his savings into a small grocery store in Baltimore. For years he conducted a successful business, and lived with pride among his white customers and neighbors.

William Canfield Marshall, the son of "Thornygood," was a dining-car waiter on the Baltimore and Ohio Railroad. He had the same proud bearing that characterized his father before him. After many years with the railroad, William became a steward at the exclusive Gibson Island Club on Chesapeake Bay. This rightfully proud father told his two sons, Thurgood and Aubrey, "If anyone calls you nigger, you not only got my permission to fight him—you got my orders to fight him." Not long after that, Thurgood was given the opportunity to obey his dad when he was pushed and called names for attempting to enter a Baltimore trolley car before a white man. He was not at fault in this incident, yet he was arrested as a result of the scuffle that followed.

It was Thurgood's mother who gave his intellectual development a forward thrust. Norma Marshall had been a schoolteacher before her marriage. She constantly pressed him to read and to work on his lessons. She was also a strict disciplinarian. Justice Marshall reminisces about her: "Mama taught me a lot. I remember how she used to say, 'Boy, you may be tall, but if you get mean, I can always reach you with a chair.' "

By the time Thurgood was ready for school, he was robust, strong, and tall for his age. In elementary school he got himself into numerous small classroom troubles. For punishment, the teacher would send him to the basement to learn a section of the United States Constitution. By the time he graduated, he knew the entire document by heart!

In 1921, the tall, eager, young Thurgood Marshall entered Douglas High School. For four years he worked and played like thousands of other high-school students in the United States. His record at Douglas was good, but it was not outstanding. His graduation in June, 1925, guaranteed only one thing—that in September he would enter Lincoln University, near Chester, Pennsylvania, as a freshman.

Thurgood's time at Lincoln was filled with the excitement of growing up. Lincoln was an all-black school with an all-white faculty. When he was a sophomore, Thurgood was expelled because he was too rough in hazing the freshmen. Later, the faculty committee that had expelled him revised their decision, and he returned to the college. One writer has summarized this period of Marshall's life with the comment: ". . . a harum-scarum youth, the loudest individual in the dormitory and apparently the least likely to succeed." Cab Calloway, the orchestra leader, who was at Lincoln with Thurgood, recently said, "He was a noisy scholar who had every student's respect."

With all his troubles, lessons, and card games, Thurgood Marshall always found time to go to church. It was while he was attending Cherry Street Memorial Church in Philadelphia that he met Miss Buster Burey. Their friendship developed into love, but they agreed to wait for five years after Thurgood's graduation before they would marry. This time period was later cut to three years—and then to one year.

The young couple were married just before he started the last semester of his senior year. So goes the vitality and fearlessness of youth.

Graduation brought with it the worry of a career plus the support of a wife, for Thurgood. At one time he had considered dentistry as his vocation. However, he had changed his mind. The move away from dentistry had not drawn him toward any other profession, though. Hard work was not his worry. He had always found it easy to undertake a task, no matter how difficult. It was his home environment that finally helped him to make up his mind. From the time that he and his brother could talk, his father had constantly urged them to discuss all issues. On returning from college, he and Aubrey found themselves sparring verbally with William Marshall. It was one long period of argumentation in which the boys learned to think straight. Thurgood Marshall explains his decision about his future career in this way, "My father had turned me into a lawyer without ever telling me what he wanted me to be."

It was almost inevitable that once the law was established as Thurgood's definite choice, he would think of the University of Maryland. His application there was rejected because of his color. That turndown caused this young, eager American to determine to do everything to "straighten out all this business about civil rights." He applied for entry at Howard University, a Washington institution that is predominantly black. He was accepted and immediately settled down to "what he wanted to do for as long as he lived."

He soon found that the easy days at Lincoln were gone forever. Law school is a hard, pressing, and constant intellectual challenge. Many times, college graduates "fail out" in law school because they realize too late its harsh demands. Marshall did not fall prey to this error. He explains his law school years in this way: "I heard law books were to dig in. So I dug, way deep. I got through simply by overwhelming the job. I was at it twenty hours a day, seven days a week."

The three years at Howard were busy ones. Thurgood would begin his day at 5 A.M. He was commuting from Baltimore to Washington. He attended classes in the morning, and then would go to the library to study, or else to work in order to help pay for his tuition. June, 1933, found Thurgood forty pounds lighter, but the recipient of his law degree. He finished at the top of his class.

Before Marshall entered Howard Law School, Charles Houston had become its dean. He was determined to make Howard a great institution of learning and at the same time to develop it as a "West Point of black leadership." It was to prepare its graduates to fight segregation in the courts. Too many cases, up until now, had been brought into the courts by Negro lawyers, "shabbily prepared and poorly argued," as Justice Brandeis has explained it.

Thurgood Marshall left Howard determined to follow a course directed toward Dean Houston's goal. Entering a Baltimore law firm in the fall of 1933, he set out to try civil rights cases fully prepared and properly orientated. In that first year he wore out an old Ford car, riding around Maryland, taking on the cases of poor Negroes. His clients were usually victims of dispossession, eviction, and the like. He assumed the responsibility for many cases, knowing full well that he would not receive a fee. His reputation spread throughout the state, so that he was soon known as the "little man's lawyer."

In 1935, Marshall was invited to join the legal staff of the National Association for the Advancement of Colored People. It was an exciting offer, because Dean Houston had resigned from Howard to assume the position of chief counsel for the NAACP. When Thurgood Marshall decided to accept the offer, little did he ever dream where the assignment would lead him and what he would be able to accomplish for the civil rights movement. Those early days with the NAACP were not filled with great prospects. It was going to be a long, hard road to follow unswervingly.

Marshall's first important victory came in 1936, in the case of *Pearson v. Murray.* Donald Murray, a Negro, had applied for enrollment in the University of Maryland Law School and was rejected. For Thurgood, this was a work that came close to his heart—he remembered his own rejection by the Maryland Law School. Marshall sought the help of Dean Houston in preparing his case. It was a well-briefed case. The proof of this was the decision of the Maryland Court of Appeals, which held that the state must afford equal educational opportunities in its institutions.

It has always been the sincere belief of Thurgood Marshall that it will be through the courts that the black man will achieve rightful equality. To this young constitutional lawyer, the Fourteenth Amendment was added to the Constitution to give the black man his full rights as an American citizen. He felt it was his duty as a lawyer to make the Supreme Court reflect the real America in civil rights cases covered by the "equal protection" clause of the Fourteenth Amendment.

Thurgood Marshall risked his life many times in the first few years of his tenure with the NAACP. He is not unwilling to admit that he was afraid during some of his experiences. After he was threatened in this way in relation to a case he was trying in Shreveport, Louisiana, he commented, "I wrapped my constitutional rights in cellophane, tucked them in my hip pocket and got out of sight. And, believe me, I caught the next train out of town." This was only a temporary setback, for, inevitably, he was around to fight again another day.

The power that kept Marshall going during this trying period was his infinite capacity for hard work. His tremendous sense of humor was a great asset, too, in helping him to keep his equilibrium. He traveled 50,000 miles a year, being away from his office most of the time. The hours he spent before the Supreme Court were filled with tension and pressure. When his court appearances were over, he became the happy, effervescent type that he had been back at Lincoln University.

All the efforts of Thurgood Marshall during his first seven years with the NAACP were not devoted to civil rights cases. Labor matters took a good percentage of his time. He won a suit against a union which used closed-shop contracts to discriminate against Negroes. He also moved into the question of discrimination in the Air Corps. His victory in this case eventually led to complete desegregation in the armed forces. It was Thurgood Marshall who fought the Democratic party of Texas until it opened its former all-white primaries to blacks.

Their interest in various areas of civil rights kept bringing the thinking Negroes back to the area of desegregation in education. Marshall and his colleagues in the NAACP decided to begin the campaign at the graduate level of education. The reason behind this was a sound one. There were fewer students involved here, so the opposition would be proportionately less. As usual, it proved to be a slow process. First, the leaders had to get someone who was willing to bring the suit, then they had to move it all the way through the lower courts until it reached the Supreme Court.

The plaintiff was found when a young man named Herman Swealt agreed to bring a suit against Texas segregation. The case was known as *Swealt v. Painter,* and in 1950 the Supreme Court ordered the plaintiff admitted to the University of Texas Law School. The decision stated that the all-black law school of Texas State University for Negroes was inferior to the all-white University of Texas Law School in such areas as community standing, tradition, and prestige. On the same day, in a case titled *McLaurin v. Oklahoma State Regents,* the Supreme Court called for the same treatment

of black students as was given to those of other races in the
University of Oklahoma Graduate School. G. W. McLaurin
was in the school, but he had been forced to attend segregated
classes.

The year 1951 was a busy one for Thurgood Marshall. He
spent many weeks in Korea, checking charges that men from
a black regiment were being discriminated against. In fact,
several had been court-martialed, and one of them had been
sentenced to death. Marshall worked on these cases and
sought evidence right up to the front lines. He was able to
get acquittals or reduced sentences for over half of the
convicted.

Arriving back in the United States, Marshall gave his
entire efforts to the school desegregation problem. Realizing
that the Supreme Court was moving they knew not where,
the southern leaders hurried to make their school systems
meet the requirements of *Plessy v. Ferguson*. Back in 1896,
the Supreme Court had declared in *Plessy v. Ferguson,* that
as long as the accommodations for whites and blacks were
equal, they could be separate. This was the theory that
Thurgood Marshall was fighting to overcome.

He felt that the sure way to kill *Plessy v. Ferguson* was
to show that desegregation in education was indeed unequal.
This could only be done by presenting a mountain of evidence from professionals. Marshall and his assistants gathered
their evidence from sociologists, psychologists, psychiatrists,
and anthropologists. Their general consensus was that the
equal but separate concept played havoc with the feelings of
members of the black race. The reports of these professionals
formed the basis for the cases eventually presented by Marshall to the Supreme Court.

These cases all arose out of separate attacks on *Plessy v.
Ferguson* in Kansas, South Carolina, Virginia, and Delaware.
The Supreme Court took these four school appeals and heard
the first argument during the October, 1962, session.

The lead-off case, which bore the name of the four suits, was known as *Brown v. Board of Education of Topeka*. Oliver Brown was the father of an eight-year-old girl who was not permitted to attend an all-white school five blocks from her home. Instead, she had to travel twenty-one blocks away, to an all-black school. Her parents were asking that this segregation be stopped. The United States District Court for Kansas refused on the "separate but equal" ruling contained in *Plessy v. Ferguson*. The other three state decisions were about the same. This left the door open for appeals to the Supreme Court.

Final arguments were heard in December, 1953. Before Thurgood Marshall walked into the Supreme Court chamber to present his case, hundreds of hours had been spent by him and by his associates in carefully gathering and sifting the facts. Lawyer Marshall realized that one small slip, the misplacing of the right word in a single instance, could wreck the case. He presented a masterful brief in which he concluded that the only reason why the South wanted to keep segregation was the "inherent determination that the people who were formerly in slavery, regardless of anything else, shall be kept as near that stage as possible."

The other side of the issue was presented by John W. Davis, an eighty-year-old constitutional lawyer who had unsuccessfully run for president in 1924. His only argument was that the school question was not a federal problem, since it was purely a state function.

It was five months before the Supreme Court spoke. On May 17, 1954, a Monday, the Court was preparing to hand down one of its last decisions of the year. Reporters were told it would be a quiet day. Then, Chief Justice Earl Warren dropped a news bomb when he announced the unanimous decision on school desegregation. He explained how the court had been persuaded by the professional testimony that the separation of the races "generates a feeling of inferiority that may affect their hearts and minds in a way unlikely ever to be undone."

These were happy times for Thurgood Marshall. He was now seeing the results of the months and months of careful, tedious planning paying off. Those lectures of Dean Houston that called for hard work and sound logic had won the day. The Supreme Court had given the southern states until October 1, 1954, to indicate how they were going to carry out the order. The NAACP was also to file its thoughts on the subject.

Between the time the order of the Court was filed and the pronouncement in the spring of 1955, tragedy struck the Marshall family. Thurgood had noticed that his wife Buster was gradually losing weight and was always complaining of being tired. The family physician informed him that his wife had terminal lung cancer. In order to spare him the shock of this sad news while he was preparing and presenting the school case, Buster would not permit the doctor to tell Thurgood until after the Supreme Court reached a decision. In the weeks that preceded her death in February, 1955, Marshall was in a state of shock. Afterwards, he remained in seclusion, refusing to leave his apartment in Harlem for weeks on end, and reliving the twenty-six years of happy married life he had shared with his wife.

Marshall's personal sorrow had added to it the realization that the southern states were in no hurry to carry out the Supreme Court's directions. This was brought home with a vengeance when Governor Orval Faubus, of Arkansas, refused to permit black students to enter all-white Center High School in Little Rock—this in spite of the Brown decision. It was only when President Eisenhower sent in Federal troops that the violence generated by segregationists was quelled.

Marshall was moved to action when the United States Court of Appeals, Eighth Circuit, issued an order to keep schools segregated for the time being. He appeared before Supreme Court Justice Charles E. Whittaker, demanding that the Court of Appeals order be revoked. He said it was about time that the Supreme Court be obeyed. Governor Faubus got the state legislature to pass a law authorizing the closing of the schools of Arkansas if the Supreme Court acted. While the nation marked time, President Eisenhower told a press conference that there should be "slower" movement toward integration in the schools. The NAACP members could not believe what they heard. Roy Wilkins, the executive secretary, could only consider the President's statement "incredible."

Following the Arkansas school decision, Marshall continued to work hard. It helped him to forget his sorrow at the loss of Buster. He continued to travel as much as 50,000 miles a year, and had his hand in as many as five or six hundred cases involving his race. Some thirty-two times he appeared to argue civil rights cases before the United States Supreme Court. In nine out of ten times, he came out the victor. He was the toast of the black community, where he was known as "Mr. Civil Rights." He was offered many lucrative private legal opportunities, but he preferred to stay with the NAACP.

The election of President John F. Kennedy made the offer of a federal judgeship to Thurgood Marshall almost a sure thing. This sort of an appointment had been suggested once before, in 1949, when the press declared that Thurgood Marshall's name was being considered for a federal judgeship. At that time, Marshall had refused to join a Democratic club in New York City, because it was suggested that this was necessary to get the appointment.

This same offer, now a firm one, was still looked upon with disdain by Marshall in 1961. In addition, he believed that if he went to the bench, he would be charged with deserting the civil rights cause. Eventually, however, he agreed to have his name presented to the Senate for confirmation. President Kennedy sent his name in on September 23, 1961, and the southerners on the Judiciary Committee announced they would not touch it until they returned from their recess, in January, 1962. To get around this deliberate delay, President Kennedy gave Marshall an interim appointment. This meant that while Congress was out of session, the President placed him on the bench. On October 24, 1961, hundreds of Thurgood Marshall's friends were present when he took the oath as a federal judge. Among those who watched with pride was Thurgood Marshall's second wife, Cecile Suyat Marshall. Cecile had been a secretary in the New York office of the NAACP. With her on this happy day were their two children, Thurgood, Jr., five, and John, three.

Congress returned in January, 1962, and the President sent to the Senate a strong endorsement of Thurgood Marshall as a federal judge, and the American Bar Association declared that he was "well qualified." In spite of all this, the Senate Judiciary Committee, led by Senator James O. Eastland, a Mississippi Democrat, did everything possible to stall the appointment. It was only after the New York Republican, Senator Kenneth B. Keating, declared, "A distinguished American jurist is being victimized," that in July, 1962, hearings on the nomination were scheduled.

Long and delaying tactics eventually forced the committee to report favorably on the appointment. When the Senate finally voted, in September 12, 1962, it was to seat Thurgood Marshall as a United States Court of Appeals Justice. It had taken almost one year to place this fighter for civil rights on the bench.

Four long years—and more than one hundred opinions—later, Thurgood Marshall was well established as a jurist. He found the bench much more restricting than his work with the NAACP. He missed the excitement of preparing and trying cases.

When President Lyndon B. Johnson telephoned Thurgood Marshall on July 7, 1965, and asked him to become Solicitor General of the United States, he accepted with alacrity and dispatch. In this position he was forced to take a cut of $4,500 in salary, but to compensate for this, he would be back before the Supreme Court, trying cases for the Government. He answered his friends who wondered why he left a lifetime job for one that could be lost with a change of administration: "The President asks you to go, you go." There was some negative southern reaction to the appointment, but not of the type that had been used to hold up his judicial appointment.

While he was Solicitor General, Thurgood Marshall performed for the Government as well as he had for the NAACP. His record shows that he won fourteen of the nineteen cases he presented to the Supreme Court. As the Government's chief appellate lawyer, when he appeared before the Court, he was listened to with attention by the justices.

It was on July 13, 1967, that President Johnson told a press conference that he intended to send the name of Thurgood Marshall to the Senate as the replacement for retiring Justice Tom C. Clark of the Supreme Court. President Johnson said of Marshall, "I believe he has already earned his place in history. But I think it will be greatly enhanced by his service on the Court . . . it is the right thing to do, the right time to do it, the right man, and the right place."

The story of prejudice was the same as before in the Senate. The southern bloc held five long hearings to decide whether Thurgood Marshall was fit to serve on the Court. On August 3, 1967, the Senate Judiciary Committee voted eleven to five to confirm the nomination. Four weeks later, the full Senate voted their approval sixty-nine to eleven. Upon receiving the news, Judge Marshall commented, "Let me take this opportunity to reaffirm my deep faith in this nation and its people, and to pledge that I shall ever be mindful of my obligation to the Constitution and to the goal of equal justice under law."

To fully understand and appreciate Thurgood Marshall's fight for civil rights, it must be remembered that it never included violence. Civil disobedience was never his way of accomplishing things. His deference for the law approached the intensity of a dedicated man. It made it impossible for him to join the civil rights demonstrators. He achieved the goal in his own fine way.

Immediately following his coming to the Supreme Court, Judge Marshall had little opportunity to participate in decision making. This was because, as Solicitor General, he had helped prepare many of the cases then being decided. It is always expected that a justice will disassociate himself from any case in which he has had a hand before it comes to the Court.

In late 1967, Thurgood Marshall traveled to Africa with Vice-President Hubert Humphrey. It was a far cry from the trip made in the opposite direction by his great-great-grandfather, the slave.

Thurgood Marshall has always been considered a moderate in the program to see black people guaranteed their civil rights. Although he votes with the liberal bloc in most instances, he sees the problems of his day being settled in a legal way: ". . . It is only by law suits and legislation that we'll ever teach reactionaries the meaning of the Fourteenth Amendment."

> If John Marshall, the United States Supreme Court's first Chief Justice, made the Court into a going concern, then one hundred and seventy-five years later, one Thurgood Marshall had a great hand in guiding the court nearer to where the Founding Fathers wanted it to go.
>
> —Russell L. Adams, *Great Negroes Past and Present*

John Hope Franklin

[1915-   ]

EDUCATOR AND HISTORIAN
OF THE BLACK RACE

> Not only does his Americanism compel the Negro to
> strive to improve his own status by demanding the rights
> that are his. It also gives him, as it gives to others com-
> mitted to the ideals set forth in the American dream, a
> burning desire to make the system work.

—John Hope Franklin, *Time* Magazine, January 11, 1963

Tulsa, Oklahoma, during World War I, was a small city that
had yet to feel the pressures that besiege a great metropolis.
The Negroes in Tulsa were in many ways treated like their
fellows in the Deep South. Oklahoma had for too long been
exposed to the immigration of southern whites into its con-
fines.

In 1913, Buck Colbert Franklin came to Tulsa with his
young bride. Mollie Lee Parker had met Buck Franklin
while they were both students at Howard University. Buck
decided he would stay on after graduation to study law. Mollie worked for the United States Government in the Capital
until Buck finished his law studies. They were married a few
days after her fiancé received his LL.B. degree.

Young Buck Franklin truly believed that success for a
young Negro lawyer was to be found in the Southwest. With
trouble brewing in Europe, the economy of the United States

would expand and the great developing Southwest would be bound to prosper.

Those first few years in Tulsa did not turn out well for the young Franklins. It took quite a bit of money for a young lawyer to go into private practice, and until he could raise it, he would have to find another kind of work. Law firms in Oklahoma were not about to hire Negro partners.

Mollie and Buck were forced to move into the black section of a small town named Rentiesville, a few miles from Tulsa. It was here that John Hope Franklin was born on January 2, 1915. The Franklins had three other children, two girls and a boy.

Buck was able to find work, and at the same time, put money in the bank in preparation for the day when he could open his own law office. He felt the sting of discrimination but faced up to it. John has explained his father's position on segregation with the comment, "He paid no attention to signs marked 'Negro' and 'White.' He went where he pleased, mingling with people like any other man."

With the United States in World War I after April, 1917, the Franklins felt some of the prosperity that touched the nation. Buck Franklin worked on an army installation in a clerical position, and found that the northern officers and men were more tolerant than the people of the Southwest, and were willing to accept him for what he was.

It was not until 1921 that Buck Franklin could afford to rent space over a candy store in Tulsa, to open his own law office. The small two rooms became his private office and reception room. The place was sparsely furnished with second-hand furniture and a rather beat-up typewriter. All of the law books that lined the walls had been purchased on the time-payment basis. When things became busy, Mollie came to type the briefs and other legal documents. The children would run up and down the stairs, playing and shouting as their parents worked.

Things appeared to be going well. There was some name-calling and heckling when Buck came down the street to his office, but he took it in stride. From time to time, he would find signs on his door reading "Nigger go home." There were notes pushed under the door that threatened violence, yet he paid them no heed.

Early one morning, about six months after he had moved into his office, Buck Franklin was called out of bed by the police. They told him that his office had been set afire and completely destroyed. The fire marshal described the origin as "suspicious." The young lawyer was more direct in his diagnosis. "It was set by race rioters."

One fire could not stop a man who believed that he was equal to all other men regardless of their race, color, or creed. A man who "scorned segregation as a mask of indignity" was bound to try again. His second attempt to establish a practice was more successful. He later became the first Negro in his state to sit on a United States district court bench. He did not sit as a judge of a United States court, but rather as a master in chancery. This is a designation sometimes given to an attorney who is to handle a specific case and also to judge it. Buck Franklin's first case involved a dispute between the congregation of a Negro church and their pastor. As the years went by, lawyer Franklin tried cases before the Oklahoma state supreme court, the Oklahoma criminal court of appeals, and the United States Supreme Court.

The Franklin children never felt the pangs of hunger nor the threat of being dispossessed. They did feel the stinging remarks of the white children in school, as well as the segregation pressures of the community. They realized early that, as Negroes, it would not be easy for them to make their mark, but they had the stamina and determination to fight that had been given to them by their sturdy parents.

John Hope Franklin entered the local public school at just about the time that his father opened his law office. His first years of formal education were not unlike those of any other young American boy. He played ball, swam in a local swimming hole, and managed to get into mischief. He was a good student but not an outstanding one. He listened as his history teachers told of the great exploits of the leaders of his country. Even then, he asked questions as to why the black heroes were never mentioned along with Washington, Lincoln, and Teddy Roosevelt.

In 1927, John entered the all-black Booker T. Washington High School in Tulsa. It was in high school that he began to find himself. He first showed an interest in extracurricular activities when he joined the debating team. At that time, the chief debate topics centered around such questions as should the United States join the World Court or not; should President Coolidge send marines to Nicaragua; and is prohibition proving successful? One classmate has declared that John Franklin demonstrated great oratorical prowess, no matter on which side of the debate he appeared. He probably spent more time in the library than any other student in the school, as he carefully did his research for the debates.

John Hope Franklin had loved to sing from the time he was a small boy. In high school he found enjoyment in this area by joining the glee club. The director summarized his performance this way: "John had a pleasant voice. When he came to us he was still a boy tenor, by the time he graduated he was a husky baritone."

As graduation time approached, in 1931, the big decision for John to make was not whether he should go to college, but to what college should he go. Because of his good academic record at Booker T. Washington, in addition to his fine work in extracurricular activities, he was awarded the Alpha Phi Alpha scholarship, plus a freshman scholarship to Fisk University. Fisk, located in Nashville, Tennessee, had the reputation of being one of the finest Negro universities in the country. John decided to accept the latter's offer, and in early

September, 1931, made the long journey from Tulsa to Nashville. It was an experience long remembered by the young student. The segregation of reservations on the train; the refusal to permit him to eat in the dining car, which necessitated his buying food in the station restaurants and eating in the black section of the waiting rooms; the back seat in the trolley car that took him to the Fisk campus—these indignities were hard to forget. It was certainly not the way an American boy should be required to travel in his own country. John Hope Franklin was determined to have the white man understand the black man's desire—and right—to advance. He arrived at Fisk convinced that if he worked hard to achieve this goal, he would succeed.

The four years at Fisk were a grand awakening for the boy from Tulsa. John's outgoing personality made him popular on campus from the first day. The Fisk debating team was his chief pleasure. Debating the same topics here that he had in high school permitted him to polish his earlier arguments and present them on the intercollegiate level. His naturally keen intellect, which developed further in college, particularly in the field of history, gave him an added advantage on the platform.

John's continued interest in singing brought him a membership in the Fisk glee club. Another member of the group was a pretty young girl from Goldsboro, North Carolina, named Aurelia Elizabeth Whittington. At first Aurelia could not stand the young baritone from Tulsa. John was a perfectionist in everything, even his music. He would attempt to suggest to Miss Whittington ways to improve her singing. However, it was not long before Aurelia and John were seen everywhere together on campus. On the warm spring evenings, they would join the other students on the steps of the Alpha Phi Alpha fraternity house to sing college songs and to listen to a string quartet. Life was happy and easy at Fisk.

John Franklin enjoyed these leisure hours with Aurelia,

but he also devoted himself seriously to work. He never believed that his education should be subsidized by his parents. There were his two sisters and a brother who had to be clothed and schooled. His scholarships paid most of his way at Fisk, but there were always things that were needed which were not covered by the grant. He waited on tables in the university dining hall for his meals. He was secretary to the librarian of the university for several semesters, as a result of his decision in high school to take typing during one of his free periods. These odd jobs made possible his trips back to Tulsa at vacation times, plus allowing him the money for his now frequent dates with Aurelia.

An excellent student in all fields, young Franklin was completely fascinated by history. When the time came for him to declare his major, it was inevitable what subject he would choose. He took every course that was available to him in this well-staffed department at Fisk. His strongest interest was in social and intellectual history, for he saw the hopeful trends and possibilities for his people in the America of tomorrow. Prior to his graduation in 1935, he was elected to Phi Beta Kappa, and when he graduated he received his B.A. degree, Magna Cum Laude. Phi Beta Kappa is the highest scholastic honor society in the academic field. To graduate Magna Cum Laude (with the greatest praise) meant that he had an overall average of A for all of his courses. There is only one step higher, and that is Summa Cum Laude (with the highest praise).

During his time at Fisk, John had grown very close to Theodore S. Currier, who was his mentor in history. Professor Currier was most insistent that Franklin go on to the Harvard Graduate School of Arts and Sciences for his M.A. in history. It was not easy for John to leave Aurelia. She planned to return home to Goldsboro, since marriage was not to be thought of until the completion of his schooling permitted him to take a job and earn a fair income to support a wife.

This was the time of the Great Depression, when youth had to curb its desires and honestly and gallantly face the facts of life.

John Hope Franklin was enrolled at Harvard for a master's degree in history. Cambridge, Massachusetts offered another new experience for him. The year spent as a graduate student was most exciting. He discovered that here in New England were to be found some of the most important documents connected with the founding of America. His courses were taught by the leading men in their field. In the history of the United States John was fortunate in having as an instructor Professor Samuel E. Morison, who, more than any other teacher, awakened the spirit of the true historian in John Franklin. Samuel Morison, the man who later wrote the history of the U.S. Navy's part in World War II, taught John to love research and gave him the desire to write.

In 1936, John Franklin left Harvard with his M.A. degree. Professor Currier invited him to join the history department at Fisk and he accepted immediately. Teaching was what he had most wanted to do ever since he had entered Fisk. Now he was to serve as a substitute at his own alma mater. His work at Fisk was minimal and probably very ordinary. A new teacher may have a great deal of enthusiasm, but he does not always have the finesse necessary to make his work outstanding.

A college teacher is never considered to have reached his majority until he has been awarded the doctor of philosophy degree. John Hope Franklin decided that one year of teaching at Fisk must be sufficient before he returned to Harvard to finish his educational studies. Probably his decision was aided by the fact that he had been awarded the Edward Austin Fellowship for the year 1937–38. Moreover, he was able to supplement the Austin Fellowship with a Julius Rosenwald Fellowship for the years 1937–39. Aurelia Whittington agreed that John must try for this important degree in his career as a teacher.

At the close of the 1939 spring semester at Harvard, John had completed all his course work for the Ph.D. degree. All that remained before the degree could be conferred was the passing of the comprehensive examinations and the writing of the thesis. These last two requirements are the real stumbling blocks for most candidates for the doctor of philosophy degree. The comprehensive examinations cover the entire area of study that the student has majored in, plus the areas of his minor. They are usually written, and take several weeks to administer. The thesis must be on a topic for which the candidate is required to do original research. Most students who arrive at this stage of their careers take teaching positions while they prepare their papers. John Hope Franklin was no exception to this usual practice.

When St. Augustine's College in Raleigh, North Carolina, offered him a position as instructor in history, he accepted. St. Augustine's was one of the many all-black colleges that had sprung up in the South following the Civil War. It was a denominational school that was founded in 1867. It had about four hundred students and was coeducational. Franklin spent four years at St. Augustine's. The willingness of this young scholar to go South to this small school was probably motivated by the fact that Raleigh was only fifty miles from Goldsboro.

Aurelia Whittington had been serving as a librarian since leaving Fisk. She had been working steadfastly to help earn the needed money that would make her marriage to John possible. With John holding down a full-time instructor's position, it was decided that they could be married by the end of the spring semester. On June 11, 1940, in a beautiful country-style church, John Hope Franklin took Aurelia Elizabeth Whittington as his bride. This earnest young scholar, six feet tall and weighing 160 pounds, towered over his dainty bride as the minister read the marriage service. Following a short but happy honeymoon, the young couple moved into a small furnished apartment in Raleigh.

The 1940–41 scholastic year proved to be a good one for the Franklins. Aurelia managed to receive a local appointment as librarian, and John found satisfactory material for his research on his doctoral thesis. Franklin had presented as a proposed topic for his thesis, "The Legal, Economic, and Social Position of the Negro in North Carolina Before the Civil War." He traveled widely during the Christmas and mid-term recesses, searching out his original sources. At the end of the academic year, he submitted his findings to the faculty at Harvard and was awarded his Ph.D. degree. He was now Dr. John Hope Franklin.

From his research on his doctoral thesis, John Franklin produced several articles that were published in popular historical journals, both white and black. His article "The Free Negro in the Economic Life of North Carolina," was published in the *North Carolina Historical Review* in 1942. The article "Slaves Virtually Free in Anti-Bellum North Carolina," was published in July, 1943, in the *Journal of Negro History*. The thrill of publishing his first book came in 1943, when the University of North Carolina Press issued *The Free Negro in North Carolina*. John Hope Franklin was indeed on his way as an historian of note. Usually it is years before a young instructor breaks into print; John established himself as an author early. George Streaton, in *Commonweal* magazine, praised Franklin's book as ". . . an admirable piece of work." He went on to comment that the author had gone ". . . deeper into social and economic factors dragging the free Negro down than many older scholars."

It was inevitable that a young instructor with John Franklin's drive and capabilities would be moving on from St. Augustine's. In 1943, he took Aurelia and their small son, John Whittington, who had been born the year before, to live in Durham, North Carolina, where, at North Carolina College, he had been offered a position as a professor of history. During his four-year stay at Durham he continued to carry on research and write. At the same time, though, he did an exemplary job in the classroom. As one of his former pupils decribes it, "He was a dynamic lecturer and an inspiration to his students."

One of the top schools in the United States has always been Howard University in Washington, D.C. For a Negro, an invitation to teach at Howard is considered a special honor. In the case of John Hope Franklin, it was also an honor for Howard when he accepted, in 1947, a full professorship in history.

John Franklin found Washington the ideal place in which to work. The Library of Congress and the National Archives gave him the opportunity to do much research that was impossible in Durham. Being in the National Capital also put him in the center of the Negroes' fight for civil rights. Dr. Franklin became an advisor to the National Association for the Advancement of Colored People. Drawn into the legal struggle which was being led by Thurgood Marshall, he helped to prepare the brief on segregation in public schools that the association submitted to the United States Supreme Court. From this case the Supreme Court outlawed, in 1954, segregation in education. (See *Constance Baker Motley* and *Thurgood Marshall,* elsewhere in this book.)

The writings that Franklin had published, up to 1947, were solid and well-researched but did not have wide circulation. However, with the publishing by Knopf and Company, of his textbook, *From Slavery to Freedom: A History of the American Negro,* Franklin's reputation as a scholar was greatly enhanced. Dedicating this volume to "Aurelia," he made clear in the preface to the first edition that, ". . . the history of the Negro in America is essentially the story of the strivings of the nameless millions who have sought adjustment in a new and sometimes hostile world." Twenty years after the first edition appeared, Knopf produced the third edition, in which Franklin commented on the change that had taken place since the last edition, "Since that time, the very pace at which events moved has discouraged any effort to prepare a revision that would inevitably be out of date at the time of its publication."

The issuing of his monumental text did not cause John Franklin to rest on his laurels. In 1956, Harvard University Press brought out his *Militant South 1800–1860*. He was the second Negro scholar ever to have a manuscript published by Harvard University Press in their historical series. The other volume was W.E.B. DuBois' study of the slave trade. Franklin's work presented material concerning the South before the Civil War that no historian had ever covered before.

In February, 1956, John Hope Franklin received an invitation to go to Brooklyn College as chairman of the department of history. Brooklyn College, a very large collegiate complex, is part of the New York City college system. New York City has, under the jurisdiction of the New York City Board of Higher Education, four senior colleges. When Dr. Franklin assumed the chairmanship at Brooklyn College, he became the first Negro to head a college department in the State of New York. His choice by his colleagues in the department was based completely on merit. In the years since receiving his Ph.D., his position in the field of history had grown steadily. He was widely known outside of Negro universities because of his teaching as a visiting professor of history at Harvard in 1950, at the University of Wisconsin in 1952, and at Cornell in 1953.

Dr. Franklin soon found that Brooklyn College was not like Harvard. He was burdened with a great amount of administrative work. His opportunities to write and to do research were limited. During every spare moment, he would be in the New York Public Library or busy at his typewriter.

In spite of the limitations, he was able to complete for publication, *Reconstruction After the Civil War* and *The Emancipation Proclamation*. In both of these works he strongly endorses the thesis that what has happened in America's past also relates to her development in the twentieth century.

Writing in behalf of his people is still what John Franklin wants most to do. For ten years he administered, taught his classes at Brooklyn College, and wrote. When the University of Chicago offered him the opportunity to get out of administration, understandably, he jumped to accept.

The University of Chicago announced in April, 1963, that Dr. John Hope Franklin would join the staff in September. At the time the announcement was made John Franklin was on sabbatical leave. This is a leave granted to teachers every seven years so that they may rest and study. He was serving as William Pitt Professor of American History and Institutions at St. John's College, Cambridge University, England. During that academic year of 1962–63 he also gave lectures at some twenty universities in Great Britain, Germany, Italy, and France. This was not his first experience lecturing in Europe, for in 1954 he had lectured in Cambridge as a Fulbright professor.

John Hope Franklin also traveled to India to represent the American Council of Learned Societies when the Indian universities celebrated their centennial in 1957. In addition, he was asked by the United States Department of State to represent his country at the independence celebration of Nigeria in 1960.

Early in John Franklin's career, he was given the opportunity to serve on the editorial board of the *Journal of Negro History*. It was this scholarly journal that published one of his first articles.

In 1962, President Kennedy appointed Dr. Franklin to a three-year term on the Board of Foreign Scholarships. In 1965, and again in 1968, President Johnson renewed the appointment. He is also a member of the United States Commission for UNESCO, and on the board of directors of the American Council on Human Rights.

John Hope Franklin has the distinction of being the first black member of Washington's Cosmos Club. His election brought him wide publicity, partly because of the furor raised some time before, when the club rejected the Negro State Department official, Carl T. Rowan. When Rowan was denied membership, Robert Kennedy resigned from the club. The election to the club of John Franklin was indeed a significant breakthrough.

The Franklins are a churchgoing family. They are parishioners of a Methodist Church close to the University of Chicago campus. In politics, John Hope Franklin is an independent. He sums up his political creed by declaring "I vote for the man who I believe understands the issues and wishes to do something about them."

As a black man, John Hope Franklin has been a perfectionist, a scholar, and a fighter for the rights of his people. This personality promises a new role for Negroes in American education, not just as representatives of a black minority but of all the people. By his classroom work, his writings, and his travels, Dr. Franklin has inspired new white attitudes. Some of the permanent bridges that have been built between the white and black worlds must be credited to this modern-day scholar.

> Dr. Franklin's future colleagues stress that he was selected for his high standing in his field. The appointment was also made because the university hopes that it will encourage Negro intellectuals and make Chicago a center for their research.

> —*The New York Times*, April 14, 1963

Augusta Baker

[1913-   ]

LIBRARIAN

More than 130 Long Beach children had a treat Tuesday afternoon at Bret Harte Library. They heard a master storyteller tell how the jaguar borrowed eyes from Mr. Vulture.

There's no mystery why the tots were spellbound. They couldn't ask for a better storyteller than Mrs. Augusta Baker, Coordinator of Children's Services, New York Public Library.

—*Press-Telegram*, Long Beach, California, February 3, 1966

The plantation was but a short carriage ride from the busy, thriving, and cosmopolitan town of Baltimore, Maryland. The year was 1857, and the uneasiness that preceded the Civil War was yet to be felt on the Fax Plantation.

Augusta Fax—the slave often carried the name of the owner —was fortunate in being the child of a mother who worked in the main residence. In the capacity of a house slave, young Augusta was given the opportunity to learn how to read and write. She attended, with her two brothers, the school provided on the plantation for the white children. Augusta loved going each day to the ornate front parlor of the master's house to learn how to read the many books on the shelves of the large room. Life was easy and slow on the plantation, so this young Negro child had the time to satisfy her thirst for knowledge.

Abraham Lincoln made good the promise contained in the Emancipation Proclamation. The day came when the Fax plantation was no longer the home of Augusta and her family. The training obtained there through the years held them in good stead, however.

The family moved into Baltimore, where they believed the opportunity for former slaves to earn a living would be greater. Young Augusta worked in a local retail store, where she was able to attend to the account books for the owner, and be generally helpful. She devoted her evenings to teaching ex-slaves and their children how to read and write.

The Faxes were considered by their neighbors to be leaders of the community. They worked hard to give aid and support to their fellow freedmen. It was inevitable that Augusta would some day meet up with a young man as independent and determined as herself.

Charles Gough had come into Baltimore from Elkton, Maryland, where he had been a field hand on a small plantation. Charles was sure that, now that he was free, he would never again work for another man. He knew that, until he could read and write, his dream might remain just a dream. In Baltimore, he met Augusta, and she taught him the alphabet and numbers. Charles was a good student and learned quickly. He did odd jobs during the day and studied by candlelight at night.

Every penny that Charles earned beyond the little needed to keep body and soul together, was saved for the business he wanted to own someday. The struggle was not an easy one for the former slave in those years immediately after the Civil War. Black men were not received with open arms by the whites. It was difficult to earn money necessary to open one's own business; it was equally difficult to have that business succeed if you were a Negro. As his granddaughter has so aptly stated the situation, ". . . he was a proud man and he did not want to work for other people."

Charles Gough managed to purchase a small trucking business. He began with two small wagons and three scrawny horses. At first, his customers were fellow black businessmen. The Negro community of Baltimore was growing and prospering. As time moved on, Charles added more trucks and horses. He bought large sleighs to move the cargo in winter. Soon he was renting horses and carriages. His business was a success.

Augusta watched and hoped as Charles strove toward his goal. She observed this determined, hard-working young man while he pored over the letters and figures on his chalk board. She liked his fierce determination to move ahead. She also liked him for his kindness and winning smile. When Charles asked Augusta to marry him, she had no difficulty in saying yes.

Charles and Augusta Gough had a happy home life. Their marriage was blessed with a little girl whom they named Mabel. They worked for one prime purpose—that Mabel would receive an education which would fit her to teach youth. Their other children, two more girls and a boy, were also educated, but their oldest, to whom they had dedicated those hard, earliest efforts, was always the favorite.

Not too far from the center of Maryland, on a large plantation that had been broken up and distributed among the former slaves, lived a man named Amos Braxston. He worked his small parcel of land during the week, and visited nearby Hammondtown on weekends. Amos had met a local girl who had much social standing, since she was a Hammond. Years before the Civil War, her father had been given his freedom and a large tract of land. Amos visited Lucy Hammond's home regularly when he came to town. Their common interests led to mutual love. They were married in the small Baptist Church in Hammondtown.

Convinced that their future would be brighter in Baltimore, the Braxstons moved into the bustling metropolis. The money Lucy had inherited from her father made life pleasant for the young couple. When a son was born, they named him Winfort.

Lucy Braxston lost her husband during a cholera epidemic a few years after Winfort was born, but not before two daughters had also blessed the union. Now she was more determined than ever to see that her son received the fine education she and Amos had wished for the boy.

Happily, Winfort Braxston showed a strong desire to learn. He loved books and the challenges they offered. He attended schools that were completely segregated, a fact that bothered him all his life. He graduated from Morgan State College, Magna Cum Laude.

Following college, Winfort obtained a position teaching industrial arts in a segregated Baltimore high school. During the summers, he went to New York, where he attended Columbia University and obtained his Master of Arts degree.

Simultaneously, Mabel Gough had fulfilled her parents' fondest dreams. She had taken to education from the very first day in school. Her work in high school placed her at the head of her class. In teachers college, she excelled in English. Her work as a student teacher convinced her that the classroom was where she could do the most for her people.

Like those engaged in other professions, teachers have a tendency to meet frequently in certain places that naturally attract them because of their mutual interests. Mabel Gough met Winfort Braxston at the theatre, in museums, and at teachers' meetings. She noticed that, although he lived on the other side of town, he managed to walk her home after church on Sundays.

These two young people were attracted to each other from their first encounter at a teachers' meeting. Their family backgrounds were similar, as were their interests. While before long, Mabel found the thought of becoming Winfort's wife a happy prospect, she realized that the rule of the school system would not permit her to remain teaching after marriage. Therefore, when he first proposed, she turned him down.

Winfort was not easily put aside. He continued to pursue Mabel . . . and finally won out. They were married in the church they had both attended during their courtship. Teacher Mabel Braxston became a housewife, and she loved her new vocation.

The Braxstons set up housekeeping just a few streets from the Frederick Douglass Junior-Senior High School, where Winfort was teaching. His work at Columbia University had given him the opportunity to qualify as a science and mathematics teacher.

Mabel was uneasy about her mother, who was now a widow, and, at Winfort's suggestion, brought her to live with them. She proved to be a great help when the baby came. Mabel had hoped for a girl and she was not disappointed. They named her Augusta, for her grandmother.

Augusta Braxston was the only child of Mabel and Winfort. Her family life was loving, calm, and dedicated to learning. From her earliest recollection, she was exposed to books. She remembers: "I was constantly demanding that my grandmother or mother read to me." Her mother sheltered the little girl, and spent a great deal of time teaching her to read and write. Apparently, Mabel Braxston still felt the urge to teach that had been taken from her when she married Winfort. As a result of her efforts, Augusta entered the second grade when she was ready to begin school.

The Henry Highland Garrett school was segregated. Augusta was not troubled by this fact, for she had had little experience with whites. She explains the problem: "Curiously enough, I knew no white people in positions which were equal to our own kind of middle-class way of life. Our doctor was a Negro, our lawyer was a Negro, all the teachers I knew were Negroes. The white people that I saw were the men who collected the garbage. I was too young to realize that these jobs only went to whites." This situation troubled Winfort Braxston. He worried that his daughter would grow up a warped person.

Augusta's school experiences were helped by the constant interest of her parents. Her father was indeed a man of letters. He read widely and was most alert to academic advances. Her mother was a teacher. The combination of the teaching mother and the scholarly father could only contribute to the development of a child to whom books became one of the most important items in life. Augusta remembers it this way: "My father was a book man, my mother was a teacher."

Augusta recalls that early in life, she had a teacher (whose name she can't remember) who awakened a strong feeling for the written word. She says, "She read aloud to the class, without any attempt at teaching. All we had to do was sit there and listen to her as she would read a chapter. I remember the book was *Beautiful Joe*. She made an impression." Much of this young girl's after-school time was spent in the children's room of the local library.

When Augusta moved up to high school, she again was forced to attend an all-black institution. She was assigned to the Frederick Douglass Junior-Senior High School. It was the same school in which her father had been teaching for some years.

Augusta was a good student. The concentration necessary to understand complicated material is made easier by the ability to read well. There was no question that Augusta had that ability. She graduated at the top of her class.

Her almost exclusive exposure to her fellow Negroes had been troubling her father for a number of years. His fear that this narrow viewpoint could act as a hindrance convinced him that only a white college would be acceptable for her.

He wanted Augusta to realize that there were all sorts of white people. Mabel Braxston would have much preferred to see her daughter attend a black college. However, she was overruled.

Winfort Braxston's sister Mary lived in East Carnegie, a suburb of Pittsburgh. It was decided that Augusta would attend the University of Pittsburgh and live with her aunt. When the time came to enter the University, the Braxstons drove their daughter to Pittsburgh. It was still difficult for Augusta's mother to realize that her little girl had grown up.

Augusta Braxston came to the University as an honor graduate from high school. She explains the situation: "My freshman year was most difficult. There is no use kidding ourselves about separate but equal schools. This is not true. When I went to college I was an honor student from high school. I soon discovered what I did not know, so I had to make up a great deal of work." This experience was not new to most black students who were forced to attend inferior segregated schools.

Augusta was but sixteen years old when she entered her first college class. Maybe she was too young to adjust fully to being in classes with boys and girls who were several years older than herself. She also found it difficult to adjust to mingling with white boys and girls who were her intellectual equals. However, she was determined to make the adjustment. She made good friends in the two years she spent at the University of Pittsburgh.

Shortly after going to the University, Augusta Braxston met James Baker. Young Baker was a graduate student at the University on a scholarship from the Urban League, intending to get a master's degree in social work. He was one of the few Negroes attending Pittsburgh on a scholarship.

Augusta was not too busy to become involved with the work of the Urban League, and in so doing she saw much of

James Baker. By the time she was finishing her sophomore year she was married to James.

The Urban League assigned James Baker to Albany, New York, to organize a branch to be called The Albany Interracial Council. Augusta was thrilled to have the opportunity to furnish their own little apartment in the State capital. The shopping for curtains, furniture, and food kept her busy during that summer of 1933. However, when the apartment was in good order and the summer was drawing to a close, she made her plans to return to college study.

Albany State Teachers College was the most logical place for Augusta to enroll. The campus was close to the Baker apartment, plus the fact that this was depression time and it was not too expensive to attend. The fact that Mrs. Baker was attending a teachers' college caused all who knew her to conclude that she was preparing to be a teacher. As Augusta Baker explains it, "There were few positions open to Negro women, and it was just taken for granted that I would be a teacher."

Entering Albany State was not as easy a task as she thought it would be. The University of Pittsburgh sent on the transcript of Augusta Braxston Baker's record to Albany State. There was reluctance to accept her. She was going to be a teacher, and, as such, would do her practice teaching at the Milne High School. The Milne School was an experimental school attached to the Albany State Teachers' College. Augusta was a Negro and they did not want her there.

Her determination to see this challenge through caused the officials at Albany State to admit her, but to demand that she practice teach in a segregated school. Augusta's cause was aided by the officials from the University of Pittsburgh, who made clear to the Albany administrators that, if she was good enough to attend their university without restrictions, she was surely good enough to go to teachers' college. There was also the possibility that the Albany Interracial Council would have taken up the issue if Albany State had refused to receive Augusta Baker without restrictions. She entered as a junior without limitations.

Augusta broke the practice of forcing Negro students to meet their academic requirements in the less scholarly segregated schools. She and her husband used this victory to encourage other Negro students to prepare for college careers, rather than to consider their high-school graduation sufficient. The Bakers visited the high schools in and around Albany, to make clear to the young Negro pupils that a free college education was at their doorstep. They invited these youngsters to the Interracial Council clubhouse, to meet Negroes who had made good in their chosen fields. They emphasized the fact that it would have been impossible for these people to succeed without an education.

The door was now open for Augusta Baker to do her practice teaching at the Milne School, the model school of Albany Teachers' College. Soon after receiving her first opportunity to appear before a class, she was convinced that she did not care for teaching. She analyzes her feelings, "I soon discovered I did not like teaching, but I did like books."

Dr. Harold Thompson, the folklore historian and a famous storyteller, was on the faculty at Albany State. Augusta talked with this kind, understanding instructor about her dislike for teaching. He introduced her to Margaret Caroline Prichett, the Director of the Library School at Albany. Miss Prichett suggested to Augusta Baker that she think seriously of becoming a librarian. This was a brand new concept for the latter and she took time in making up her mind. When she did, she moved into the Library School.

It was difficult to avoid the school atmosphere, even in library studies. Augusta found herself still closely aligned with scholastic routines because of the work that frequently took her to the school library. She chafed under the necessary restrictions due to school curriculums, so Miss Prichett made a special arrangement for her to do her practical work in the Albany Public Library. Here Augusta Baker had her first experience in public library work and she found it most stimulating.

Augusta Baker graduated with a degree in library science in 1934, but it was not possible for her to secure a position in a public library. Some months before the end of her senior year she was aware that she was to be a mother. The summer of 1934 was spent in reading and sewing as she awaited the birth of her first child. The baby was named James, Junior. For three years Augusta Baker kept house and watched her baby grow strong and healthy.

The depression was far from over in 1937, so when an opportunity came to begin work for the New York Public Library, Mrs. Baker jumped at the chance. Moving to New York City was not easy, for her husband could not come with her. His work with the Urban League had him continually traveling around the country. During the hours when his mother was in the library, little Jimmy was watched over by the staff of a local nursery school.

Augusta Baker's first assignment took her to the Children's Room of the Countee Cullen Branch, in Harlem. In this predominantly Negro section of New York City, Mrs. Baker recalls: "When I started I couldn't find books that did not portray the Negro as a servant. They were always shown as racial stereotypes."

Talking with Augusta Baker thirty years after her first experience as a librarian, you feel the intense determination that moved her to change the image of her people in the books to be circulated among white as well as black people. The Harlem branch, named after the man who carried Negro poetry to a peak which was unsurpassed during the early years of this century, was a challenge for Augusta Baker. Her dismay at finding so very few books which dealt with Negro culture, or, indeed, with Negro life at all, was the catalyst that sparked her resolution.

Mrs. Baker worked to compile a bibliography of children's books which presented Negro life. She gathered as many volumes on the subject as were available. She explains her task, "So, we set out to find books and urge publishers to print stories which would strengthen the Negro child's pride in his race and, in turn, show the Caucasian child his Negro counterpart also has a background."

To help fill the gap made by the lack of written material, Augusta Baker held storytelling sessions for the children. Her work with Dr. Harold Thompson and the storytelling of her grandmother and mother, plus her reading sessions with her son, made her most proficient.

Four years after Augusta Baker arrived in New York City she founded the James Weldon Johnson Memorial Collection. It was one of the first truly substantial collections of children's books about Negro life in any library in the United States. Mrs. Baker chose to name the collection for "a gentleman of letters." James Weldon Johnson, as a novelist and a poet, NAACP official and diplomat, has left a lasting impression on the cultural and social life of the Negro in America. It was Johnson's essays on the roots of the Negro's cultural contribution that helped to explain the foundation of the achievements of the black race in literature.

In the meanwhile, Jimmy Baker was growing up. He attended the local public school and was doing well. His mother took him with her whenever possible, so that he could listen to her tell her stories. In the summer, the boy visited with his Grandmother Braxston. Mrs. Braxston had returned to teaching after her husband died, which was shortly after Augusta finished her freshman year at Pittsburgh. She was always happy to have her grandson with her during vacations. Jimmy enjoyed Baltimore, so when it came time to choose a college, it was logical that he would pick Johns Hopkins University.

Augusta Baker worked hard to develop her specialty, that of a children's storyteller. She is a true believer in the fact that "A good storyteller is made as well as born." Her interest and constant striving for excellence were rewarded, in 1953, with the position of Assistant Coordinator of Children's Services and Storytelling Specialist with the New York Public Library. In this same year, she received the first Dutton-Macrae Award for "advanced study in the field of library work with children and young people." She took a year off from her work at the library to study the role of the children's library in intercultural education, with specific emphasis on the Negro. Part of her study was a cross-country survey on the extent of material available about Negro life. With this award came a $1,000 stipend, which she used to complete a bibliography of books about Negro life. Her work is considered a substantial contribution on the subject.

No one knew better than Augusta Baker that she might very well complain about the lack of literature in the Negro field, but the one sure way to remedy it was to try to write. In 1955, Lippincott and Company published her first book. It was *The Talking Tree*, well received by several reviewers. Five years later, the same publisher brought out *The Golden Lynx*, a collection of folk tales for children.

By the 1950's, Mrs. Baker's fame had begun to spread. She was invited to spend one month in Trinidad, organizing library work with children for the Trinidad Public Library. Columbia University, in 1956, asked Augusta Baker to join the faculty of their School of Library Science. She accepted and is, at present, a lecturer at that school. Invitations took her to the campuses of Syracuse and Nevada Universities, as workshop director and special lecturer.

Jimmy Baker had proven to be a good student so that, when he finished high school, he was readily accepted at Johns Hopkins University. His four years there were happy ones, for he was able to live with his grandmother, and, whenever possible, his mother would spend time with them. His graduation was an event of joy for Augusta Baker. It was another milestone in a long list of achievements for this dynamic woman.

Jimmy, who had been a member of the R.O.T.C. unit at the university, entered the Army as a second lieutenant. During his tour of duty, he served at the Infantry Replacement Center, Fort Jackson, South Carolina. While in the service, he worked with soldiers with difficulties. When he left the Army, he settled in Columbia, South Carolina, with his wife, whom he had met while at Fort Jackson. At present, he works for the State of South Carolina, in a department that attempts to rehabilitate the physically and mentally handicapped. Not unlike his mother, he tried his hand at teaching in high school for one year, but gave it up. Augusta Baker always looks forward to seeing her granddaughter, and the young girl looks forward to coming to the big city at vacation time.

The sixties opened on a note of satisfaction when it was announced that Augusta Baker had been promoted to the position of Coordinator of Children's Services for the New York Public Library. Her responsibilities include administrating the children's services in the library's eighty neighborhood branches and four bookmobiles, She is responsible for the maintenance of the standards of taste, intellectual content, and cultural quality of the library's juvenile book collections and its programs for boys and girls.

Mrs. Baker, in her calm and masterful manner, engages daily in what, to almost anyone else, would be a monumental task. She coordinates and suggests policy for all work with children in all of the five counties that make up New York City. It is one of the largest public library systems in the world. She approves material and trains librarians in book reviewing. She plans and conducts programs, and maintains liaison with other library offices.

With all her daily activity in New York, Augusta Baker

finds time to work closely with the American Library Association. Twice in the last ten years she has served on the Board of Directors, Children's Services Division of the ALA. As a Councillor and President of the Children's Services Division, she has been instrumental in many innovations.

President John F. Kennedy, always aware and alert to the matter of civil rights, invited Mrs. Augusta Baker to the White House the day he sent his Civil Rights message to Congress. As a member of the Intellectual Freedom Committee of the ALA, Augusta Baker assured the President that library programs in the field of the advancement of human relations would be strengthened.

Never willing to rest on her laurels, this pleasant, compassionate woman has continued to write and lecture on her favorite topic—children and books. In 1963 and 1964, she published *Books About Negro Life for Children, Young Years: Anthology of Children's Literature,* and *Once Upon a Time.*

Each Thursday and Saturday during the school year, Augusta Baker goes to a New York TV station to moderate her program "It's Fun to Read." Mrs. Baker brings authors and illustrators from the world of children's books to speak directly to boys and girls. She believes that these programs have helped to improve the treatment of minorities in children's literature. She explains, "The important thing is for children to understand—if they are old enough—that *Oliver Twist* gives a false picture of Jews in general, and Jim in *Huckleberry Finn* isn't a typical Negro. Chances are that a younger child won't even be aware of the distortion."

In June, 1968, the American Library Association conferred on Augusta Baker the Grolier Award, voted by the executive board for her continued fine service in the field. For librarians, this is one of the most prized tributes because it is given only to those who have made an unusual contribution to children and young people.

Two years before the bestowing of the Grolier Award, *Parents' Magazine* had voted Mrs. Baker their annual medal for outstanding service to the nation's children.

Always alert to the importance of children and books, this woman who has devoted her life to both of them advises parents: "Have books around, not just as decorations, but to read and to talk about. In summer, tuck a book into your picnic basket. Read aloud. Share books. Some parents share books with small children. Then, as soon as the children can read, they're sent ahead on their own. The family sharing should continue. No one is ever too old or too advanced to share the pleasure of reading." Some of this thinking was stimulated by a story told to her by her son Jimmy when he was a college freshman. He told his mother that, to his amazement, he discovered that some of his classmates had been brought up on a literary diet of comic books. They had never read a youthful classic and were only now reading *Alice's Adventures in Wonderland* and *Treasure Island.*

Mrs. Baker's first husband died some ten years ago. She is now married to Gordon Alexander and they reside in St. Albans, Queens, an outlying area of New York City. Mr. Alexander is engaged in service work in New York. He finds his wife as active and as dedicated as she was the first time he met her. He knows that one can never really grow old or world-weary while married to such a vibrant spouse.

Always ready to grasp everything that will aid her in her work, Augusta Baker has made a thorough study of African folklore. She sees folklore ". . . as one of the ways we can realize we are all related. Folklore makes one aware of the brotherhood of man." The great lack of collections of African tales, poetry, and proverbs has caused her to turn her efforts to this area. She has already noted the change: "And, ten years ago, the black man in America had no pride. Now he does. A people must have pride—if not, they're crushed and resentful. Black kids used to giggle and be embarrassed at the mention of Africa in school or anywhere. They didn't know anything about their own heritage. Now they have a better chance to learn."

Since 1937, Mrs. Baker has also used her skills on the job of teaching boys and girls the need to read and read well. Since 1961, she and her one hundred and ten staff members have attempted to maintain a continuous literary dialogue with children, their teachers, and their parents. Their efforts go toward planning story hours, films, puppet shows, and as many innovative and imaginative library programs as possible.

Augusta Baker's work has been successful because she loves what she is doing for the children of today—who will be the parents of tomorrow.

> "I can't ever remember getting up one morning dreading work. I just love it."

> —Augusta Baker comment to the author, August, 1969

Anthony Overton

[1864-1946]

> Anthony Overton never permitted himself to suffer be-
> cause of his color. He believed that a man who feels sorry
> for himself fails to make much progress.
>
> —Abram Harris, *The Negro as Capitalist*

On the slave rolls of James Masterson's plantation in Monroe, Louisiana, Jessie Overton was listed as the father, and Ollie Storm as the mother of a baby boy named Anthony. The Civil War was almost over when this black child was born into the slavery that men were fighting to abolish.

On June 24, 1864, the day of Anthony Overton's birth, the Masterson plantation was in a turmoil. The Union soldiers were only ten miles from Monroe, and moving rapidly. Most of the slaves on this plantation were aware of the war and what it meant. However, James Masterson was a good master, as masters went, and many were worried about what freedom could mean for them. Jessie Overton, one of Masterson's house slaves, was more concerned about his wife Ollie than about the freedom that was supposed to be coming.

Shortly after Anthony's birth, Masterson called his slaves together and explained to them that soon they would be on their own. He recommended that they remain on the planta-tion, saying that he would give each family a sixty-acre piece of land. Lest one might consider that this action by Masterson was a pure act of charity, it is to be remembered that, if he had not made the move himself, the government would have made it for him.

Jessie, Ollie, and little Anthony remained in Monroe. As the child grew, and with him, the size of the Overton family, times became increasingly difficult. The only education Anthony received was from a young Negro woman, a neighbor, who could read and write. Soon she had taught this bright little boy all she knew.

When Anthony was seven years of age, a one-room schoolhouse was set up in town. His father was determined that he should attend the classes there. The teacher was a fine, well-educated, young Negro from Boston, Massachusetts. Edward Johnson had been trained in Northern schools and came to his position in Decatur well prepared. Johnson saw in Anthony Overton a great potential. The boy responded by co-operating with his teacher in every way. When Anthony had moved up the education ladder as far as the one-room school permitted, it appeared as if his training was over. There was no Negro high school within one hundred miles of Decatur.

Fortunately for Anthony, his father decided to pull up stakes and move the family to Kansas. Mr. Overton believed that in Kansas a black man's chances would be greater than in Louisiana. His work on the land in Decatur was not giving the family much better than a pauper's existence. Carrying the several hundred dollars he received for his land, he hitched the family mule to the old farm wagon and started out. It was a long, hard trek, but Jessie knew that things just had to be better. After all, he was moving to the state for which John Brown had fought, to keep it free.

Topeka, Kansas, in 1877, was a bustling, lively, growing metropolis. It was into this atmosphere that Jessie brought his family. A small house was acquired in the south end of town, and Mr. Overton found work as a clerk in a local retail shop.

Anthony was enrolled in South Side High School. The State of Kansas, while not segregating the school system per se, did separate the whites from the blacks by the way in which they drew their school lines. South Side High School had no white students.

For four years Anthony worked hard. He was an average student who was forced to give much time to his books if he was to pass. With all this, he was able to find a job helping in a grocery store after classes. Even this early, his keen sense of business began to show.

The owner of the little store where Anthony worked was an easy-going type. As a result, instead of making a good living, he was just about existing. He never bothered to weigh the butter or the other products, so that he was constantly giving customers more of an item than they paid for. He would extend credit and fail to put the transaction in his book. His purchasing procedures permitted his dealers to cheat him when he took their products. Anthony was appalled at his happy-go-lucky attitude. The first thing young Overton did was to put in a bookkeeping system. He then sent out bills to the delinquent customers, much to their annoyance. With the store owner's permission, he dickered with the wholesalers on the prices of the goods to be bought. He purchased a scale with some of the money that was saved, and made his boss use it. Before long, the store began to show a reasonable profit.

Anthony Overton might well have shown his leanings toward business at an early age, but he also showed that he was a real boy. Sports were his favorite pastime. He was not always able to play baseball because of his job, but when he was free, he was often to be found with other pupils of South Side High on the local diamond. He had a natural flair for the game. One of his classmates remarked, "If Anthony did not think so much about business, I am sure he would have become a professional ball player."

The Overton home was not always a happy one. Anthony's mother was a sickly woman who spent most of her time in bed. The other children—there were three more—were too young to help with the work, so their father came home to a job of housecleaning and cooking. Anthony helped as much as possible, but his aid was slight because of his many interests. Bickering and arguments, brought on by tiredness and short tempers, made life for the boy a bit trying. His father wanted him to get ahead in the world, yet he wanted more help at home from his eldest child.

The records at South Side High School are sparse for the years that Anthony attended classes there. They do show that Anthony Overton passed the subjects he took. They also show that his grades were just average. It is fair to suppose that carrying the burden of home chores plus his job played some part in his average academic performance. He graduated in 1881, eighth in a class of nineteen.

A high school graduate was a unique individual in 1881, and a black high school graduate was a miracle. This does not mean to say that Negroes could not master the work the same as whites. Very few boys, black or white, finished high school during this period. It was felt that education beyond the elementary level was for the children of the rich. When even middle-class white families just naturally sent their children to work early, it can be taken for granted how inevitably true this was in the case of black families.

With high school behind him, Anthony sought to establish himself in business. Topeka, as a growing city, needed young, energetic, and foresighted businessmen. Overton filled that prescription perfectly. He managed to find a partner with some ready cash, and they started a wholesale fruit business. This proved a most successful venture, again because of Anthony's shrewd and capable handling. He was not yet twenty years of age, and he was making more annually than most men twice his age. He did not wait for farmers to come to him, he went to the farmers. He bought up the entire yearly crop of an orchard before it was picked. In this way, he got the best selection before his competitors realized what was happening. This is a practice that has since been followed by all the big supermarket chains in the United States.

Two years after Anthony's graduation from South Side High, his mother died. Jessie, who had missed his friends in Monroe, decided to move himself and the younger children back to Louisiana. Anthony was left on his own, but being the self-sufficient lad that he was, he did not seem to mind. He made sure that his family was well provided for by sending them money each month. This enabled his dad to live in semi-retirement, while his two sisters and a brother could continue in school. Even after his father's death, his sisters and brother received a monthly check until they married.

Romance seemed to pass Anthony by. It is generally true that a man who becomes completely taken with business usually has little time for romance. However, Anthony Overton did eventually meet a young lady who caught his fancy. Anna Tone was the daughter of a local farmer with whom Anthony had been doing business. Each time he went to the farm for a transaction with the father, he managed to see Anna.

In time, he found himself driving his team miles out of his way, just to pass the Tone farm. Anna was fond of Anthony but she did not want to lead him on because she knew for some time that she had tuberculosis.

Anthony, at twenty-three, was most anxious to get married. Each time that he mentioned the subject, Anna found another excuse for postponing the decision. Finally, her father felt impelled to tell Anthony the truth. It was a great shock for the young lover. At first, he wanted to marry Anna in spite of her sickness. Wiser heads convinced him to wait. On June 16, 1887, Anna died.

Anna Tone's death brought a turning point in Anthony's

life. He seemed to lose interest in the fruit business, and, finally, his partner offered to buy out his share. He sold this for a large sum of money and took a long trip to California, Florida, and New York. When he returned to Topeka, he enrolled in the University of Kansas Law School.

Up until quite recent times, it was possible for a high school graduate to attend a law school without ever having gone to college. Today, most law schools in the United States will not accept a student unless he or she has already received a bachelor's degree. Anthony's high school diploma gave him the right to attend a school of law.

Law school was a great challenge to this ex-businessman. Many erroneous things that he had learned about the law in business had to be unlearned in law school. His younger classmates had a great advantage over him in this area.

The University of Kansas Law School, in the late 1880's, was integrated. Anthony got on well with his classmates, who all looked up to him for his keen sense of humor and his businesslike manner. There was only one instance of trouble, and that came in a class in contracts. Anthony was explaining to the professor his theory on the rights of both parties to a contract. A member of the class shouted out, "Niggers have no rights." Overton turned around slowly, identified the man who made the remark and replied, "Son, we had better all have rights, or the day will come when none of us will have them."

It was June of 1890 when Anthony Overton received his LL.B. degree. He prepared himself for the bar examination, which would permit him to practice law. Graduation from law school does not automatically permit a person to practice law. A law school graduate takes a long written examination that is prepared by the bar association. When the test is passed, the student is certified to practice law by the court system of the state in which he took the examination.

Overton had no difficulty with the bar examination, passing

it the first time. He was not especially desirous of opening a law office, but there was little else he could do. Soon he had a rather large practice consisting at first of members of the Negro business community. However, his reputation for honesty and fair play soon helped to attract white clients as well. He was considered a successful attorney.

Not unlike most Negroes of that period, Anthony joined the local Republican Club. The members of the black race would not soon forget what the party of Abraham Lincoln had done for them. It is from the local club that political appointments come. In early 1892, Anthony Overton was appointed a judge in the Topeka Municipal Court.

Consider the great honor it was for this ex-slave to be serving on the bench as a municipal judge. All types of minor infractions were brought before him. Domestic relations, misdemeanors, accident cases, and arraignments for felonies all came into his courtroom. The same reputation he had enjoyed as an honest attorney was his as a judge. Most attorneys wanted their clients brought before him. All those in trouble got the same fair treatment regardless of color. This was not always true in the courtrooms of the white justices.

Although Anthony Overton enjoyed his work in the court, he was not completely happy. He had been searching around, while on vacation, for some business venture that he could invest in and operate. In the summer of 1907, he traveled to Oklahoma City, Oklahoma, where he discovered a modest wholesale business in hardware material that was for sale. He put down a small deposit, returned to Topeka and re-signed his judgeship.

During the years 1907 to 1909, the Overton Hardware Corporation did well. The Oklahoma settlers were willing to pay any price to obtain the shovels, hammers, wire, rakes, and nails that they needed to set up their homesteads. Overton knew how to buy, and, above all, he knew that success came by putting profits back into the business to give it strength.

It was in Oklahoma that Anthony met the girl he eventually married. He had thought that no one could ever take Anna's place. Loneliness in a strange location can play peculiar tricks. Edith Dunbar had recently come to Oklahoma from California, to act as a companion to an elderly lady. She was visiting at the home of a mutual friend while Anthony was there and, at the end of the evening, he walked her home.

In the months that followed, Edith and Anthony saw much of one another. They were both far from familiar places and people. It was almost inevitable that they would be attracted in loneliness. Their wedding took place on February 14, 1901, in the Baptist Church, in Oklahoma City. It was truly a St. Valentine's Day lovers' match. The marriage proved to be a lasting and understanding tie. One son was born to Edith and Anthony. They named him Anthony, Junior.

In 1909, an old friend from Kansas visited Anthony. John Forbes had been a successful coal dealer in Topeka. Like Anthony, a Negro, Forbes was known as a clever businessman. He came to Overton to suggest a partnership in a new type of business. Pointing out that the women of the United States pretty much controlled the wealth of this country, he suggested that Anthony and he open a plant that could supply the ladies with materials for use in their kitchens and for the enhancement of their beauty. Forbes suggested manufacturing and selling baking powder, flavor extracts, and toiletries.

Anthony Overton was willing to take a chance on this new venture. He realized that the markets of the United States were changing. The materials that at one time the housewife prepared for herself were now going to be purchased already packaged. Women were seeking to be liberated from the kitchen and were demanding more equality with men. No longer would they spend long hours over a hot stove, cooking up appetizing foods which could now be bought in a can, jar, or box. The American woman wanted to be seen more frequently in public, and therefore she wanted those toiletries that would help make her look beautiful. Corn starch was not to be used to powder the face when Overton's Face Powder could be bought. Not only could you purchase Overton's Face Powder, but you could get it in several shades!

Back in Topeka, Anthony founded the Overton Hygienic Products Company. Forbes made a financial contribution to the company, but was not interested in its workings. Overton was the prime mover in all facets of this business, which proved a huge success from the first. In fact, by 1910, he had bought out Forbes' interest and ran the business alone.

Chicago was, and still is, the hub of the national railroad system of the United States. Railroads from all sections of the country have their terminals in the Windy City. Anthony Overton soon realized that a company that depended for better than ninety per cent of its business on distant customers must be where ease of transportation existed. Consequently, in 1911, he moved his business operations to Chicago. Here he was not only able to ship his products around the country with greater ease, he was also able to hire the kind of help that was not always available in Topeka. Anthony Overton never refused a man a job on the basis of his color. While the firm had a basic policy of employing Negroes, it did not exclude white men from its payroll. It has been said that the Overton Hygienic Products Company was a well-integrated business. During the long years of its existence the labor relations of the organization were among the best in the United States.

Overton believed in paying a living wage. Henry Ford takes credit for developing the policy of paying all his employees five dollars a day. At least two years before Ford established his formula, Overton was doing the very same thing.

It was only fair that Anthony should strive to give to the

Negroes of Chicago the opportunities that they seldom received at the hands of other businessmen. He felt that in an organization that was earning, by 1920, over one million dollars a year, the black citizens should play a major role. Many of those items that the company produced were used in great amounts by Negro purchasers. Overton certainly realized his obligation to see that the people who produced his products should be the same color as those who used them. He never forgot that his people deserved an opportunity to live and prosper in this land of plenty, just like other Americans.

Aware that the black man, because of his general economic plight, found it almost impossible to borrow the necessary capital to do business, in 1922 Overton opened a bank. Negroes have always been and still are the victims of unscrupulous lending agencies. When in need of money, they often have to take out loans at higher interest rates than those charged to white clients. As a result, many black businessmen have found it almost impossible to raise the necessary money to capitalize even a small business.

The Douglass National Bank, named for the "Golden Trombone of Abolition," Frederick A. Douglass, was opened by Anthony Overton. It was located in the Overton Building, at 36th and State Streets, in Chicago. This was Overton's way of saying to the Negroes of Chicago, "Deposit your money with us so that you may help your people by extending loans to them at low rates in order to start them on the road to success."

The bank did well in those years of prosperity during the 1920's. However, like many other banks in the United States, Douglass National was being swept along on the tide of speculation and prosperity. When the "crash" came in 1929, Overton's bank was hit a crushing blow. It staggered along, attempting to liquidate its loans, but its borrowers were also badly off and could not pay. In 1932, it closed its doors, never to reopen. There was no stigma on Anthony Overton. This same thing had happened to larger and more well-established banks. An indication of how well run a bank it was is seen in the fact that, when the assets were sold, depositors received thirty-eight cents on a dollar. This was the highest amount paid by any bank in the Chicago area that had been forced to close its doors.

Anthony Overton, Junior, never proved to be the business-man that his father had hoped he would be. He was interested, competent, and reliable, but lacked imagination. He held a responsible position in the Overton Company and carried his share of the load. When he married, he chose a fine girl who became an excellent wife and mother. They had one son whom they named Anthony III. When, in 1934, Anthony Overton, Senior, decided to start the Victory Mutual Life Insurance Company, he picked his grandson to work for the new venture.

Just as Negroes found it difficult to borrow money from banks, they also had difficulty in obtaining life insurance at a reasonable rate. Overton, like Charles C. Spaulding, saw the need for providing his people with adequate coverage at low premiums. This business has proved to be a success. At the present time, Anthony Overton III is president of the Victory Mutual Life Insurance Company.

Anthony Senior was never a person who felt strongly about his being black. He had been very successful, and had met white people who treated him as an equal. Nevertheless, he became increasingly aware of the unhappy plight of many of his people after he arrived in Chicago. His actions in opening a "friendly" bank and, subsequently, in establishing an insurance business with low-cost premiums, pointed up his desire to relieve the financial pressures of the blacks.

Overton also realized that, if the Negroes in Chicago were to be able to hold their own, they must receive accurate news in all areas. The white press, written and edited for white readers, did not tell the story of the black community. In

1940, he purchased a Negro newspaper called the *Chicago Bee*. He published this paper the way he did everything else. It was well written, it carried articles of international and national interest, and, above all, gave the black readers a sense of belonging. It was only a short time before the circulation almost doubled. The Negroes living on Chicago's South Side were among its most avid readers.

When the year 1946 rolled around, Anthony Overton had been working for better than sixty years. He had always been an energetic man, but he was also a frugal man. His home was a modest one, and his wife Edith had been careful not to be extravagant, no matter how prosperous they were. The time seemed to be at hand to turn his many projects over to others to handle. Before he had the opportunity to retire fully, his heart gave out. On September 16, 1946, Anthony Overton died. This quiet little man of business and letters had lived a full life. He understood the needs of his people and attempted to meet them. He left a very modest estate to his family because he always believed in "putting profits back into the business." He did leave them the rich remembrance of a man of honor who knew no color, but never forgot his obligation to his fellow black man.

Make each day count for more than the previous day.

—Anthony Overton's motto

John Roosevelt Robinson

[1919-   ]

ATHLETE

Jackie Robinson is in a unique position as the first of his
race in organized baseball, his will be the hardest job—
to open a door for those who will come later. I believe
he can do it. I believe he's player enough to do it and I
know he's man enough to do it.

—Branch Rickey, General Manager, Brooklyn Dodgers

August 28, 1945, was a hot day in New York City. World
War II was over just two weeks, and the United States was
attempting to get back on its normal routine. Jackie Robinson had been asked to come to Brooklyn to see the general
manager of the Dodgers baseball team. He was disgruntled
about being forced to make the long ride to Ebbets Field on
a hot subway train.

Robinson had been playing baseball professionally since
he left the army earlier in the year. He had signed a contract,
in April, 1945, to play at $400 a month with the Kansas City
Monarchs, a team in the Negro American League.

Jackie was not happy with the Monarchs. Experience had
taught him that playing ball in any but one of the major
leagues was a difficult job at best. The schedules were un-
predictable, and the players lived like gypsies. They were
moved from place to place in a bus that appeared to be
rolling along on its last cylinder. However, the worst problem

faced by these young athletes was the feeling of complete frustration at knowing that the major leagues had not hired a black player in seventy years. Jackie summarized his feelings concerning the Monarchs with the comment, "I was disgusted with the sweatshop game that was played in the Negro leagues, and had made up my mind to return to California to try for a job as a high-school coach."

As Robinson rode to Brooklyn in that hot New York City subway car, his mind went back to the long, hard road that had brought him to where he found himself this day. Jackie's mother must be given the credit for encouraging in him the fighting spirit he has always shown. It is true that when a man displays a fighting spirit and strength of character, he very frequently has acquired these assets from his mother.

Mallie McGriff's father was an emancipated slave. She lived all her early life in a small town near Cairo, Georgia, located on the Georgia-Florida border. Her marriage to Jerry Robinson, a farm hand like her father, did not help to make her place in life any more pleasant. In fact, Mallie's father and mother never wanted her to marry Jerry Robinson. He was neither aggressive nor determined in his desire to fight for the rights of his people. The McGriffs were a fighting family, and their daughter was the strongest fighter of them all. Mallie was forever calling out for equality for her people on the land where they were tenants. When the landlord failed to give his tenants their basic rights, Jerry Robinson was constantly being pushed by Mallie to stand up to the tyrant. Because Jerry failed to respond to her urgings, his wife felt that he had lost his sense of responsibility as a father and a husband, and that she must step into the family leadership.

Jackie's mother finally gave up her attempts to get her husband to farm his own land as a share-cropper. He just could not bear up under the pressure of this responsibility. The marriage produced five children—Jackie Roosevelt

Robinson was the youngest. He was born on January 31, 1919. In the summer of that same year, Jerry Robinson disappeared to Florida, leaving his wife to care for the children.

Discouraged and alone, Mallie decided that rural Georgia was not the place in which to bring up her children. On May 21, 1920, at the age of thirty, she moved the family to California. Mallie's sister and her husband went with them. Jackie was just sixteen months old—too young to recall the transfer. The trip was made by train, and it was a tiresome one. The miserable little group spent four days and nights on the cars before they arrived in Pasadena, California. Pasadena was chosen as a residence because Mallie's brother had been living there since the end of World War I.

At that time, California was no more a haven for blacks than was Georgia, and Mallie Robinson discovered this very quickly. The living conditions there were almost as bad as those back in the South. The best housing that could be obtained was a three-room apartment. Into these crowded quarters Mallie and her five children moved—plus her sister and brother-in-law. All eight of them slept in one room!

Having obtained employment as a domestic, Mallie moved with her children to a larger house in a white neighborhood within a short period of time. Here she was to feel discrimination, Northern style. The neighbors complained of the noise the children made, and demonstrated clearly that they did not like blacks. Things were very difficult in other ways, too. Mallie's meager wages did not permit even the purchase of decent food for her family. Most of the time they existed on beans and bacon. Only on rare occasions could they afford a slice of salt pork.

At an early age, Jackie began to feel the rod of discrimination and prejudice. Because he was black, he was not permitted to use the public pool, except for one day a week

He was not to enter restaurants where white people ate, nor could he join the local YMCA.

Things began to look up on the day that Mallie, seeking work, went to the public welfare office. The people there, after hearing her story, gave her clothing and saw to it that she would receive thirty dollars a month for rent, fuel, and other needs. About the same time, Jackie discovered that he would no longer have to bring his own sparse lunch to school, because his fine baseball playing got him bountiful free lunches from his teammates. Jackie also found work after school delivering newspapers and collecting junk which he sold at a profit. In addition, he acted as a candy butcher at the Rose Bowl, vending pop and hot dogs.

Jackie's older brother, Mack, played a very significant part in the development of his career. Mack was Jackie's boyhood idol. He was a born athlete, and his admiring young brother so wanted to be like him. For hours, Jackie would watch in awe as Mack batted and fielded a baseball. With all the watching, it is a wonder he ever learned to play himself. He did discover quickly, though, that he could run faster than all the other fellows—except his brother Mack.

Mrs. Robinson was constantly after Jackie to spend more time at his books because she had dreams of his going to college. He was torn between his desire to be an athlete like his brother and his wanting to please his mother. His decision to do both proved to be the best possible one.

In 1936, Mack was chosen to run for the United States in the Olympic games, to be held in Germany. Hitler, who was Chancellor in Germany, had declared that these games would prove the superiority of the German "master race." To Jackie and his friends this was a personal insult. The Pepper Street gang, to which Jackie belonged, was made up of Mexican, Japanese, black and Jewish boys who saw Hitler for what he was. By the time the Olympics were over, Jessie Owens, who won several first-place medals, and Mack Robinson, who came in right behind Owens, proved beyond the shadow of a doubt that Hitler's theory was nonsense.

Not unlike many young American boys all over the nation, Jackie's gang, looking for an outlet, since there was so little athletic or sociable activity available in their neighborhood, found themselves in trouble with the police. Their favorite sport was raiding local farms for the delicious plums, oranges, and grapes that grew on them. They also threw dirt at passing cars, and, when they could fill pails and old pots, threw water on the passers-by. The local juvenile officer would warn them sternly . . . but they would barely wait until he left before they began their mischief all over again.

It is very possible that, had it not been for a young black neighbor named Carl Anderson, Jackie might have found himself serving time in a local prison. Anderson talked sense into Jackie and his friends, convincing them that, if they continued their lawlessness, it could only mean ruined future lives for them. Jackie described the influence of Carl Anderson in this way: "There was no more trouble with the police. Carl organized athletic games. When we weren't busy with sports, we'd go to somebody's house and play cards or parlor games, or we'd give a party to raise money for charity. Thanks to Carl, we grew up with the right ideas."

Another person who played an important part in keeping Robinson on a straight course was the Reverend Karl Downs. Pastor Downs presided over the Scotts Methodist Church. Jackie listened to this man of God, and agreed to help with the work of the parish. This interest in things religious only came after the young man went to college, however.

While he was in high school, Jackie Robinson went all out for sports. He ran for the track team and soon became one of its stars. In football, he was a shining light. It was in baseball, though, that he really showed his athletic ability (Muir Technical High School never had such an all-around athlete on its roles). Probably because of his brother Mack, who was still his great hero, Jackie devoted all his sports time to track when he went on to Pasadena Junior College. His extreme speed made it possible for him to break his brother's broad-jumping record of twenty-five feet by making a leap of twenty-five feet, six and one-half inches. Jackie was very strong by now and had reached the height of six feet. Along with his physical prowess came an aggressiveness that got him the reputation of being "arrogant."

It was inevitable that a youngster who could excel in almost any sport would be offered an athletic scholarship when he finished his two years at Pasadena Junior College. Many colleges hoped that Jackie would see his way clear to come to their campuses to finish his scholastic career. It is told—but the truth of the story has never been verified—that Jackie was offered a large sum of money by a wealthy alumnus of a western college if he would go to a school not scheduled to play this man's alma mater. Robinson finally picked the University of California, at Los Angeles (UCLA), feeling it was a rare privilege for him to be able to attend such a fine university.

Even with his scholarship, it was necessary for Robinson to work while he attended UCLA, if he wanted to have a little extra cash. He served as a valet at some of the motion pictures studios that were located nearby. With this added to all the time he spent on the athletic field, his studies suffered. However, he managed to keep a respectable scholastic average.

During Robinson's stay at UCLA, football was the most popular sport on college campuses all over the United States. Great crowds flocked to the many stadiums on Saturday afternoons to watch and cheer their favorite teams and players. Many of the large number of fans at the UCLA games were drawn there by Jackie Robinson and Kenny Washington. These two were known around the football circuit as the "Touchdown Twins."

Busy with football, studies, and work though he was, this did not prevent Jackie from finding the girl he would later make his wife. Miss Rachel Isum was a student nurse when Jackie first met her. From the beginning of their friendship, she exerted a good influence on him.

During these successful days on the football field, Jackie had just about made up his mind to go into professional football. In 1939, he was the leading college football ground-gainer in the country. It was Rachel who prevailed upon him to give up this idea for one that had always appealed to him—coaching boys in sports.

Robinson was within two weeks of graduation, in 1941, when he decided to leave the university and join the National Youth Administration. There have been several versions as to why he reached this decision at such a critical time. However, the real reason was a simple one. He had not forgotten what Carl Anderson had done for the Pepper Street gang, and he, too, wanted to help youth to grow up strong and good. Mallie was sick from overwork, yet she continued to work hard to keep Jackie in school until he had graduated. His eligibility had run out, so his scholarship had stopped. Even when the Reverend Downs joined Jackie's mother in pleading with him to remain until graduation, he turned them both down. In the National Youth Administration he was able to work with orphans and children from broken homes—boys and girls of every race and creed.

The money Jackie was earning as an athletic director was not sufficient for him to support his mother in the manner that he wanted for her. He realized he must find other work. It was at this time that he was offered the opportunity to play professional football with the Los Angeles Bulldogs. Rachel had been forced to relinquish her dreams for him to the economic demands on a son who wanted most of all to help his sickly mother who had supported him for so long.

War came to the United States on December 7, 1941. The

following day, President Roosevelt went to the Congress and requested the formal declaration. Shortly after, Jackie enlisted in the army. His first assignment was to Fort Riley, Kansas, where he felt the real hard-core discrimination which he had only known about from hearsay previously. As a college man, Jackie sought entrance into Officers' Candidate School. His application was turned down. He discovered that this was true for all black soldiers. The excuse given in each case was that the black candidate was not leadership material. Shortly after Robinson arrived at Fort Riley, Joe Louis, world's heavyweight boxing champion, was assigned to the same base. Robinson told the story of his rejection to Louis, who promptly notified Washington. Just one week later, Jackie was in O.C.S.

The gold bars of a second lieutenant were pinned on Robinson in January, 1943. From that moment, he worked to get fellow black soldiers their rights as American servicemen. He pushed for the right of Negroes to be treated equally in Army PX's. Even in the Post Exchanges, Negro soldiers encountered discrimination when they went to buy Cokes and hot dogs. His work in this area brought him a transfer to Camp Hood, Texas.

At Camp Hood, Robinson joined the 761st Tank Battalion. He explains now that he knew nothing about tanks but was determined, nevertheless, to have the best platoon in the battalion. His intense interest in his work was partly due to his commanding officer, Colonel Bates. Bates saw in Robinson a leader of men. He asked the young lieutenant to come with him when the battalion moved to Europe.

During the period when Robinson was playing professional football he had broken his ankle. If he was to go overseas with Colonel Bates, he would have had to sign a paper (a waiver) declaring that, if he should hurt this ankle again, it would not be the government's responsibility. In the course of this medical problem he was transferred to a base hospital some thirty miles from Camp Hood for further examination. While waiting for his release—for he was not sick—he decided to visit his friends at Camp Hood.

Back at Camp Hood, Jackie discovered that the 761st Tank Battalion was out in the field for a few days. At that point Robinson decided to take a bus running within the base, back to the officers' club. On the bus, he met the wife of a fellow black officer and sat next to her. She was light enough to pass for a white person. The bus driver demanded that Jackie move to the back of the bus. Robinson attempted to explain that the Army had only recently issued orders that there was no longer to be racial segregation on any Army base. In the melee that followed, Jackie Robinson was taken into custody by the military police and was finally given a court-martial. His court-martial proved, beyond the shadow of a doubt, that he was right. It was now too late to join Colonel Bates. His outfit had already left for overseas duty. Jackie had had his fill of discrimination. He decided that he did not want to be assigned to another outfit, so he refused to sign the waiver after all. He requested the Adjutant General, in Washington, D.C., to give him his release from the Army. Within a short time Jackie Robinson received word that he was to be given a medical discharge.

The subway train was pulling into the Flatbush Avenue station in Brooklyn, and Jackie Robinson was shaken out of his daydreaming. Was this interview with General Manager Branch Rickey to be more of the same thing that he had been turning over in his mind during this long, hot ride? He had heard that Rickey did not understand the black problem. Well, one might just as well take a chance and discover the real facts.

As he walked into Rickey's office, the baseball leader rose and, shaking Robinson's hand, asked, "Tell me, Jackie, do you have any idea why I want to talk to you?" Jackie answered in the negative, but said he thought it might be to ask him to join a new black league that was being formed. Rickey quickly cleared this puzzle up by explaining that he wanted Robinson to join the Brooklyn organization by going first to the Montreal team.

Jackie was taken back! Rickey was not at all the type of man he had expected to meet. This white man had for years been quietly fighting to bring Negroes into major league baseball. Some have said Branch Rickey's desire to bring players into major league baseball was motivated simply by the fact that he was a master showman. This charge is unfair, because Rickey was a highly religious person who genuinely believed that all men are created equal.

Rickey had seen discrimination in action when he had coached baseball at Ohio Wesleyan University. He had had his difficulties in getting his black players accepted as his teams moved through the South to meet their schedules.

Branch Rickey had spent much time and money in scouting black baseball players. His scouts had reported to him that, after watching Negroes play in Cuba, Puerto Rico, and Mexico, they had decided that the best ones were playing in the United States.

The scouts had also told Rickey that the most promising of the home-grown players was John Roosevelt Robinson. He could hit, field, and certainly run. He was ideal on other counts also. He neither drank nor smoked, he kept out of trouble, and attended church regularly. The one thing that continued to worry Rickey was whether Robinson could take the abuse from the white fans that he would inevitably face. Could he control himself sufficiently not to fight back? When Jackie walked into Rickey's office, the general manager was prepared to find out for himself what kind of control this young man had.

The general manager put Jackie on his mettle by challenging him with all types of possible nasty situations that a Negro player could expect to encounter.

Finally, Jackie asked, "Mr. Rickey, do you want a ball-player who's afraid to fight?"

Rickey answered him with, "No, I want a ballplayer with guts enough not to fight back."

It was a tense three-hour meeting, but by the time it was over, Rickey knew that at last he had the right man to break the black barrier in a major league baseball team. Robinson signed a contract to play ball for Montreal, a minor league club, at $600.00 a month. For signing the contract he received a $3,500 bonus. The subway ride back to Manhattan was a pleasure!

The fall of 1945 found Robinson playing ball in Venezuela. He was doing what many ballplayers do when the regular season ends in the United States—barnstorming. Following his work in South America, he returned to California to marry Rachel Isum. Miss Isum had patiently waited for Jackie all this time. Their friendship had blossomed into love, but they were not really prepared for the practical problems of life. They had become engaged while they were both still students at UCLA, but had decided not to marry until after the war. This charming and capable young woman became Mrs. J. R. Robinson, on February 10, 1946, in Los Angeles. The couple were married by their old friend, Reverend Karl Downs.

The honeymoon was short and sweet because Jackie was to report for spring training in Florida. Jackie's mother was at the airport to see her son and his bride off. She was worried about their going South. Her worry was well-founded, for it took the newlyweds two days to make the trip, since they were constantly pushed off planes and forced to wait around for later flights. They finally arrived in Fort Lauderdale by bus.

On reaching the Montreal training camp, Robinson was

faced with many troubles. The manager of the team was Clay Hopper. Mr. Hopper came from Mississippi, and it did not take long for Jackie to know how he felt about black baseball players. No matter how well the young Negro performed, Hopper never had a good word for him.

While he was with the Montreals, Robinson hit .349 for the season. With that batting average, he led the International League. This record becomes more impressive when you realize that it was made while Jackie played in 100 games, hit safely 133 times, stole 33 bases, and scored 100 runs. Due in great part to Robinson's contribution, Montreal won the pennant in the International League. This meant that his team would play in the Little World Series. Their opponents would be the Louisville Colonels of the American Association.

The first game of the series was played in Kentucky. The blacks admitted to the park were limited on the theory that the fewer the Negroes, the less chance of trouble. The white fans quickly showed their strong racial feelings toward Jackie Robinson. The stands rocked with cries of, "Hey, black boy, go back to Canada. Take all your nigger-loving friends with you." The last part of the suggestion was directed toward the newspapermen. The sports writers had for years fought to bring an end to the color line in baseball. The heckling had a strong effect on Jackie. In the two games played in Louisville, Robinson got only one hit during eleven times at bat. Montreal left Louisville trailing two games to one.

The remaining games of the series were played in Montreal. In every game, Robinson has to be given the credit for his team's victory. When Montreal won the sixth game and the series, the response of the fans was fabulous. Robinson was carried on the shoulders of the enthusiasts while youngsters tugged at his clothes. The one result of the victory that pleased Jackie the most was the comment by Clay Hopper to Branch Rickey, "There never has been a faster-breaking two way player on the base paths. He's a player who must go to the majors. He's a big-league ballplayer, a good team hustler, and a real gentleman."

Rickey was ready to bring Robinson to Brooklyn, but he was not sure that the public was ready for Robinson, the first black man to play on a big league team. He decided to ask some thirty prominent blacks to dinner, and express to them his concern over what could happen if Robinson were to play in Brooklyn. He explained that overreaction by the black community could do harm to Jackie's big chance. When he had received the assurance from the leaders that everything possible would be done to make Jackie's entrance into the big leagues a smooth one, Rickey decided to move.

On April 11, 1947, back in the office of Branch Rickey, Jackie Robinson signed his first major league contract. The sum was for $5,000, and it was approved four days later by Ford Frick, President of the National League.

Robinson soon found that a big league berth did not necessarily mean that his racial troubles were all over. In fact, he faced more problems from his teammates than from the fans. Two members of the Dodgers' squad asked to be traded rather than to play on the same team with a black man. Bobby Bragan and Dixie Walker, both popular players in Brooklyn, requested that Rickey trade them. The general manager attempted to meet their demands, but was not successful, so they played the first season with Jackie. When the season was over, Bragan told Rickey he had begun to like Robinson.

That first year was a nightmare, not only for Jackie, but for his wife Rachel as well. One point that Rickey had made quite clear to Robinson was that under no circumstance was he to lose his temper. So no matter how he was heckled from the stands, ignored by his teammates, or pressured by a slump in his batting, he had to control his temper and speech. Rachel said later, "I became extremely worried about

Jack. I knew nobody could go along day after day . . . bottling up his emotion. . . . He couldn't eat, and at night he'd toss constantly in his sleep. I insisted that Jack consult a doctor, who warned him if he didn't stay away from the ball park he would surely suffer a nervous breakdown. . . . In two days, he was back, playing ball."

The real test of Jackie's success during that first season was his performance on the diamond. When the fall of 1947 came around, Robinson had played in more games than any other Dodger. He had scored 125 runs and hit safely 174 times. His batting average was .297. In that first season, he hit 12 home runs. The crowning tribute was when the Baseball Writers' Association voted Jackie Robinson the outstanding rookie of the year. *Time* and *Life* placed his picture on their covers after he won the Rookie of the Year Award. Now the favorable comments were beginning to appear that were so unhappily slow in coming earlier in the season. Leo Durocher stated, "He can beat you in more ways than any player I know."

Rickey could now tell Robinson to act naturally, for the period of trial and error was over. With the freedom to react, the tension was lifted from Jackie's shoulders and his already good game improved. Robinson stood toe-to-toe and argued with an umpire until he was thrown out of a game. He could then comment, "Now I feel I belong in the big leagues."

It was not until 1949 that this first black baseball player to make the big leagues reached his peak. In that year, he was named to the All-Star team. In the fall, the Dodgers played in the World Series, and Jackie outdid himself in the field and at bat. Birdie Tebbetts, one of the great managers in modern baseball, summed up Jackie's performance with: "In one spot, in one ball game, where I need the one big base hit, I'd rather have Jackie Robinson up there for me than any other man in baseball."

Jackie was playing great ball in 1950, 1951, and 1952. However, it was in 1951 that he showed his prowess as a true professional. During most of the season the Dodgers were playing superbly and had a lead of thirteen and one-half games over their nearest rival, the New York Giants. As the season wore on, the Dodgers seemed to tire. Down at the wire, with but one game left in the season, they were tied for the league lead with the Giants. The championship would be decided by what the Giants could do with Boston, and what the Dodgers would do with Philadelphia. The pennant would be garnered with a win by one and a loss by the other. The Giants beat Boston 3–2.

In Philadelphia, the Dodgers were losing in the early innings, 6–1, but by the eighth inning they had tied the score 8–8. The game went to fourteen innings, until Jackie broke it with a left-field home run. The Giants and Brooklyn went on to a playoff to decide the championship. A *New York Post* sports writer stated that Robinson proved himself to be "one of the greatest clutch players of all times."

The years were beginning to mount up on Robinson. In the 1955 World Series he played fine ball. In fact, for the first time since he had joined the Dodgers, they defeated the Yankees in the Series. When the 1956 season opened, Jackie found that somehow it took more of an effort to show the same spark that had made him the great hitter and runner he had been in previous years. He was now thirty-eight years old and his announcement to the press told the whole story: "I've got to think of my future. . . . At my age a man doesn't have much of a future in baseball and very little security. I'm quitting the game for good."

When Robinson had made his decision to retire he looked about for some type of employment that could use his talents as a leading black in the United States. In New York, a restaurant owner by the name of William Black needed a troubleshooter for his large staff of employees. Black, the owner of a chain of snack shops called Chock Full O' Nuts, employed over one thousand people, most of them black. Robinson felt that this type of work was just what he would like. His title would be vice-president for personnel affairs. On the very day that he signed a contract with William Black, he was notified by the Dodger front office that he had been traded to the New York Giants. Robinson was sure then that his move out of baseball had been well timed.

At Chock Full O' Nuts Jackie Robinson was kept busy handling the financial problems, salaries, and recreation of the employees. His name did much to attract job seekers to the organization. As an example of the type of employer-employee relationship in which Robinson engaged, when he thought the workers were being exploited by loan companies, he offered to lend them money, interest free.

While at Chock Full O' Nuts, Jackie continued his interest in affairs that would aid his people. He became active in the NAACP, the National Association for the Advancement of Colored People, to such a degree that in 1956, they presented their highest award to him, the Spingarn Medal. He later wrote a column in the *New York Post* that covered the baseball scene primarily, but it also touched on problems concerning civil rights. He took a strong stand against President Eisenhower's weak position on civil rights, and chided Bing Crosby for his failure to integrate the famous Crosby Golf Tournaments.

The presidential campaign of 1960 found Jackie supporting Richard Nixon. To Robinson, John Kennedy was the "fair-haired boy of the Southern segregationists." The failure of Nixon to win in 1960, as seen by Jackie, was due to the Republican standard bearer's refusal to hit hard on the civil rights issue.

Jackie has always claimed that he was not a Republican. He declares flatly that he votes for the man, not the party. When it appeared that the Republicans would nominate

Barry Goldwater in 1964, he resigned from his $50,000 a year job at Chock Full O' Nuts to work for Nelson Rockefeller. When the New York Governor failed to get the nomination, Jackie took a job in his administration dealing with community relations.

The 1968 election found Jackie on the Humphrey team. The failure once more of Rockefeller to nail down the Republican nomination made it impossible for Robinson to support the party of Abraham Lincoln.

Jackie Robinson is prouder of what he has done as a civil rights activist than he is of all his baseball achievements. When, in 1962, the possibility of his being named to the Baseball Hall of Fame was being debated, Robinson said: "The Hall of Fame is tremendously important to me, but if it meant I had to give up anything I did or said, the Hall of Fame would have to go its own way. I did what I thought was right and, to me, right is more important than any honor." He was elected to the Hall of Fame.

His work with Governor Rockefeller is not very pressing, and Jackie Robinson is not the type of man who can sit idly by and watch life move on. Consequently, he is also chairman of the board of Freedom National Bank and vice-president of a new project, the Proteus Company, which provides business opportunities for blacks.

A giant in the arena of civil rights, a man who has never forgotten his trials and tribulations while growing up as a black in America, Jackie Robinson will continue to fight for the civil rights of all peoples as he has done in the past.

> When it came to the key spot of winning or losing a ball game, Robinson was the one man I feared most.
>
> —Leo Durocher

Edward W. Brooke

[1919-   ]

UNITED STATES SENATOR

". . . that's the biggest news in the country!"

—President Kennedy, on hearing of Edward W. Brooke's election as attorney general.

Born into a middle-class Negro family on October 26, 1919, Edward William Brooke was not conscious of being black while he was a child. His father was a practicing attorney working for the Veterans Administration in Washington, D.C. His mother, Helen Seldon Brooke, imposed her strong personality on him. From her he acquired a spirit of independence and a determination to rise above white bigotry once he discovered its existence.

Edward was educated in the city of his birth. He attended Dunlap High School and, upon graduation, enrolled at Howard University. Seven years before he entered Howard, his sister Helene had graduated from this famous Negro institution.

Edward was not a good student. He was more interested in the social functions on campus. He fought to be recognized for election to Alpha Phi Alpha, the oldest Negro social fraternity in the United States. He finally made it—but failed in organic chemistry. This failure held him back for another semester. When he graduated, in 1941, he had given up the thought he had entertained earlier of going to medical school.

The attack on Pearl Harbor took care of Edward's school problems. He had been an ROTC student at Howard. On December 8, 1941, he was called into service as a second lieutenant. His assignment was to the all-black 366th Combat Infantry Regiment at Fort Devens, Massachusetts. Here he did a great deal of work on courts-martial for the enlisted men. It was this work that later convinced him that law was the career he really wanted.

Edward Brooke had an exciting tour of duty in Europe. He fought with General Mark Clark's Fifth Army as it moved to drive Hitler's forces out of Italy. Brooke was awarded a Bronze Star for a courageous daylight attack on an artillery battery, during which he was wounded.

While waiting to be shipped home after V-E day, Lieutenant Brooke decided to spend his leave at Viareggio, an Italian seashore town. While on the beach there, he met Remigia Ferrari-Gracio, the daughter of a wealthy white Genovese merchant. They had only seen each other three times when Edward asked her to marry him. She refused him, and he returned home with just a memory.

Back in Washington, Edward Brooke realized that he had to settle down and decide definitely on a career. Thanks to the advice of two friends from the army, he made up his mind to enter Boston University Law School. He moved to Boston in the fall of 1946 and secured an apartment in the Italian section there. He had heard from Remigia. She wrote that she was coming to the United States and would marry him.

Edward's mother was deeply concerned about her son. She worried, too, about the effect that the reaction of Americans toward a white girl's coming to a strange country to marry a black man might have on Remigia. Edward Brooke was aware of the discrimination that Negroes suffered at the hands of whites in the United States, although he himself had experienced little direct bigotry. When Remigia arrived, however, she was received with open arms by Mrs. Brooke. The young couple were married and moved to Roxbury, Boston's Harlem, to begin a new life together.

Remigia had a good effect on Edward. He had not studied much at Howard—he did nothing but study at Boston University Law School. He became editor of the law review and he graduated with honors. The following autumn he returned to the University to take his master's degree in law.

After passing the bar examinations, he opened a combined law and real estate office in Roxbury. His partner was a wartime buddy, Al Brother. The two made many friends at a time when thousands of Negroes were moving up from the South to seek jobs. Each one of these new residents was a potential voter.

Brooke and his associates decided to take advantage of the friendships he had made by having him run for the state legislature. He ran as a Republican—and lost. In 1952, he ran for the office of judge of the general court in the Roxbury area. He lost the election again, but only by a slight margin.

Edward Brooke decided to stop seeking public elective office. Instead, he became active with the American Veterans of World War II (AMVETS). He was elected Massachusetts State Commander and, later, the National Judge Advocate.

Edward had withdrawn from politics at the right time, as far as Remigia was concerned. She could only remember what happened to politicians under Mussolini. She was also convinced that he should give up seeking elective office because, "He was doing well with the law, and I wanted him close."

For seven years, Edward Brooke built up his reputation in the community. He was named by the Junior Chamber of Commerce, along with John F. Kennedy, one of Boston's "outstanding young men." He was elected to membership on sixteen boards of trustees, including those of Boston University and the Opera Company of Boston, which he later headed.

By 1960, the Republican Party in Massachusetts realized that, if it hoped to succeed, it must pick a state ticket composed of candidates that would get the vote of all the ethnic groups. For too long they had supported only Anglo-Saxon office seekers—and the Democrats, with a variety of office-seekers, had won all the elections. As a result, the Republican leadership selected an Italian Catholic to run for governor, and Edward Brooke for secretary of state. Both were readily nominated. This was the first time in the history of the United States that a black man had been nominated by a major party for a statewide office.

The Brooke campaign was run on the sole issue that he was an American. He stated it this way, "I honestly believe that people will vote for a man on the basis of his qualifications for public office."

Election day was not one of happy triumph for the Brooke family. The Democratic tidal wave, led by John F. Kennedy, defeated Edward Brooke, but he had polled over one million ballots, having lost by less than 12,000 votes. Edward Brooke had lost the election, but he had won the support of the Republican leadership as a vote-getter.

Governor Volpe, who had been the only Republican on the state ticket to win, chose Brooke to head up the powerful Boston Finance Committee. It was the duty of this committee to uncover any graft and corruption in Massachusetts—if there was any. Everyone waited to see what Edward Brooke was going to do with his new responsibility.

Remigia was proud of her husband. Although busy with their two little girls, Remi and Edwina, she found time to be at his side at most public functions. She was fast becoming accustomed to the responsibilities faced by a politician's wife.

As chairman of the Finance Committee, Edward Brooke

opened up a hornet's nest of corruption in both state and city government. His investigations were not limited to Democrats, as members of his own party soon discovered. He was truly a successful prosecutor.

In 1962, Brooke decided to run for attorney general of Massachusetts. There were many within his own party who would have preferred to have him take a judgeship and forget another election. However, he was determined to go ahead.

He secured the nomination over a powerful, well-known member of his own party, and won the election with a total vote of 1,143,065. It was his first victory out of four tries.

Brooke, not like the majority of Negro leaders, refused to be identified as black. He was not ashamed of his heritage, but he argued that he should be taken as anyone else in American society. After his election as attorney general, he believed his family was entitled to better living conditions. He bought a house in a stylish suburb of Boston and moved out of Roxbury, where he had lived for ten years.

When his two years were up as attorney general, he decided to run for reelection. This was a difficult year, for in 1964, the Republicans nominated Barry Goldwater for president. Brooke felt he could not support Goldwater, and said so. In spite of the tremendous vote that President Johnson received in Massachusetts, Edward Brooke won with a majority of 800,000 votes.

Brooke was questioned, following his victory, by a reporter from *U.S. News and World Report:* "Have you in mind running for a higher office someday?" Brooke answered: "I guess I wouldn't be a politician if I didn't, and I certainly plead guilty to being a politician."

Edward Brooke made the leap into national politics in 1966. His book, *The Challenge of Change,* was published that same year. In it he took his party to task for not keeping up with the times. Many believed this would hinder him from obtaining a higher office in the Republican party. This was not the case, however, for he went on to win the nomination for the United States Senate, followed by the election in November.

When the Congress convened on January 6, 1967, Senator Brooke was escorted by his senior colleague, Senator Edward M. Kennedy, to be sworn in before Vice-President Hubert Humphrey. Here was a black man who represented one of the most conservative of states. He was a dependable, religious, and dedicated public official.

Edward Brooke presented a personality that was to establish a new role for the Negro minority. He was a black man who represented not only his own people, but the other cultures in his state as well, with the firm conviction that America was for everybody.

Remigia and the children made the move to Washington with great expectations. They, like Edward Brooke, know that the day must come when a man's color will not be the determination of his rights as an American.

> Concerning Brooke's election: ". . . the most exciting step forward for Negroes in politics since Abraham Lincoln freed the slaves."
>
> —Clarence Mitchell,
> NAACP Washington Bureau Director

Reverend Martin Luther King, Jr.

[1929-1968]

CLERGYMAN

He has an indescribable capacity for empathy that is the touchstone of leadership.

—*Time,* January 3, 1964

Standing in the middle aisle of the Dexter Avenue Baptist Church, in late September, 1954, Martin Luther King, Jr., wondered why he had decided to come to Montgomery, Alabama. He was still working on his dissertation for his doctor of philosophy degree at Boston University. He believed that until he received this degree, he should not undertake any other work. However, he could not forget that in Montgomery there was a challenge, and to Martin there was nothing more persuasive than a good challenge. His people needed him—his degree could wait.

Martin Luther King, Jr., was born on January 15, 1929, in Atlanta, Georgia. The prophetic name of Martin Luther was given to King, not at birth but at the age of six, about the time that his father also changed his name. Originally, it was Michael Luther King. There were two other children in the family: an older sister, Christine, and a younger brother, Albert Daniel.

The mother of this outstanding boy had been a school-teacher before her marriage. Her father was the Reverend

Adam Daniel Williams, who was pastor of the Ebenezer
Baptist Church, in Atlanta. When Alberta Williams married
Martin Luther King, Sr., he was serving as an assistant to his
father-in-law. King took over the pastorage on the death of
Reverend Williams, in 1931. He continued his pioneering
work in resisting discrimination against the black race.

The King family was not economically deprived. Young
Martin did not suffer from want the way so many of his race
have. He had a good home, a twelve-room structure, and
plenty to eat. However, he learned early what segregation
meant, and felt deeply the emotional pangs that it brought.
He was only six years old when he discovered that two white
boys whom he had known quite well were forbidden to play
with him because he was black.

When Martin began school at the Young Street Grade
School, which was an all-Negro institution, he learned more
about segregation. White students would cross to the opposite
side of the street when passing his school. The whites, when
they came upon the black students, would call them harsh
names and pelt them with refuse.

Pastor King saw that young Martin had a keen mind and
was a fine student. It was decided to transfer him from the
local public school to the private laboratory school at the
University of Atlanta. This school took only the most promising of students.

When Martin was ready for junior high school, he was sent
to the Booker T. Washington High School in Atlanta.
During his time there, he carried on his studies so well that
he skipped the ninth and twelfth grades and graduated at
the age of fifteen.

When, in 1944, Martin entered Morehouse College, in
Atlanta, he had no intention of following in his father's
footsteps. Although his father and grandfather had gone to
Morehouse and entered the ministry, Martin's interests did
not lean in the direction of the church. The studious, calm,

and quiet young man felt he was not geared to the excitement and activity of church leadership. This was the way he expressed his feelings many years later, after he had changed his mind on the subject: "I felt that the life of a clergyman was beyond my reach."

The president of Morehouse College was Benjamin Mays, who had known Martin's father when he attended the college. Mays took a special interest in this bright fifteen-year-old boy. Rev. George Kelsey taught Martin his courses in philosophy. The impact that this man of God had on his young student was tremendous. It was Kelsey who impressed Martin with the belief that a career in the ministry could be intellectually as well as spiritually satisfying. As Martin Luther King said later, "Professor Kelsey had more to do with making me the man I am than anyone else I have ever known." How frequently a dedicated teacher should receive the credit for many promising careers of those who studied under him—and yet how frequently that teacher never knows of his success.

It was a proud day for the Reverend and Mrs. Martin Luther King, Sr., when, in June, 1947, their eldest son was ordained a minister in his father's church. While presiding at the ordination, the happy father told the assembled congregation, "This is truly a day of joy. Mrs. King and myself have prayed for this day for many years." Martin was named as assistant pastor to his father. However, he had yet to earn his degree from Morehouse. In September, he returned to college and managed to maintain a B average. At the same time, he sang in the college glee club and became active in the National Association for the Advancement of Colored People.

Martin Luther King received his degree in June, 1948, and immediately made plans to further his religious training by attending Crozer Theological Seminary, in Chester, Pennsylvania. This move proved most significant for the young minister. It was the first time that Martin had been so far from home. He also realized that, at Crozer, he would be on trial. He was one of only six black students in a student body of some one hundred. He threw himself into his studies with dedication and enthusiasm.

Young King was keenly aware that President Truman was fighting an uphill battle for a "strong" civil rights bill. He was also alert to the fact that the black man in America was beginning to lose patience. Little did he suspect, at this time, that he was actually preparing himself to lead his people toward their rightful place in American life.

Martin did well at Crozer. He was an excellent student, maintaining an A average for the three-year course. He even took additional courses in philosophy at the University of Pennsylvania. It was while he was at Crozer that he read widely in philosophy and political science. One strong attraction for him was the career of Gandhi, the Indian non-violent civil rights leader who did so much to free India from British rule.

King was graduated in June, 1951, from Crozer Theological Seminary. He left the school with a fine record. He won the Plafker Award as the most outstanding student, was president of the senior class, and received the J. Lewis Crozer fellowship of $1,200 for graduate study at a university of his choice. He came away from Crozer with more than material things. He was now a mature, determined, and dedicated man for the cause of his people.

Martin knew that, to be more effective, he must continue his formal education. He enrolled in Boston University as a graduate student in philosophy. He arrived in Boston in a new green Chevrolet that was his dad's graduation present to his son. Here, the young graduate student would achieve some of his most singular triumphs.

Miss Coretta Scott was studying at Boston's New England Conservatory of Music when Martin Luther King, Jr., was working at Boston University. Unlike Martin, Coretta had faced much hardship before arriving in Boston. Her family, from Heiberger, Alabama, were truly victims of the depression. This young girl had to fight every inch of the way to finally reach her goal—the New England Conservatory of Music.

When Martin met Coretta, he was quite sure that his "plans for the future" did not include marriage. Coretta, like most young women, was waiting for her knight in shining armor and she was sure that there could be little stirring romance in a minister.

It was not long, however, before Coretta would be admitting, "The more I see of him, the more I like him." She was impressed by the fact that "he talked so often about what he planned to do with his life, of what he hoped to contribute to the race and to humanity at large. . . ." She knew that it would only be a question of time before she would marry Martin. So, on June 18, 1953, Coretta Scott said "yes" to God and to Martin Luther King, Jr., in a lovely garden wedding in Heiberger, Alabama. Martin Luther King, Sr., officiated.

Martin was finishing his work toward the degree of doctor of philosophy that year. He believed that, as a married man with responsibilities, he must now find some type of employment. He had had many offers that ranged from teaching to pastorates at several churches. He would have welcomed the opportunity to teach and, at the same time to be a pastor of his own church.

When, with the complete approval of his wife, he finally decided to accept an offer, it was from the Dexter Avenue Baptist Church of Montgomery, Alabama. The decision to go to Montgomery marked a sharp break in King's life. He had spent twenty-one years in school; now he was free to make his way in the world. He stood on the brink of a new existence. He was prepared physically and mentally to do the work God had chosen for him.

Montgomery, Alabama, proved to be a battleground for Martin Luther King. The Montgomery City Lines, a northern-owned bus company, brought young King into national prominence. The struggle in Montgomery began with the Kings' arrival, on September 1, 1954, and reached its high point on December 5, 1955. During this same period, Martin managed to finish his degree requirements, and he received his Ph.D. in June, 1955.

During the first few months following their arrival in Montgomery, Coretta and Martin King were extremely happy. In their home were love and congeniality, and the congregation was most receptive to the new pastor and his wife. This serene way of living did not last, for, after the Supreme Court's May 31, 1955, order for school desegregation with "all deliberate speed," the atmosphere in the South became increasingly difficult.

Montgomery became the center of black protest when, on December 1, 1955, a young black woman refused to give up her seat on a bus to a white person. She was arrested, and that arrest unified the entire black community. This young black woman had formerly been the secretary of the local NAACP branch.

Martin Luther King, Jr., and the Reverend Ralph D. Abernathy worked out a program to stage a one-day boycott against the Montgomery City Lines. This was supported by the black community.

December 5th dawned warm and cloudy. It was the day of the boycott and Dr. King was up early, for he was not sure how much support the black people of Montgomery would give to this protest. Watching from his living room window, he received his answer when he saw that the first bus that passed his door was completely empty. He quickly realized that a "miracle" had happened. The boycott was almost totally effective. It remained so for an entire year.

From this first effective action came Martin's opportunity.

The black leaders of Montgomery had formed the Montgomery Improvement Association and elected Martin Luther King its president. He had accepted the post because no one wanted the honor, being uncertain about what might happen. Dr. King met the challenge with one of the greatest speeches of his life when he addressed a mass meeting on that fateful night of December 5th at the Holt Street Baptist Church. He declared in a firm voice to his associates, "I must make a speech that will be militant enough to keep my people aroused to positive action and yet moderate enough to keep their fervor within controllable and Christian bounds." This would be his basic philosophy from then until his life was ended. He told his audience, "Our method will be that of persuasion, not coercion. We will only say to the people, 'Let your conscience be your guide.' Love must be our regulating ideal. Once again we must hear the words of Jesus echoing across the centuries: 'Love your enemies, bless them that curse you, and pray for them that despitefully use you.' As Booker T. Washington said, 'Let no man pull you so low as to make you hate him.' "

With Ralph D. Abernathy to assist him, King put together a working organization. The boycott was functioning, while money poured in from all over the country to aid the cause. Some three hundred automobiles were making regular runs from forty-six pick-up stations in the area.

Dr. King was catapulted into undisputed leadership of the Montgomery boycott when he was arrested on January 26, 1956. The charge was ludicrous—"driving thirty miles an hour in a twenty-five mile zone." He was placed in a cell and remained there until the authorities, fearing the large crowd that surrounded the jail, released him after he signed his own bond.

Four days later, on January 30, while Dr. King was addressing a mass meeting, his home was bombed. Mrs. King, fortunately, was not injured, nor was her baby, who was asleep in a back bedroom. When Martin returned home, he found almost one thousand of his people in a violent mood, milling about outside his house. It was clear that the crowd was on the verge of a violent outbreak. If it came, Montgomery would go through a blood bath.

This moment changed the course of the racial protest and made Martin Luther King a living symbol. Standing on his front porch, he quietly addressed the crowd: "Don't get panicky. Don't do anything panicky at all. Don't get your weapons. He who lives by the sword will perish by the sword. We are not advocating violence, I want you to love our enemies. Be good to them. Love them and let them know you love them." When he finished, the crowd quietly began to disperse, its anger deflected, under control.

In November, 1956, the United States Supreme Court ruled that a decision of a lower court, sanctioning the Alabama laws requiring segregation on buses, was unconstitutional. On December 21st, blacks and whites rode for the first time together in desegregated buses in Montgomery, Alabama.

Black leaders from ten Southern states met in the Ebenezer Baptist Church in January, 1957, to form what has since been known as the Southern Christian Leadership Conference. The following month, Dr. King was elected its president. The work of the Conference was concentrated on eliminating discrimination in transportation and voter registration.

By now, Dr. King was in demand to appear all over the world. His prominence in the black protest movement caused him to travel some 78,000 miles to make well over 208 speeches in 1957. During the next year, he visited Ghana as a guest of the new government. He also completed his first book, which he entitled *Stride Toward Freedom*. It told the story of the Montgomery boycott. While he was in a bookstore in Harlem, late in September, 1958, promoting the sale

of his book, he was stabbed by a deranged woman. His reaction to this incident was that it indicated "a climate of
violence, hatred and bitterness" that was spreading throughout the country.

In early 1959, Martin Luther King fulfilled a long-time
dream. Ever since he had first read the works of Gandhi he
had wanted to visit India. He had a long-standing invitation
from Prime Minister Nehru but had never been able to get
away. Now he was determined to go. Receiving a grant from
the American Friends Service, he made the long trip, accompanied by his wife and several close friends. His comment
at the airport, upon his arrival in India, showed his true
feelings, "To other countries I may go as a tourist, but to
India, I come as a pilgrim." His visit to Nehru was a most
satisfying experience. To Martin, Nehru was a man of great
perception and feeling.

After returning from India, Martin devoted most of his
time to attending demonstrations throughout the United
States in behalf of desegregation. He realized that his national
commitment made it impossible for him to do justice to his
pastorage in Montgomery, so in January, 1960, he resigned,
moved from Montgomery to Atlanta, and became assistant
to his father in the Ebenezer Baptist Church.

Following the sit-in by four young blacks in a lunch
counter in Greensboro, North Carolina, in early 1960, Dr.
King realized this was the turning point in race relations in
America. He is known as the father of the sit-in because he
inspired and encouraged this civil-disobedience type of
demonstration.

Events in 1961 and 1962—especially the Freedom Ride
crisis—caused Martin Luther King to realize the seriousness
of the moral crisis facing the country. His role with the
Freedom Riders was more passive than active. He went to
Montgomery, Alabama, in May, 1961, to speak at a mass
meeting being held by this organization. Some of its mem-

bers had been assaulted a few days before, and Attorney General Robert F. Kennedy had sent four hundred U.S. marshals to the city to maintain public order. Dr. King told his audience that night, "The law may not be able to make a man love me, but it can keep him from lynching me."

While Martin Luther King sang and prayed in the First Baptist Church, U. S. marshals, aided by the National Guard, battled the crowd that fought to enter the building. When the authorities managed to evacuate the Freedom Riders, the latter formed a Coordinating Committee with Dr. King as their spokesman.

In October, 1962, Dr. King was invited to the White House to talk with President Kennedy. When John F. Kennedy had run for office in 1960, Martin Luther King saw him as "a leader unafraid of change, a young, bold, questing spirit." However, Martin was not too sure of his man during his first two years in office. He went to Washington to press for a more decisive stand on civil rights from Kennedy's administration. He had to wait until 1963 before a member of the Kennedy family emerged who would press hard for civil rights—the President's brother, Robert.

The Southern Christian Leadership Conference ran into trouble during late 1961. They continued to experience difficulty when, in Birmingham, Alabama, in 1963, Dr. King moved to set up fair living practices and also the desegregation of facilities in department stores. A court order had barred demonstrations; King defied the order and was jailed. While in prison, he wrote his famous "Letter from Birmingham Jail." This was his answer to his fellow clergymen who criticized him for what they called his "unwise and untimely" action. Dr. King said in part, "In no sense do I advocate evading or defying the law as the rabid segregationist would do. This would lead to anarchy."

Coretta would have wished to have played a more active part during this period, but she now had a growing family to take up most of her time. The oldest girl, Yolanda Denise, could keep an eye on the younger children, but they needed the steady attention of a mother. In quiet succession Coretta presented Martin with Martin Luther III, Dexter, and Bernice. The King family was growing.

King's work in Birmingham paid worthwhile dividends. Following his sojourn in jail, the interracial crisis lessened. Whites and blacks negotiated an agreement for a program of desegregation that would gradually bring Birmingham into line. The fight for civil rights in that city had been won. King tells the story of this hard-fought victory in his second book, *Why We Can't Wait.*

Birmingham was the beginning. In some 800 towns and cities all over the United States similar action was undertaken on a less spectacular scale. On October 28, 1963, the largest civil rights demonstration in the history of the United States took place. Over 250,000 marchers, of whom 60,000 were white, moved on Washington to press for the passage of the civil rights bill then under consideration by Congress. It was at this gathering, in front of the Lincoln Memorial, that Martin Luther King gave his "I Have a Dream" speech. The speech echoed the Bible, the Constitution, and the National Anthem to prove to this large gathering that the freedom for blacks would yet come true. Dr. King gazed over the vast sea of faces and spoke: "I have a dream that one day every valley shall be exalted, every hill and mountain shall be made low, the rough places will be made plain, and the crooked places will be made straight, and the glory of the Lord shall be revealed, and all flesh shall see it together." In 1963 Dr. Martin Luther King was awarded the St. Francis Peace Medal by the North American Federation of the Third Order of Saint Francis, a Layman's Order in the Catholic Church. In accepting the Peace Medal Dr. King said that it was the first time he had been honored by a

Catholic organization, and that this added a new significant dimension to his role in the non-violent movement.

The year 1964 was a trying one for Dr. King. It was the year during which Congress passed a civil rights act that Martin felt did not go far enough toward giving minorities their just privileges. It was also the year that saw the minorities in northern urban areas riot for their basic rights. Leaders of the fight for civil rights were beginning to question whether the nonviolence thesis of Dr. King was the answer to the problem. It was during the summer of 1964 that Martin Luther King, for the first time, moved directly into the national political arena. The nomination of Barry Goldwater by the Republicans determined Martin to campaign actively for his defeat. Martin's decision to get into the campaign came after he testified on civil rights before the platform committee of both major parties.

All of King's experiences in 1964 were not negative, however. In March he heard that eight members of the Swedish Parliament had nominated him for the Nobel Peace Prize. He was almost certain that he would not be chosen, even though he had received many honors in the previous year. In 1963, *Time* magazine had named him "Man of the Year." In its comments, *Time* declared: "King was selected as a man but also as the representative of his people, for whom 1963 was perhaps the most important year in their history. The American Negro made 1963 the year of his outcry for equality, of massive demonstrations, of sit-ins and speeches and street fighting, of soul searching in the suburbs and psalm singing in the jails." Many more honors were added as 1964 progressed.

In September, 1964, Dr. King toured Europe. His decision to go abroad came with an invitation to visit West Berlin -Sex from Willy Brandt, the mayor. After talking with Protestant leaders in both East and West Berlin, Martin flew with his good friend Reverend Abernathy to Rome for a private audience with Pope Paul VI. His talk with the Pope appears to have been most beneficial. King explained the meeting as a "profound encouragement for all Christians in the world and particularly in the United States who are involved in the civil rights struggle with us."

Upon arriving back in the United States, Dr. King was privately informed that he had been selected as the Nobel Peace Prize winner for 1964. On October 14, the world was given the news of the selection. When Martin Luther King was nominated, the press release declared: ". . . he has succeeded in keeping his followers to the principle of non-violence. Without King's confirmed effectiveness . . . demonstrations and marches could easily have become violent and ended with the spilling of blood."

The choice of Dr. Martin Luther King, Jr., as the Nobel Peace Prize winner was most significant. It can be stated with emphasis that the choice showed international concern for America's racial struggle. King was the twelfth American to receive the award, and the youngest person ever chosen.

Martin Luther King went to Oslo to receive the award and showed his modest and self-effacing strain by seeing the Prize "as a sign that world public opinion was on the side of those struggling for freedom and dignity." The point was made again when he received the plaque and stated: "I accept the Nobel Prize for Peace at a moment when twenty-two million Negroes of the United States of America are engaged in a creative battle to end the long night of racial injustice."

The King family was now at the apex of its long trail. When Martin came home to his modest red brick house in Atlanta, his four children, Yolanda Denise, Martin III, Dexter, and Bernice Albertine, greeted him enthusiastically and hoped he would remain with them for a long time. When their dad had time to play with them, he showed a great interest in their favorite amusements. He was forever taking Martin III to baseball games, and many evenings found the children with their parents, listening to famous operas. The King home was a happy home where Mother and Dad prayed and played with their youngsters as a natural part of their lives.

Martin Luther King was not an ascetic, yet his ability to mingle with all types of people did not take away from his detached elusive quality—a quality that explained his strength.

From Oslo, Martin went on to receive more and more honors. On December 7, 1965, the Judaism and World Peace Award of the Synagogue Council of America was bestowed on him. His campaign to get his people their rights was not allowed to falter. He moved back and forth across the South in his quest for fair play and justice.

Civil servants all over America strove to improve their working conditions as the sixties moved toward a close. The inflation that plagued the United States called for workers' action. In Memphis, Tennessee, on February 12, 1968, some 1,300 sanitation employees walked off their jobs in a dispute over wages, union recognition, and a dues-checkoff arrangement. The strike continued, and on Thursday, March 30th, Martin Luther King went to Memphis to give his support to the strikers. A peaceful march was held, led by Dr. King. Unfortunately, the march ended in violence that took the life of a sixteen-year-old black youth.

As a result of the strife, the city officials sought a Federal injunction. It was granted on April 3rd, prohibiting the Reverend Dr. Martin Luther King, Jr., from leading a civil rights march that was scheduled to be held on Monday, April 8, in Memphis. Dr. King planned to appeal the court order.

While his attorneys prepared their appeal, he waited in Memphis. He and his associates were staying at the Lorraine Motel, and all day on April 4th, he worked on plans for the march that he knew would come. At a few minutes past

6 P.M., Dr. King stepped out on the motel balcony facing the street. He was leaning over the rail to talk to some of his friends below when the crack of a rifle was heard over the din of the city. Dr. King reached for his throat and swayed into the arms of one of his assistants. Within an hour, the hospital to which the injured leader had been rushed notified his associates, who were waiting anxiously, that Dr. Martin Luther King, Jr., was dead.

The great leader in the struggle for true freedom for his people was gone—but not his ideals and hopes. The nation mourned and wondered. Carl Sandburg, Lincoln's biographer, once said that "a tree is measured best when it is down;" but it is certainly true, also, that standing trees can tell us things that fallen trees cannot. Martin Luther King had fallen, and with his fall his greatness could truly be measured.

Coretta King was a tower of strength to Martin. All through the years of their marriage this young woman worked closely with the man who was to do so much to make the black man's cause a success. Coretta King read and edited her husband's speeches. She accompanied him, when she could leave her children, on his important assignments. Her closeness to the cause of Martin Luther King, Jr., has made her a distinct asset to his assistants since his death.

> Dr. King dedicated himself to justice and love between his fellow human beings. He gave his life for that principle, and it is up to those of us who are here . . . to carry out that dream . . .
>
> —Robert F. Kennedy, April 4, 1968

James Howard Meredith

[1933-   ]

CIVIL RIGHTS LEADER

> He wanted to break the system that had oppressed him.
> He was bitter, a real crusader (who) wanted to get back
> at society. He was fighting the battle all the time—in
> everything he said, in everything he did.
>
> —A close friend of James Meredith

Moses Meredith was the son of a slave who ran an eighty-four-acre cotton and corn farm near Kosciusko, in the rocky bottomland of Attala County, in North Central Mississippi. "Cap" Meredith, as Moses was known to his friends, married Roxie Smith in the early 1920's. By the time Franklin D. Roosevelt entered the White House, this couple had six children, with a seventh on the way.

On June 25, 1933, Roxie presented Moses with their seventh child, a boy. They named him James Howard. There were to be six more children for the Merediths, making a total of thirteen. James, as the seventh child, always declared that he was born "between things. . . . It was like being an only child. I got used to taking care of things myself." He was forced to become independent very quickly.

Moses was a fighter against the domination white southerners held over the black population. The influence "Cap" had over James was tremendous. James's father was so anti-white that he would have absolutely nothing to do with his neighbors. Moses Meredith kept his family so far from any contact with whites that James, when he first left Mississippi at the age of sixteen, had never been in a white person's home.

Home life for the Merediths was hard. Their house was poorly constructed, so that the rain and wind blew through the boards. There were no bath, no toilet, and no running water in the building. The few beds for this large family had been acquired many years before by Moses, when he was a sharecropper. However, the young Merediths were a proud group that had the leadership of a strong mother and father.

As has been pointed out, during most of his growing years James Meredith had little or nothing to do with white folks. The stand-off attitude of his dad made his young life one of almost complete isolation. Even when he went into town, he shunned the white stores and movie theaters.

It took James some time before he realized that his was not the best of all worlds. He attended Tipton High School in Kosciusko. Each day he walked the four miles to and from school while the white children rode. The inequality was not in transportation alone, for the white teachers received higher pay than the black teachers. The State of Mississippi was paying three times as much to educate a white child as a black youngster. The Supreme Court had ruled, in *Plessy v. Ferguson,* that schooling should be "separate but equal." All the Negroes received in the way of education was everything "separate" but nothing "equal."

Even with all of this unfairness, the questions of discrimination and opportunity differences did not strike Meredith until he was fifteen, and visited relatives in Detroit. On his way home on the train, the conductor made all of the Negroes move into a "Jim Crow" car when the train reached Memphis. ("Jim Crow" is an expression used to indicate a segregated place.)

From then on, James Meredith knew what he wanted to do in life. He was determined to fight white domination. He realized that if that goal was to be reached, he must have a better education. Kosciusko was not the place in which to get quality education, so he went to St. Petersburg, Florida, where an aunt lived, to complete high school studies.

It is not to be supposed that because of his serious, intense nature, James had no fun as a boy. He fished and hiked with his friends. He learned to use a .22 rifle so well that he was considered an excellent marksman. He was fond of reading, and perused everything that the Tipton High School library contained, even the cook books.

When he graduated in June, 1951, from Gibbs High School, he wanted overwhelmingly to go to college, but there wasn't any money for tuition. He had heard that the University of Mississippi would soon be admitting Negroes. Most southern colleges had begun to change their policy of admissions. When that change would actually come, he was not sure, so he decided to enlist in the United States Air Force. Thanks to the work of General Benjamin O. Davis, Jr., the Air Force was the most integrated of the three armed services. (See *General Benjamin O. Davis, Senior and Junior* elsewhere in this book.) Meredith enlisted on July 28, 1951.

During his period of service, he was known as a careful person with his money. By the time he was promoted to sergeant, he had actually saved thousands of dollars. He explained his saving like this: "I knew what I wanted to do when I got out, so I saved."

His time in the Air Force was not all occupied with military work. He took a series of college extension courses at the University of Kansas and at Washburn University in Topeka. During the years from 1954 to 1960, he elected several of the courses that are offered to service personnel by universities and colleges throughout the United States, which accept them for credit. Meredith carried on these studies during the time that he served within the United States, as well as when he was assigned to Japan.

In 1955, Meredith was assigned to the Bunker Hill Air Base. While there, he met Mary June Wiggins. Mary June was from Gary, Indiana, and had spent some time at Howard University before going to Boston University. She met James at a USO dance. Their friendship was, at first, very casual. However, the intense desire that James had for education and advancement attracted Mary June. They were married in 1956.

When James Meredith transferred to Japan, Mary June accompanied him. It was here that their daughter Mary was born. Meanwhile, both were experiencing an entirely new feeling. In the eyes of the Japanese, that these two young Americans were black made no difference whatever.

Discharge came for James Meredith in 1960 at Memphis, Tennessee. He promptly drove back to Mississippi. It was the first time that he had returned to his native state in nine years. During all his tour of duty with the Air Force, he had lost none of his zeal to fight against white supremacy. He states it clearly: "Victory over discrimination, oppression, the unequal applications of the law was my goal." He felt that he had a divine mission to accomplish this task.

Both James and Mary knew that, to reach their mutual objective, they must complete their education. They could not, as yet, enter the University of Mississippi, so they arranged to enter all-black Jackson State College. While at Jackson, Meredith became convinced, "that only a power struggle between state and the Federal Government could make it possible . . . to gain admission to the University of Mississippi."

James Meredith, in 1961, believed that President Kennedy would stand by him as he sought to see his mission fulfilled. John Kennedy, James believed, owed a great debt to the black man for his narrow margin of victory. The day after John F.

Kennedy took the oath of office, Meredith wrote the University of Mississippi for an application.

The application was forwarded to James, and he returned it to the registrar on January 31, 1961. With the application, he sent a picture of himself, plus the statement, "I am an American—Mississippi—Negro citizen." Two days before registration, he received a telegram declaring he "was not eligible" because his application "was received after January 25th, the deadline date"!

In anticipation of trouble, Meredith had already seen Medgar Evers, Mississippi field secretary for the NAACP. A long, involved court fight with the State of Mississippi would cost a great deal of money. Evers, with no direct authority, agreed to help. (See *Medgar Evers* elsewhere in this book.)

Evers suggested that a letter to Thurgood Marshall, attorney for the NAACP Legal Defense and Educational Fund, could prove helpful. (See *Thurgood Marshall* elsewhere in this book.) James's letter told Marshall of the problem and declared that this, for him, would be a fight to the finish.

Marshall and Meredith did not hit it off too well at first. Marshall wanted to be sure of his man, and he requested documents to prove Meredith's position. Meredith resented being asked to prove his sincerity. If it had not been for Evers, the entire matter would have died. Evers calmed Meredith down and induced him to collect the documents Thurgood Marshall wanted. Marshall then wrote, "I think it should go without saying that we are vitally interested in what you propose."

A staff member of the NAACP was assigned to the case. The lawyer selected was Constance Baker Motley. (See *Constance Baker Motley* elsewhere in this book.) Her effective work on cases involving southern discrimination was well known. James Meredith saw her appointment as "the best possible thing that could have happened. I do not believe that anyone else could have survived two and a half years of Mississippi courts."

All types of persuasion were used to discourage Meredith in his determination to enter the University of Mississippi. Neighbors in Kosciusko were pressed to tell unfavorable stories about him. His records in high school, the Air Force, and Jackson State College were combed for any possible negative evidence that they might contain.

James Meredith and Constance Baker Motley brought the suit against the University of Mississippi into Federal Court in Biloxi. Judge Mize ruled that the registrar of the University of Mississippi had not denied Meredith admission because of color. The argument was that James Meredith failed to qualify academically. It took Mize a total of 118 days to reach this decision. It was now a year since James had sent in his first application.

Mrs. Motley turned to the United States Fifth Circuit Court of Appeals. She was hoping to get an injunction that would permit Meredith to attend the winter semester. The appeals court agreed to the fact that the University of Mississippi discriminated against blacks. However, it upheld Judge Mize because they wanted him to proceed with a full trial. This would permit James Meredith, if successful, to enter the school in the February term.

The judicial byplay that followed reads like a novel. Judge Mize moved quickly to restate his previous decision. Mrs. Motley returned to the Court of Appeals and won a two-to-one decision that ordered the admission of James Meredith to the University. At that point, one of the judges of the appeals court issued a stay order.

The appeals court, which previously had declared, "We find that James H. Meredith's application for transfer to the University of Mississippi was turned down solely because he was a Negro," was not to be stopped now. However, the harder they struggled, the more they were frustrated.

Mrs. Motley took the only road now open to her—the United States Supreme Court. The Court was in recess, so the request went to Justice Hugo L. Black. The assignment fell to Judge Black because he was in Washington and was in charge of the Fifth Circuit business. Black reviewed the case and upheld the decision of the Fifth Circuit. Judge Mize issued the order for the University to admit Meredith. It was all over—or so Mrs. Motley thought, when she declared, "This is the end of the road for the University."

She had failed to reckon with Governor Ross Barnett of Mississippi. He took over when the courts had spoken. He declared that he would not accept the Federal Government order.

The Department of Justice decided to look into the matter on the theory that it might have to act. Little did it realize how quickly it would be drawn into the struggle. When Judge Mize issued his new order, Governor Barnett declared that Mississippi would operate its own schools, regardless of what the Federal Government did or said.

The United States Department of Justice sent marshals to Mississippi to enforce the court's order. They escorted James Meredith to the University campus. Governor Barnett was there personally to prevent the Negro student's entrance. He was able to turn back Meredith and the marshals.

The Department of Justice moved to force obedience to the court order. It was unfortunate that the fight to get Meredith his rights had now turned into a struggle over states' rights. The fight that the NAACP had begun—a fight to permit a black man to attend a white-dominated school—seemed to have been lost.

After several more attempts to move Governor Barnett, the federal marshals were ordered to use force to get James

Meredith on campus. Attorney General Robert Kennedy, brother of President John Kennedy, had had his fill of Ross Barnett and his clique. Action was now the order of the day. When again it was impossible to force entrance to the campus with marshals, President Kennedy ordered the Secretary of Defense to take the necessary steps to enforce the Fifth Circuit Court's order.

This action brought units of the Mississippi National Guard to the scene. After a wild night of white student revolting, the marshals and National Guard managed to have James Howard Meredith admitted to the campus of the University of Mississippi. However, before that task was accomplished, two men had died in the melee.

James Meredith realized that he had been responsible for breaking the wall of discrimination at the University of Mississippi. However, after ten days of constant pressure, and living surrounded by federal marshals day and night, he decided to quit. It was only after great pressure on the part of his friends that he finally decided to stay on until graduation.

On August 18, 1963, James Meredith received his diploma from the University of Mississippi. He could look proudly down on his family, especially his dad, and know that this day was one of triumph for them all. It was also a day of triumph for all Negroes. It was especially a victory for Thurgood Marshall, Constance Baker Motley, and the NAACP.

James Meredith had had enough of Mississippi. Mary June, who had stayed close to her husband during these years of trouble, was only too pleased to move to New York with him.

Since going to New York, James Meredith has joined freedom marches in the South. He was wounded on one of these marches. He has made tours all over the United States, preaching his cause. At one time, he declared himself a candidate to oppose Adam Clayton Powell for his Harlem congressional seat, but later he withdrew. His book, *Three Years in Mississippi,* had made him a successful author.

James Howard Meredith will always be known as the hero who broke the color line in Mississippi at great physical risk.

> There is no dramatic sprint and slam-bang in Meredith's sort of heroism. He is more nearly the marathoner, a man plodding step by step, pacing himself, not looking to right or left, but just managing to get one foot in front of the other over the long course. . . .

> —*Saturday Review,* June, 1963

John B. King

[1908-   ]

EDUCATOR

> John King was a tower of strength to me while he served
> in the New York City school system. This cool, calm,
> and capable educator must be credited with much of the
> advancement in our school system.
>
> —Dr. Bernard Donovan,
> Superintendent of Schools, New York City

Dr. John B. King sat facing me in his office in the new Leon
Lowenstein Building of Fordham University's Lincoln Center compound, on the West Side of the Borough of Manhattan, in New York City. He was reminiscing on his early childhood, his family, and his growing up in a large city. Looking
out on the beautiful Center of the Performing Arts, John
King talked of his mother and father, his brothers and sisters,
but especially of his famous brother, "Dolly" King, the All-
American athlete.

John King is a distinguished-looking, six-foot professional
educator. Meeting him for the first time, he impresses you
with his quiet, sincere manner. He is the type of individual
that you like the minute you shake his hand. He speaks in a
low tone, yet you feel the determination and intenseness
which helped raise him to second in command of the New
York City school system.

As John King talked, the afternoon sun began to sink behind the large buildings that surround Lincoln Center. For the past four hours, he had been reliving for me a childhood and youth that read like a modern novel.

Charles King married Estelle Livingston Stansberry just as the twentieth century moved onto the scene of history. Her father was the presiding elder of a church in Philadelphia.

Charles and Estelle King moved into an apartment on the West Side of Manhattan. The young husband was full of ambition and immediately enrolled in the New York University Law School, but he continued to work to support his rapidly growing family. Before long, the family outgrew his ability to support them and still continue in law school.

It was during the couple's residence on West 66th Street that their first child, a son, was born. He was named John. When he was three years old, the Kings moved to New Brunswick, New Jersey. During the time the Kings lived in the Garden State, Charles was a United States Marshal. A marshal is a person who acts as a federal police officer for the attorney-general. This is a position appointed by the President of the United States.

Realizing that his job as marshal could end when a new administration took over in Washington, Charles King sought employment of greater permanance. He obtained a position with Batten, Barton, Durstine & Osborn, a public relations firm in New York City, as a receptionist. He moved his family to Brooklyn, New York, and for the next twenty-six years, worked for BBD&O without ever missing a day's work. That type of reliability he would inculcate in his children.

Young John B. King was first exposed to a formal education in Brooklyn. He was six years old when his mother took him by the hand and led him to Public School 26 to be enrolled.

When John reached the sixth grade, he was transferred to Junior High School 85. This school was called Halsey Junior High School, and it is still one of the best known of the schools in Brooklyn. He was thirteen when he entered Boys' High School.

As stated elsewhere, it was not the usual thing for a boy to go to high school in the 1920's. In many homes of the lower middle class, the boys who finished junior high school were considered to have sufficient education and were sent out to work. However, with a boy from a Negro family, it was usually the rule that he would go to work after finishing elementary school. The economic problems of people with low incomes in post-World-War-I America called for the children to help maintain the family. Even minor advanced education was for the offspring of the rich only. A boy's inherent ability had nothing to do with whether he could continue in school or not.

John had one outstanding trait when he arrived as a freshman at Boys' High School—he was the smallest boy in the school. As a result, his interest in sports was limited to serving as manager for the football, baseball, and basketball teams. During all this time, while his enthusiasm for sports never ceased, his marks, which indicated that he was the leader in his class, kept him busy.

Happily for John King, his interest in athletics was satisfied to a great degree by his having a younger brother who excelled in many sports. William "Dolly" King entered Alexander Hamilton High School in Brooklyn, while his older brother John was in college. In high school, Dolly received the athletic award for general excellence, and the all-scholastic award for activities in basketball, football, and baseball. He was captain of all three of these teams. During one baseball game, Dolly hit two balls out of the largest high-school park in New York City, a feat no one had ever accomplished before. He played a most important part in the life of John B. King, and, as a result, will be inseparably entwined throughout this entire life's story of his brother.

John graduated from Boys' High School at the age of fifteen. By now, he believed he knew what he wanted to do for the remainder of his life. His desire was to be a doctor. He longed to help his fellow men and felt that this was the best way to fulfill his wish. As he looks back on this period of his life now, John King believes that his desire to study medicine had come long before he graduated from high school. He remembers that, as a youngster living in New Jersey, he was constantly attempting to operate on various injured animals that came under his sympathetic control. His desire would have to wait. College and medicine school were expensive, and the King family was a large one. John did not feel that he had the right to expect his father to bear the full brunt of keeping the family, and, at the same time, sending him to college.

By 1924, the postwar recession was on the wane and the national economy of the United States was on the move toward one of the greatest periods of prosperity in its history. John found little difficulty in getting a job. He worked for the Florence Stove Company, in Manhattan. He was expected to travel daily from the office of the company to its factory in the Bush Terminal section of Brooklyn. This was a distance of some twenty miles that John had to cover by subway and trolley car. In the factory, he worked on stove parts; then, later in the day, he returned to the company's office to do clerical work. In the evening, he attended the College of the City of New York.

The Florence Stove Company was owned by Thomas A. Shanahan. Mr. Shanahan was a graduate of Exeter Academy and Harvard University, and he was anxious to see his ambitious young employee attend college on a full-time basis. Meanwhile, John had begun to have second thoughts about studying medicine. On his rides to Manhattan he had noticed a poster in the subway cars that called for high-school graduates to become teachers, and suggesting that they attend Maxwell Training School for Teachers, located in Brooklyn. Over ninety per cent of all the men and women who taught in New York City schools during that postwar period were graduates of Maxwell Training, which was to that generation what the schools of education are to the teachers of today. From this outstanding institution dedicated men and women came to the New York City school system to teach the future politicians, clergymen, business leaders, and college professors. The faculty was superb. Their devotion and determination helped greatly to staff the largest school system in the world with first-rate classroom instructors.

Mr. Shanahan told John King that he would underwrite his college education if he wanted to attend full time. By then, John had been sold completely on this idea of becoming a teacher, so he chose Maxwell Training. He told me, "Once I entered Maxwell I never again considered medicine as a career. I was to devote my life to the teaching profession." At Maxwell, he was assigned to a special progress class. This meant that he would move more rapidly in the study of his liberal arts courses, as well as in his courses in pedagogy. King was an excellent student because he was an eager student. A course that normally took three years to complete, he finished in two and one-half years. Yet, with so much of his energy concentrated on his studies, he still found time to be president of the student body and editor of the school paper in 1927–1928. When he graduated, in 1928, he received the Campbell Award for school service. He graduated with honors, receiving first rank in General Fitness for Teaching. This was considered the most valuable award by all students at Maxwell Training.

John King was nineteen years old when he was assigned as a substitute teacher to Public School 26, in Brooklyn. It was February 2, 1928, when he walked into the principal's office for assignment to a class. He remembers that morning as if it were yesterday. He had been a student in that same school just nine years before. P.S. 26 is located in the Bedford-

Stuyvesant section of Brooklyn. This is the area where a large
number of Negroes reside, so that John had the opportunity
to teach a number of his own people. He remained as a substitute teacher for three years, because when the depression
set in, there were no regular appointments.

The salary of a substitute teacher was not great. John decided to add to his small income by working as a teacher of
Health Education and Recreation. Always interested in
athletics, and now a young man of over six feet, he worked
with his brother Dolly to perfect his body. He was agile, and,
above all, very keen about sports, so that his activities in this
area were both lucrative and interesting. During the summers, he acted as a teacher-in-charge and principal in various
playgrounds and community centers. He continued this work
until 1941, even after he moved up the academic ladder. This
is indeed proof of his great interest in the building of strong
bodies as well as strong minds.

It was during this period of John's life that his link to
his brother became even closer. Dolly decided to enroll at
Long Island University in the 1930's. Today, this is one of
the largest universities in the New York metropolitan area,
but when he made the varsity basketball team, it was not a
well-known institution. He played a key role in lifting that
team from the obscurity of a tiny gym to national prominence. While he was with the team, he and his fellow players
were the Varsity National Invitation champs for three years.
He was captain of the team, and won All-American honors
at Madison Square Garden. He also played on the college
football team. He once played a complete football game at
Ebbets Field in Brooklyn, went over to Madison Square
Garden to play a full basketball game, and was high scorer
in both games. It is this All-American brother of whom John
King is so very proud.

In 1931, John King was appointed under an elementary
school license as a permanent teacher. He remained in Public

School 26 because it was here that he was given the opportunity to help the children of the deprived and underprivileged.

It was not in John King to rest on his academic laurels. From the beginning, he realized that his Maxwell Training education would have to be supplemented. Back to school he went in 1928, and by 1931 had earned a Bachelor of Science degree in Education from New York University. He continued studying at New York University until 1936, when he was awarded his Master of Arts degree.

In the teaching field John King also made progress. The public school system, in the 1930's, was establishing some additional schools as junior high schools. These would prepare their pupils from the sixth to the ninth grades for the work of senior high. P.S. 26 was designated as a new junior high, making it necessary for John King to seek a teaching license in a specific subject. English had always been his chief interest, so he chose to be licensed in that field. He continued to teach in *his* school.

All public school teachers do not hope for the day when they will qualify with a senior high school license. However, during this period, teachers in New York City who held senior-high licenses were placed in a higher wage bracket. In 1939, John King received a senior high school English license, and was assigned to the Brooklyn Technical High School. This is a special high school, to which the academically proficient students are sent in preparation for college engineering courses. The faculty is, like its student body, chosen from the elite.

John King, always a strong family man, had met a beautiful young girl in 1931. Elizabeth Bundick had much in common with John. She was an English major in college, and it was in an English class at New York University that they met. For two years they saw much of each other. They loved to stroll in Brooklyn's Prospect Park, go to the local movie houses on Saturday nights, and visit museums on Sunday afternoons. In 1933, Elizabeth Bundick became Mrs. John B. King. The marriage was blessed with two lovely daughters, Joan and Lynne.

Brooklyn Technical High School lost John King after one year. War had come to Europe and was well on its way toward its second year when King became an assistant principal—and was assigned back at P.S. 26. In 1944, he became an assistant in the office of the Assistant Superintendent in one of the districts into which the New York City public school system was divided. These included a number of elementary, junior high, and senior high schools. An assistant superintendent coordinated and supervised each of these city areas for the school superintendent. The system operated in this way until the new decentralized program was set up.

Prior to his assignment to the district office, where for a year he was able to get the feel of the largest public school system in the world, John King had taken the examination for principal of an elementary school. In 1945, he was sent to P.S. 70 as junior principal, the designation of anyone who runs a school with less than twenty-five classes. P.S. 70, like P.S. 26, was in the Bedford-Stuyvesant section of Brooklyn. John King soon sensed that one of his biggest challenges was to see that the pupils under his charge had all the advantages of those in the more prosperous sections of the city. His interest was in human relations—and in presenting the correct general principles and methods of teaching, insofar as he was able. He realized, however, in this underprivileged area, that special techniques in meeting the special-pupil needs would be required, and had to be worked out if he was to achieve his goal. His work was so well received that by 1946, after only one year of effort, P.S. 70 was raised to the position of an elementary school, with John King as principal. Three years later he was transferred to P.S. 25, so that he might, to quote the Superintendent of Schools, ". . . broaden his supervisory experience." This was a sign of things to come for John King. P.S. 25 was the largest elementary school in the country.

While these giant academic steps were being made by John King, he felt more pride in what his brother Dolly was doing in professional athletics than he did in his own accomplishments. He was also watching carefully the progress of another brother, Haldane King, who was making his mark in the United States Army Air Corps.

Dolly was involved as a professional in baseball, basketball, and football. He played baseball with the Homestead Group of the Negro National League for three years, and was with the world's champion Litchman Bears in Washington, D.C., for two years. He was the first Negro player in the National Baseball League, and it has been said by those who know, that had he continued in that sport, he would have been the first black man in the big leagues, for he had the talent. As one sports writer stated it recently, ". . . he was one of the greatest catchers baseball ever saw." He was his brother John's pride and joy.

His excellent record at P.S. 25 brought John King an appointment as an Assistant Superintendent of Schools. His district covered one of the most deprived sections of New York City. Difficult work was cut out for him, but he was ready to meet the responsibilities. He strove to raise academic standards by strengthening certain programs in order to greatly improve the teaching on all levels. He gave of his talents personally by instructing in a course at Long Island University, at the graduate level, on teaching speech to handicapped and disadvantaged pupils. His work on curriculum gained for him membership on the City-Wide Curriculum Council. The large number of Puerto Ricans in his district stimulated his interest in arranging an exchange-teacher program with Puerto Rico.

It has often been said that, if you want something done, ask a busy man to do it. John King, busy with his family and his district, still had time for the community. Between 1942 and 1951 he served as an officer of the Brooklyn Citizens' Committee of the *Amsterdam News,* which conducted a wide variety of activities for the benefit of deserving Negro charities. He was Chairman of the Brooklyn Urban League Campaign in 1946. That same year, and again in 1949, he was elected in the *Amsterdam News* poll as the Leading Citizen. In 1951, he was the recipient of the Salvation Army Red Shield Club scroll for community service. These awards continued and became more varied. On May 9, 1967, John King received one of his most cherished tokens. He was awarded the gold medal of the New York Academy of Public Education.

Time was moving on for Leading Citizen King. His two daughters were grown and well educated. It was not long before he was walking with Joan down the long aisle of St. Thomas Aquinas Church, to give her away in marriage. Shortly after that, Lynne announced that she too, was getting married. The years seemed to fly, and soon grandchildren were calling for their much-loved Grandpa and Grandma. The senior Kings looked forward eagerly to having their daughters bring their youngsters over for a day. Each daughter has two children. When listening to John King talk he seems to come alive in a special way when he speaks of John, Dawn, Keith and Kim—he is a devoted grandfather.

For eight years John King worked as an Assistant Superintendent. He was the first Negro to have come so far in the public school system. In 1959, he was named an Associate Superintendent, and was assigned to the Division of Child Welfare. In this work he administered programs for physically, mentally, and emotionally handicapped children. This was a monumental job, and John King came to it with the same determination that he always brought to a new task. He did not stay long in this position, however, because a vacancy came in the area of elementary schools, and this was his first love.

September, 1960, found him planning for those changes that the elementary schools were going to need. For the three years that he served in this field, he did much to strengthen the programs and services in the elementary division. Reading, the major problem, received new programs to improve greatly the teaching of this important subject. All of John King's new programs were not directed in behalf of the academically deprived, though. King also established programs for intellectually gifted pupils. They were particularly devoted to foreign language instruction. In order to insure a competent teaching staff, the Government of the United States made arrangements with French officials that resulted in sending about sixty of New York City's elementary French teachers to Paris.

All this time, Dolly King was moving along in his chosen field—athletics. He automatically became a referee, and was the first Negro basketball official in the College Basketball Officials Association. Later, he was made Recreational Director for a housing development on the East Side of New York City. In 1964, the Board of Higher Education of the City of New York opened Manhattan Community College. Dolly King was appointed Chairman of the Health and Physical Education Department. As basketball coach, he led his team to a record of fifty-five wins and eleven losses in four and one-half years. His progress was proudly watched by his older brother John. The career of Haldane King was also moving upward. It was now Lieutenant Colonel Haldane King, stationed at the Pentagon as an expert in data processing.

A man with the educational experience, skill, and warm humanity of John King was bound to continue moving up the ladder. Early in 1963, his promotion to Deputy Superintendent of Schools was announced to the people of New York City. He was now in charge of instruction for the entire school system. Two and one half years later, he moved to the second spot in the system—Executive Deputy Superintendent of Schools. As a prime policy maker with the Superintendent, he held the responsibility for a wide variety of board, staff, and community matters. It was a long way from the segregated Negro boy who saw that subway ad for teachers, to the second in command of the largest public school system in the world.

John King served for forty years in the New York City school system. In all that time, he was never absent. He told me that his determination to maintain that unusual record came to him from his father, who worked for twenty-six years without ever missing a day. John King finally decided reluctantly that he really should retire and devote more attention to his wife and his grandchildren. He retired in February, 1967, shortly after his wife, Elizabeth, died. It was a harsh emotional shock for this kind, quiet, devoted, scholarly man.

After the initial reaction to his loss, John King began to search around for something to occupy his time and talents. For several years he had been teaching in the Fordham University School of Education as a part-time professor. Fordham was more than pleased to employ this knowledgeable man of education as a full professor. Since June 1962, he had been known as Dr. John B. King, for he then received from St. John's University of New York City an honorary Doctor of Pedagogy degree.

Still vitally interested in his family, John King was always seen in the stands when Dolly's team from Manhattan Community College met a rival. On weekends he visited with his daughters. From time to time, Colonel King came to New York, or John would run down to Washington for a reunion with his brother. Life was beginning to look busier—and hence brighter—for John King.

January 29, 1969, was special—on that day Dolly took his basketball team to Binghamton, New York. In the early afternoon he complained of pains in his chest. When he was taken to the local hospital, it appeared as though this great athlete, who had never before suffered one day of sickness, would survive his first heart seizure. He asked that his team be brought to his bedside. He told them "go and play and win." One hour before the game William "Dolly" King died. The team came on the court wearing black armbands—they played, and they won.

John B. King has found the death of Dolly almost too much to bear. Yet he carries on unswervingly with the work he does best. In March, 1969, he accepted the chair as the John Mosler Professor of Urban Education at Fordham University, effective as of September, 1969.

Dr. King is indeed a man for all peoples. He has managed to come far in his chosen profession, and, consequently, to heap praise on his race. He has made it very clear that, when a man has a purpose and is determined in seeing that his hopes are fulfilled, his color, creed or race make little or no difference to him in carrying his dream through to success.

John King looked out on the West Side of New York City as the sunshine gave way to twilight; there was a glint of tears in his eyes. He asked me, "Why do you want to write about me? You should be writing about a great man—Dolly. This scholar has not lost his humility with the acquisition of many honors. He has all the marks of a great human being— one who has done much, not only for his own people, but for all children in the great urban complex of New York City—and, inevitably, beyond. . . .

> We not only are honoring an unusually capable educator who thoroughly merits the designation of John Mosler

Professor, but we also are indicating that in our search for excellence we include our faculty among those to be considered.

—Dr. Harry N. Rivlin,
Dean, Fordham School of Education

Robert Teague

[1929-   ]

NEWS CORRESPONDENT AND BROADCASTER

> If there is a secret to success, it might be an understand-
> ing of the fact that no one achieves success on his own.
> Everybody needs help along the way. The secret then is
> to develop attitudes that can make you the kind of person
> others are willing to help.
>
> —Robert Teague, *Letters to a Black Boy*

Milwaukee, Wisconsin, not unlike other cities in the United
States, was basking in the sunlight of prosperity in the early
months of 1929. On Veliet Street in Milwaukee, Nancy
Teague was awaiting the birth of her first child, and Robert,
her husband, was proud in the belief that it would be a boy.

Nancy Teague had her baby, but she did not live to know
him. Baptized Robert, the baby knew only Aunt Letty as
"Mother." Aunt Letty was Nancy's sister. She came to Milwaukee from Detroit after her sister's death, to take care of
her nephew. The Teague home became a lively place for
little Robert as he grew up, for Aunt Letty taught the boy
to "dream beyond your blackness." She made sure he never
forgot that "life is much larger than the limits imposed on us
for the color of our skins; and the world is bigger than the
boundaries of the ghetto . . ."

School was indeed a thrill for Bob. He was most anxious
to know about everything that the teacher had to offer. He

asked more questions than all the other boys and girls together. Then he would rush home excitedly to tell Aunt
Letty and his dad about the wonders he had discovered in
his classes and books.

High school opened up the wide world of sports. Football
became the all-demanding interest of Bob's life. He had
grown into a handsome, strong, and agile young man. Each
fall, when the football season opened, Robert Teague was
first to report for practice. By this time he had experienced
many of the heartbreaking incidents that Negroes know too
well.

Pressed by Aunt Letty to improve his speech patterns, Bob
practiced regularly on word pronunciation. As she told him,
"Confucius say, boy who speak like hobo soon grow from
boy to tramp." One of the methods he used to improve his
speech was by singing. Soon he became an excellent singer.

Milwaukee had a popular entertainment center, the Clarion
Theater. Here, an amateur talent contest was held. A prize
of five hundred dollars in cash and a trip to Hollywood for
a screen test was to be awarded to the winner. It was being
conducted as part of a public relations stunt to advertise a
Shirley Temple movie. This child movie star was the rage
of Hollywood during those days of the depression, which had
followed close on the heels of the prosperity of early 1929.

Bob Teague was convinced by his family and friends that
he had an excellent chance to take first prize. He wondered
what it would be like to "wind up being a black boy Shirley
Temple." After practicing his favorite song intensively, he
went around to the stage door to enter his name in the contest.

A tall, white usher in the dashing blue theater uniform
made the issue very clear for the applicant when he stated
flatly, "Go home, boy. It's for whites only."

Bob knew then the frustration and rage that were to be his
many times in the years to come. To lose the contest was one

thing, but not to be permitted even to compete was indeed another.

Football was different. Out on the field, color made no difference. It was the strong desire to win that drew these young athletes close together as a team. When Bob was told by a doctor that his playing days were over because his "heart valves had gone bad," he believed his life was devastated. However, Teague decided he was not going to be stopped by a doctor's stethoscope. He went on playing . . . and soon forgot what appears to have been a doctor's mistaking an active boy's jumpy heartbeat for a bad heart condition.

High-school football had its special compensation for a Negro. When Bob graduated, in 1946, he immediately entered the University of Wisconsin on an athletic scholarship. He knew what he wanted to accomplish from the very first day that he set foot on the campus. He would play football so well that his name would become a household word, and at the same time, he would receive good grades in his journalism courses.

In 1949, during his junior year, Bob realized the first of his desires. He won All Big Ten as Wisconsin's famous grid star. Football had been good to him; now, he decided it was time to concentrate on his academic pursuits.

Graduation with a Bachelor of Science degree in journalism did not mean a job or a future as a reporter for Robert Teague. His dad was concerned that he was dreaming about a career that would never come true, for in 1950 there were less than a half-dozen Negro reporters in the United States. Bob's father advised him to play professional football.

Bob Teague knew what he wanted to do, however. He remembers his father's comment when he told him he would not play pro football: "Are you crazy? The Packers are ready to pay you five thousand seven hundred dollars a season. That's as much as I make all year."

Teague found his chance in the field of his choice on *The*

Minneapolis Journal. He was hired as a sports writer, mainly because of his football career. The work was pleasant and the experience was most necessary. During the next six years, he worked the sports beat on the *Journal* in addition to serving his two-year stint in the Army.

While in the service, he again felt the pressures of being black. He was barred from theaters, restaurants, and a baseball park while on furlough in Louisville, Kentucky. His reaction tells the whole poignant story, "My patriotism was drowned in Louisville in my tears of helpless rage."

Shortly after returning to Minneapolis, Bob Teague was offered a position on *The New York Times.* It had been a struggle to get the *Times* to accept him, and when he talks about it now, he smiles as he recalls: "But I filed my fifty-first application. . . . They called me two weeks later." He worked on the paper for six and a half years, until he decided to go into broadcasting.

New York was a new experience for Bob Teague. The bright lights, theaters, rushing taxicabs, and eight million people fascinated the young man from Milwaukee. This was 1955, and the world was at peace, for the time being. Bob Teague made his rounds as a *New York Times* sports writer. From time to time, the news department borrowed him to write special articles on integration, politics, and economics. He was beginning to find his wider niche in the news game.

Romance had touched Bob while he was a senior in college. Following the last game in his junior year, he was invited to a party at a classmate's home. There he was introduced to Matt Turney, a Milwaukee girl who was a co-ed with him at the University. They had never met before, but it was evident that they would see much of each other after their first meeting.

When Bob Teague came to New York, Matt Turney came also, to study dancing. Bob was assigned to handle the first Liston-Patterson fight in Chicago. Before he left town, he told

Matt that when he returned he would have a question to ask her. Matt knew what the question would be and she knew how she would answer. The two were married late in 1955 and moved into a small apartment on the fringe of Harlem.

Matt Teague continued to follow her career in dancing. She was given a part in the Broadway show "Milk and Honey," as a solo dancer. She appeared in "Siddartha," an opera that premiered in Boston. But Matt made sure that she was with her Bob a great deal of the time. She sat with her husband on that Saturday in the fall of 1956 when he covered the Giants' football game and watched Y. A. Tittle toss seven touchdown passes.

As newlyweds, it was inevitable that Bob and Matt would be looking for a more comfortable apartment, now that more money was coming their way. The struggle to rent the type of apartment they liked became almost a crusade.

Time after time, they found an "ad" in the apartments-for-rent section of a newspaper and went to inspect the place, only to be told that it was rented—after the landlord discovered they were Negroes. One day, they were pleasantly surprised to find the ideal apartment and a landlord who was willing to rent to the Teagues. Bob has told it this way, "We lived in his building quite happily ever after for five and a half years, until we bought the cooperative apartment we live in now. Our landlord proved to be not only a fair man, but a good friend as well."

With his initiative, personality and talents, Bob Teague was bound to move up in the field of reporting. In late 1962, the National Broadcasting Company offered him a job as a radio news writer. He had no difficulty in making up his mind because he was sure it was not his color that had prompted the offer. He evaluates it like this: "As a matter of fact, I had been hired before they knew the color of my skin. . . . Furthermore, once I accepted the job, they treated me no differently from white writers hired about the same time."

Teague's early experience at NBC was finding himself at the lowest rung of the broadcasting business. As a fledgling, he was placed into "the pool." This meant writing half a dozen scripts a day or night for other people to read on the air—over radio. He was told that, with luck, great effort, and devotion to duty, he could work his way up to writing for television. There might even be the possibility of his becoming a street reporter for radio or TV.

It took Bob Teague the better part of a year to make the grade in radio writing and advance to writing for television. With all his concentrated effort, it required about a year and a half to qualify as a full-time street reporter.

Some of the stories that Bob Teague covered brought home to him experiences that he remembered from his youth. One in particular was an assignment to check a story where an all-white building trade union was charged with cheating Negroes who received high marks in an examination given by the union. Bob Teague looked pensive as he explained to me, when I interviewed him with my tape recorder, "I couldn't say so in my television newscast, but that story brought back vividly the summer of 1937, in Milwaukee. My Aunt Letty . . . helped my daddy study for a written test for a white union. Finally, a few days before the test, she said daddy knew enough to pass. . . . On the day of the test, however, my daddy returned home sputtering and cursing. 'The man said I passed,' he told us. 'Then he tore up the papers and dropped 'em on the floor. He claims he seen me cheating. The man lied, I never done no such thing.' "

Soon after Bob Teague began to appear on news reporting assignments for NBC-TV, Matt presented him with a son. His parents decided to name the boy Adam. His dad was determined to leave the little fellow a legacy that would start him on his way under proper circumstances. Teague is quick to point out, "It is possible that I may not be around when my young son has grown up enough to hear some sensible things he ought to know." Bob Teague's gift to Adam was a book he called *Letters to a Black Boy*.

It was two years and nine months after he was employed by the National Broadcasting Company before Bob was assigned a nightly fifteen-minute newscast. It was necessary that he learn how to speak all over again in the approved TV manner. It meant that he had to take elocution lessons, breathing exercises, and memory tests.

After four and half years with NBC, Bob Teague was promoted to half-hour newscasts. He was given his own weekly television program, "Sunday Afternoon Report." With all of this TV exposure, he continues to function on radio by handling "News-on-the-Hour" broadcasts on Saturdays for "Monitor."

Bob Teague, in his early forties, seems geared for a promising future. The strident tempo of "On Wisconsin" seems to have been a prophetic theme for the forecasting of his career as a newsman.

> Have I shown that you can reach the sky if you believe you can
> Have I helped you toward the courage to stand up and be a man
> And have I made it obvious in anecdote or rhyme
> That what I wish for all black men is freedom in your time
>
> —Robert Teague, *Letters to a Black Boy*

Asa T. Spaulding

[1902-   ]

BUSINESSMAN

> A man with a purpose, who proves that, as a Negro, a
> chance is all a person needs. Good luck, Asa! New York
> will miss you.
>
> —*New York University Yearbook,* June, 1930

When Asa Spaulding was born, in 1902, the company that
he would later head was struggling to keep alive. Asa's uncle,
Charles C. Spaulding, must receive the credit for establishing
the North Carolina Mutual Life Insurance Company.

Charles C. Spaulding, the son of an ex-slave, met two
enterprising young businessmen named John Merrick and
A. M. Moore, in Durham, North Carolina. These two Negro
men had organized a burial-aid association. This was an attempt to make possible a decent burial for poor black people.
By paying a few cents a week, a subscriber could get a certain
sum of money to bury his dead when the time came. The
people running the association just hoped they had collected
enough money before someone else died. It was a very un-
businesslike way of operating.

In 1898, Merrick and Moore converted their association
into a mutual life insurance company. However, it was
Charles Clinton Spaulding who built the company into the
successful, sound organization that it has become through
the years.

The company was so small when Spaulding joined his two partners that when they had to pay out a $40.00 claim, they almost went bankrupt. Charles was the jack-of-all-trades for the organization. He was the bookkeeper, janitor, salesman, and advertising manager. For years he walked over the highways of North Carolina, searching out new business. It was during this period that Asa, nephew of Charles, was born.

The plain whitewashed shack in the poorer Negro section of Durham, North Carolina, was where Asa Spaulding was born on July 22, 1902. The Spauldings were poor, and Asa's father was not the go-getter that his brother Charles proved to be.

Those early years for Asa were no more difficult than they were for the other children in the neighborhood. When the time came for him to attend school, he was only too pleased to go. Here he learned to read and write, but, more importantly, his teacher gave him hot soup and fresh milk.

From time to time, Uncle Charles would come to Asa's home. After he left, the family always seemed to be able to buy meat and some needed clothes. Uncle Charlie made a point of seeking out Asa and making clear that he must stay in school if he was ever to amount to anything.

Fortunately, Asa was a good student, and when he finished elementary school he enrolled at the National Training School in Durham. This school is now North Carolina College.

The years spent at National were happy ones. Asa had always loved to play ball, and National had a championship baseball team. He went out for the freshman team and nailed down the center-field spot. When he was a sophomore, he made the varsity, and batted 320 that year.

Baseball had to be forgotten in favor of business in his junior year, however. Uncle Charlie made clear to his nephew that if he wanted to stay in school, he would have to help at the insurance office.

Asa became a salesman for Mutual Life. His uncle was a leader in the saturation advertising theory. Asa covered every barbershop, store, lodge hall, and farm in his quest for new customers. The company provided its young salesman with pens, paper weights, fans, and calendars to win over signatures on policies. All of these modern methods of selling were a great help to Asa as he became more and more convinced that business was to be his life career.

Finishing at the National Training School, Asa was promoted to an inside position with the company. It was his job to place advertisements in the black press and to hire schoolteachers to act as salesmen. The use of schoolteachers as agents gave the company a most respectable group to sell their policies, and at the same time establish confidence in the policy holder. It was not long before Mutual Life Insurance Company was known up and down the East Coast. For the first time, Negroes were given the opportunity to acquire a measure of security for a very small premium.

Asa Spaulding knew, as well as his uncle, that further education was necessary if he was to be a real asset to the company. It was decided that he would go to New York and attend the New York University School of Commerce, Accounts, and Finance. Asa was now twenty-five and determined to work at top speed to acquire his degree.

New York City held a fascination for young Spaulding. He was constantly on the move around the big metropolis, when he wasn't busy with his class work. He visited all of the museums, the parks, and the Stock Exchange. His special business interest led him to Wall Street, into the Federal Reserve Bank, and other big banks throughout the city.

One of the most surprising discoveries that Asa made in New York was a strong anti-black feeling in the midst of so-called equality. After many futile attempts to find a room near the University, he was forced to take lodgings in Harlem. Some of the "better" restaurants managed to make it very clear that black clients were not welcome. In North Carolina, Asa had not only expected to find this type of treatment, he had lived with it. But he had heard that New York City was different. It was in some ways, but the basic resentment was always under the surface.

At the University, Asa discovered that his classmates accepted him for what he was. He enjoyed the companionship of many of them, and made some lasting friendships.

It was decided that Spaulding should remain in New York until he completed his work for his degree. He continued attending classes during the summers and finished all his courses in June, 1930. He graduated Magna Cum Laude. This was quite an accomplishment for a young man who was so far from home, and who had come to college after several years of working. His degree was in accounting, and with that background, he became a distinct asset to the North Carolina Mutual Insurance Company.

Many students, during their time in college, constantly declare that, once they get their bachelors' degree, they will never go back to school, but when they finish, quite a few continue on for the graduate degree. Asa Spaulding was no exception to this desire for more knowledge. On finishing at NYU, he went on to the University of Michigan for his master's degree in business.

He had found that a northern university would give him a better education. In the South, the fight by the NAACP to open the state universities to black students had not yet begun. Spaulding, like many other Negroes, knew well that separate and equal education in the South did not mean quality education.

When he had earned his M.A. degree in 1932, Asa returned to Durham and the North Carolina Mutual Life Insurance Company. He was now thirty years old, and it was time for him to think of taking a bride.

Elra Bridgeforth, a friend of an old schoolmate, had met

Asa Spaulding before he left Durham for New York City. At first, it always seemed as if Elra and Asa were quarreling. Elra had an aggravating faculty of challenging statements made by Asa. Apparently, he was so determined to make her see his point of view that he deliberately sought her out for dates. It was only a question of time when they were seen everywhere together. While he was in New York and Michigan, the two corresponded. When Asa came home for vacations or the holidays, he always made sure that he spent a good deal of time with Elra. They were married a few months after he received his M.A. degree and returned to Durham.

Uncle Charlie had waited eagerly for his nephew to return so that he could assume an important position in the insurance company. Charles Spaulding had been president of North Carolina Mutual since 1923. The organization had grown steadily until the depression struck it in 1929. One of the reasons why Asa could take the time to go to graduate school was because business was slow in this period. The greatest compliment that can be paid to Charles Spaulding is through an appreciation of the ability and ingenuity he displayed in keeping his company solvent and operating throughout the depression. It was possible for North Carolina Mutual to keep going only because of the sound business policy followed by its leader.

In 1933, Asa Spaulding became the treasurer of Mutual. His educational background made him the most logical man for the job. He continued to follow the sound investment policy that had been established by his uncle.

The North Carolina Mutual Life Insurance Company became a financial success. The Spauldings were able to live well. Elra finally convinced Asa that they should build their own home. It was, however, not just a question of constructing a house wherever you pleased. It meant building in a segregated area of the city. Successful though a Negro might be—a business genius who had proved himself—he still must live inside the segregated area. The Spauldings were proud to be black and to live with their own people. However, as Americans, they resented the very idea of segregation in this country of opportunity. A beautiful home was built for Elra, Asa, and the children—in a black area. The Spauldings had been blessed with four fine children. Asa, Jr., like his father, was a student with a leaning toward business. He joined Mutual following his graduation from college. The younger son, Aaron Lowery, decided that his interest was in teaching. Kenneth, after finishing college, joined his brother Asa in the Mutual business. It now appears that the Spaulding name will continue to carry on the North Carolina Mutual Insurance Company with the traditional high standards. The one daughter, Elra Bridgeforth, married a young attorney from Durham. The big house often rings with the laughter of the grandchildren. Grandfather and Grandmother are always happy to see them.

Charles C. Spaulding had gradually given more and more administrative responsibility to his nephew as they moved into the nineteen forties. He was getting on in years, and he now felt assured that the company would remain in the family—and be properly directed.

North Carolina Mutual Life Insurance was successful because Charles Spaulding had infused it with those habits of hard work, dependability and thrift that he had practiced all his life. He knew that these same principles would be maintained with Asa heading the company.

Charles Spaulding, born in comparative poverty, one of fourteen children, was now a man of wealth and influence. Schools, parks, and playgrounds had been named after him. His story is indeed another of those encouraging, authentic success stories with which American history abounds.

However, Charles would not relinquish his hold on the

business as long as he was physically capable of running things.

In the meantime, Asa Spaulding was making his own mark as a business executive of national fame. More and more, he was being invited to business seminars and college campuses to deliver lectures and papers on current financial and monetary questions. In 1958, he was awarded an honorary LL.D. degree from Shaw University in Raleigh, North Carolina, where he delivered the commencement address.

During the years since Asa had received his M.A. degree from the University of Michigan, he had been taking courses at Morgan State College. He used every possible opportunity for studies that would eventually secure for him his Ph.D. degree. In 1961, Morgan State College named him a doctor of business administration.

Charles Spaulding was seventy-eight in 1952. He was working just as hard then as he had twenty years before. However, it was quite evident that he was not too well. He had a reputation of never being late for an appointment or of missing a directors' meeting. As 1952 wore on, there were mornings when he did not go to the office at all. He missed several directors' meetings. Late one night in June, the telephone rang in Asa's home. It was the housekeeper at his uncle's home. She asked Asa to hurry over because Mr. Spaulding was extremely ill.

When Asa, accompanied by Elra, arrived at Charlie's bedside, he had lapsed into a coma. He was rushed to a hospital, but before morning, he had died. The local press, both white and black, praised this strong, honest man of business. Newspapers throughout the nation carried laudatory obituary notices of his passing.

Asa Spaulding was not promptly elected president of the company. The reason for this was not a lack of confidence in Asa, but the normal procedure followed by big business. When Charles Spaulding died, Asa was one of Mutual's vice-presidents. The choice of a president was to be determined by the board of directors. There had been other men around Charles who had seniority over Asa. These men had every right to succeed to the leadership just then. In time, Asa would get his chance. It came, following proper procedure, in 1959, when the board elected him president. He is, at this writing, holding down this important post.

With his election as president of the North Carolina Mutual Life Insurance Company, Asa Spaulding became a member of the board of directors of the company. In this position, he is now not only an officer of the company, but also one who helps decide the policies to be followed. The board of directors of a business determines what the company will charge for its product, how much it will sell, and when it will sell, etc. Officers of a company carry out the policies upon which the board of directors has decided.

Business organizations elect to their boards of directors men who have experience and know-how. They need not be in the same line of business as the companies that elect them to their boards. All that a board member must have is business ability. At times, banks will place men on their boards of directors from companies that have borrowed large sums from them. This presents an opportunity to keep a close eye on their investments. It is also true that banks place on their boards men who can aid them in their business transactions.

Asa Spaulding is also a director of the Mechanics and Farmers Bank and the Mutual Savings and Loan Association; and he is chairman of the board of the Bankers Fire and Casualty Insurance Company.

When a man becomes a business success, he will naturally be called upon to share his ability and his checkbook with charitable, brotherhood, and educational projects. Asa Spaulding has proven himself a true humanitarian by accepting the responsibility of heading up many charitable organizations and drives. He is a trustee of the James E.

Shepard Memorial Foundation, which was developed for the purpose of supplying money to send needy black students to college. As a member of the board of directors of the John Avery Boys' Club, he has seen to it that the black youngsters of Durham, North Carolina, have been given the opportunity to go to camp and to have a fully equipped gym. As one of the few Negro members of the United Fund of Durham, he has made certain that his people get their rightful share of the monies collected.

Insurance companies have as their prime responsibility the preparation of tables that determine the life spans of people of various ages. A company could not afford to insure a client for a large sum if that person's age was such that the tables indicated he would not live very long. The people who figure out these statistics are called actuaries. They must have great facility with mathematics. There are special examinations that must be passed before one can become an actuary. Asa Spaulding is an actuary, a position he has held at Mutual for over thirty years. The results of his careful work in this sensitive area are seen in a quotation from a publication of the United States Department of Commerce titled *Causes of Negro Insurance Company Failures*. This pamphlet declares: "The North Carolina Mutual Life Insurance Company is one Negro insurance group that computes its premiums from tables that reflect the true mortality of the Negro population." This quotation simply means that Asa Spaulding knows how to determine how much a client pays for insurance based on his chances of living. Other black insurance companies have failed because they have neglected to do just this.

The respect in which Asa Spaulding is held by his fellow insurance executives is seen in the fact that he was elected First Actuary of the National Negro Insurance Association in 1934 and 1936. He was again chosen for this position in 1938 and 1940.

In 1966, the W.T. Grant Company elected Asa Spaulding as a member of its board of directors. The significant importance of this election is that W.T. Grant Company is a nationwide business corporation. It is one of America's largest five-and-dime chain stores. That the company realizes the need for a Negro on its board because of the pressure for proper recognition by such organizations as the NAACP, does not take away from the fact that a worthwhile company will naturally seek the most capable people as its leaders.

Educational institutions, like business, look for the *best* qualified people to sit on their boards of trustees. (Granted that there are examples where colleges and universities have elected members to their boards because of the possibility of receiving large contributions, nevertheless, they prefer men of ability and loyalty.) Asa Spaulding serves on the boards of Howard and Shaw Universities as a man of ability and loyalty.

His own people have not been unaware of Spaulding's ability. For the past few years, he has had the honor and distinction of being on the board of the National Urban League. Throughout the United States, there are numerous local urban leagues whose responsibility is to the black community in all areas of social work. They touch problems of home and neighborhood, problems of youth, housing, health, education, and many other vital areas. The National Urban League works like a general staff for all of this work. Asa Spaulding is an active member of this general board of strategy.

This short biography of a successful Negro businessman has necessitated the inclusion of some extended explanations of business procedures. It was necessary in order that Asa Spaulding and his contributions to black history may be properly understood. Asa Spaulding has arrived at the apex of business success by the principles set down by his Uncle Charles. There is no short cut to the success that Asa and his family have known. Education is the key factor in most of the biographies in this volume. Asa Spaulding's has not been an exception.

The North Carolina Mutual Life Insurance Company has, at the present time, over 800 agents and over 400,000 outstanding policies, and it has paid its policy holders more than $20,000,000 since its founding. This is the most telling and humanitarian tribute to Charles C. Spaulding and his most capable nephew—Asa T. Spaulding.

> The push to improve the opportunities of black businessmen is on. . . . Essentially, the aim of government must be to speed loans to black businessmen and to offer them counsel.
>
> —Roy Wilkins, *Negro Businessmen Can Make It*

Shirley Anita Chisholm

[1924-   ]

> But she will have no truck with black extremists such as
> the Black Panthers and some spear-carrying agitators who
> once came to her door to urge her to be more "free
> thinking."
>
> —David English, *Divided They Stand*

Calvin Coolidge had just been elected to the Presidency of
the United States. The whole country was traveling along
a pleasant road of prosperity when, in a small apartment in
Brooklyn, Ruby St. Hill gave birth to a daughter, Shirley
Anita, on November 20, 1924. It was a cold, windy, depressing type of day. For Charlie St. Hill, the baby's father,
the weather, plus the realization that there was one more
mouth to feed sent a cold chill down his spine.

Charles and Ruby had come from the West Indies convinced that New York would provide them with the riches
that they had dreamed of since their marriage. The best employment that was available to Charlie was a job in a burlap-
bag factory in New York. Ruby sought work as a cleaning
woman, but she could only help now and then, the children
came along so quickly. Life was not easy for the St. Hills.

Shirley was three when it was decided that she and her
two younger sisters should be sent to their grandmother in
Barbados. It broke their parents' hearts to part with the little

girls. However, what could they look forward to in Brooklyn, with the pre-depression inflation eating into the small income that was coming into their home? It was better that the three grow up in a climate where they would not know the freezing winters and boiling summers of New York.

The liner *Vulcania* carried not only Shirley and her two sisters to Barbados, but also four of their cousins whose parents had discovered, along with the St. Hills, that America was not the Promised Land. Grandmother Emmaline Seales was suddenly acquiring a ready-made family of seven!

Mrs. Seales had raised her own family. Now a woman in her mid-fifties, she assumed an almost monumental task, but she did much to mold well the characters of her charges. They walked each Sunday the two miles to the Parish Church. Shirley, dressed in starched frills and ribbons, walked tall and proud at the head of the little band. Grandma Seales taught the children to have confidence and courage, but she also made them understand that *she* made the decisions.

Barbados, an English colony, gave Shirley a fine basic education in reading, writing, and mathematics. These fundamentals served her in good stead when she returned to Brooklyn. She talked many times as she grew older about the British system of education that made sure that every youngster could read and write. She compared this with the New York City ghetto schools wherein children grow to be teenagers and still cannot read or write.

For seven years the three St. Hill girls frolicked and played on their paradise island in the Caribbean. Shirley was ten when her mother came to take her and her sisters back to Brooklyn. Grandmother Seales hoped to convince her daughter Ruby that the girls should remain in Barbados, but mother love was too strong. The St. Hills wanted their girls home with them and with the new sister that had been born since they left Brooklyn.

Returning to Brooklyn was not a happy experience for

Shirley. When you are ten years old and have tasted life on a Caribbean island, the paved streets of New York offer little to cheer about. However, the difficulty of adjusting to their new surroundings did not prevent Shirley and her sisters from doing well in school. The foundation of an English system of education enabled them to move ahead of their classmates. Shirley was advanced one full year ahead of the children in her age bracket, and was still able to perform better than the others in her class.

Shirley St. Hill went on to attend Girls' High School in Brooklyn. While she was attending this school that was rated very highly academically, she realized her intellectual ability and determined to develop her advantages. This is the motive that has driven her on to the pinnacle of success she enjoys today.

Graduation from Girls' High brought with it the offer of four college scholarships. She was forced to accept the offer from Brooklyn College because this permitted her to live at home. Had she gone elsewhere, it would have meant living in a dormitory, and this added cost she wanted to save her family.

College opened up a whole new life for Miss St. Hill. She majored in sociology and began to see the place among their fellow Americans that Negroes were seeking in order to meet their aspirations. As a member of the Harriet Tubman Society on campus, this young Brooklyn girl attempted to emulate the courageous slave woman for whom the organization was named. In the debating society, she found the opportunity to prove to herself that she could think straight and speak well.

Shirley did not spend all of her time on her books. As a teen-ager, she loved to dance. However, her mother, as a person born in Barbados, could only see dancing as one of the major misleading temptations in a large city. This attitude troubled Shirley. She became an excellent dancer, winning contests for the lindy hop, jitterbug, and applejack. Hoping to keep her daughter at home and take her mind off dancing, Mrs. St. Hill bought her a piano. She had nothing to fear, for her Shirley was not going to become a professional dancer.

Shirley was twenty-one when her father bought the family a house on Prospect Place, in Brooklyn. Their new home was more elegant than any in which the St. Hills had lived previously. The neighborhood was very different—for Brooklyn. The street was lined with beautiful trees. The St. Hills were the third Negro family to move into the neighborhood. Today, the section is completely Negro and Puerto Rican. It was a good investment that Charlie St. Hill made then; for today the place is worth three times what he paid for it originally.

Graduation from Brooklyn College did not quiet Shirley's desire for education. She secured a position as a teacher in a Harlem day nursery, and in the evenings traveled to Columbia University, where she took courses toward her M.A. degree. Her interest in men was limited to that of dancing partners. She explains her attitude toward boys at that time in her usual clear manner: "I had no time for them because all I wanted was to get an education. Besides, boys shied away from me because I was too brainy. . . . One boy danced with me only on condition I never talked to him about my lectures."

In 1948, Shirley met Conrad Chisholm. He was a graduate student who had recently emigrated from Jamaica. He noticed the ambitious young lady and marveled at her activity. The first time he spoke to her he pointed out that life was made up of other things besides work. He asked if she ever thought of just having fun. Shirley thought that he was terribly fresh. The one attribute of Conrad's that particularly caught Shirley's fancy was his ability to get her to give up her day-to-day plans in order to be with him. To her, any man who dominated her that way deserved more than a passing interest. In 1949 they were married; she was twenty-five.

Marriage did not slow down this vibrant young woman. She continued her work as a teacher of nursery school. As the director of the largest and most recently established day nursery in New York, she learned the way to be an executive and administrator. The school was located just under the Brooklyn Bridge, on the lower East Side of Manhattan. Here, Shirley worked with more than 150 Negro and Puerto Rican children. Determined to make the importance of her work understood by all levels of New York society, she began a campaign that gave her local prominence.

It was her first real move into politics. Her actions and words were not always received with enthusiasm, even by her own people.

Shirley Chisholm tried her hand at politics once more when the Negroes of Bedford-Stuyvesant decided to fight the regular Democratic leadership of Brooklyn. Bedford-Stuyvesant, the largest single Negro section in all New York City, is located in the Borough of Brooklyn. For years, the Negroes of this area had been represented at all levels of the political ladder by white officer holders chosen by the party leadership. In 1953, the Negroes of Brooklyn decided to break this stranglehold.

Mrs. Chisholm joined the new independent organization known as the Bedford-Stuyvesant Political League. Led by a capable Negro named Wesley Holder, who had immigrated from British Guiana to Brooklyn, the fight for political rights was launched. Backing their own man for a judgeship, they defeated the white candidate whom the Democratic machine had tried to force on them. At the victory dinner, Wesley Holder made a prediction that he would keep fighting until Negroes from Brooklyn held office at every level of government up to the United States Congress. Little did Shirley

Chisholm, who was listening enthusiastically, realize she would be the one to make that prediction come true.

Once Mrs. Chisholm moved actively into Brooklyn politics, she worked with her usual dedication and determination. Bedford-Stuyvesant was an area that badly needed the attention of a vibrant woman of her knowledge and desire. In 1955, she was thirty-one. Slender—never weighing over 117 pounds—her five-feet-four-inch frame carried her with speed as she made her rounds of social groups, political gatherings, and church festivals to bring the people her message. This message was always the same—"Respect yourself as an individual and have a sense of belonging, a sense of power."

After a number of years on the campaign trail, working for the election of fellow Negroes, Shirley Chisholm's own chance finally came in 1964. This was her year to try her own political wings. A seat in the New York State Assembly was her goal. The primary fight in opposition to the machine candidate tested—and proved—her vote-getting ability. She went on in November to win the election.

Shirley Chisholm's years before the election had been filled with honors and hard work. In 1957 she received an award for her outstanding contributions in the field of child welfare. That award came as the result of the consulting work she had done for the bureau of Child Welfare. She continued as director of the day nursery in Manhattan. In 1960, she became the Chief Educational Consultant for all of New York City's day nurseries.

Albany, the capital of New York State, is some 150 miles from New York City. On January 1, 1965, Shirley Chisholm stood in the assembly chamber to take the oath as an assemblywoman. She had resigned her position as Chief Educational Consultant to devote all her attention to the problems of her district.

As a freshman in the Assembly, she was expected to sit

back and listen. Shirley Chisholm was not a listener; she was a doer. She remembers those early days in Albany: "I quickly made my maiden speech, and when I had finished they came over and said, 'Sister, where did you learn all that stuff?' "

For four long years Assemblywoman Shirley Chisholm worked to get legislation on the statute books that aided the impoverished people of the state. Three of the six bills she sponsored were passed—a tremendous record. One law gave more money to her favorite interest—day nurseries. The act that provided unemployment payments to domestics had been long overdue. Many Negro women engaged in cleaning work received no unemployment payments when out of a job. Shirley Chisholm's law benefited thousands of New York women.

The third law passed under her sponsorship, and the one in which she takes the greatest pride, brought about the establishment of the SEEK program. SEEK stands for Search for Education, Elevation, and Knowledge. It provides funds to young Negroes and Puerto Rican students who have potential so that they may have the opportunity to go to college.

SEEK offers an examination to those Negro and Puerto Rican students who feel that, even though their high-school training was not adequate, they could still make it in college. If they pass this test, they are given the opportunity to attend college, providing they will take extra courses to catch up to their classmates. Shirley Chisholm tells of the success of the program: "I held a series of public hearings about SEEK up and down the state. Many of the young people said that, without it, they would never have dreamed of becoming anything in America."

It was inevitable that Shirley Chisholm would move on up the political ladder. In 1968, the primary for the Democratic nomination to Congress from Bedford-Stuyvesant had three contestants. All the candidates were Negroes, but only William Thompson was a threat to Shirley. Thompson had been with the New York State Department of Labor. He had strong connections with Robert Kennedy. An assassin stepped in to remove Bobby Kennedy as a supporter of Thompson.

Wesley Holder, the man who had predicted that a Negro from Brooklyn would sit in Congress, was sparking Shirley Chisholm's campaign. He saw her as the victor because there were more women voters than men in the district. A small turnout of voters in the primary gave her 5,680 votes. William Thompson received 4,907.

The primary was but the initial roadblock to pass. The general election was the major hurdle. James Farmer received the Republican nomination. Farmer was a truly formidable opponent. He was nationally known as a Negro leader and civil rights worker. To add to Shirley Chisholm's campaign troubles, she was obliged to undergo a major operation that her opponents attributed to nervous tension.

Farmer's campaign pointed out that while Shirley Chisholm was a gracious lady, the district needed a strong man to do the job. Holder continued with his plan to make his candidate's appeal touch the broad base of the average voter. He felt that Farmer's approach would reach only the one or two per cent at the top of the pyramid.

Shirley Chisholm's real break came at the Democratic National convention in Chicago. She had been chosen by her fellow Democrats as one of the two members from New York on the National Committee. She was the first National Committeewoman of the party. Television cameras picked her out of the crowd on the floor, newspaper reporters sought interviews, national magazines wrote special articles on her unique career.

The campaign back in Brooklyn brought Farmer and Chisolm into several face-to-face debates. Thousands of dollars were spent by both candidates on TV time, newspaper advertisements, and street signs. It was a contest between two Negroes within the two-party system, without resource to violence or arson. Yet when the vote was tallied, the number who went to the polls was discouraging, to say the least. Shirley Chisholm received 34,885 votes to Farmer's 8,923.

Shirley Chisholm fully understands the havoc that a political career can play on one's personal life. She and Conrad have no children, which in itself has put a strain on their family life, although it has given Shirley more time to devote to her work and political tasks. Her marriage has been a good one but she and Conrad see little of one another. She feels that he has stood up well under the pressure of being the husband of a prominent woman.

The Chisholms live a few streets away from the old St. Hill house in Brooklyn, where Mrs. St. Hill and two of her daughters continue to live. A strain between Shirley and her family came about when her father provided in his will for a trust fund of $11,000 for her alone.

Washington has proved to be a new arena for Shirley Chisholm to conquer. Almost daily she makes headlines with political moves that prove her aggressiveness in behalf of her favorite causes. Never willing to remain loyal to her party simply because it is expected, she is more often supporting candidates other than Democrats. In the 1969 New York City mayoralty campaign, she turned her back on the Democratic candidate to support the Fusion leader. Even though her action could have caused her the loss of her party's National Committee position, she persisted in her stand.

The Shirley Chisholm success story is another one in which the prime theme is a good education. The two major assets that will help the Negro to overcome his racial imbalance are education and example in achievement. Along with thousands of other Negroes who have been successful, Shirley Chisholm has set her own special example. It is the responsibility of the United States Government, on all levels, to provide the best possible educational opportunities.

I have learned that independence and integrity are not the most desirable attributes in politicans—although they should be.

—Shirley Chisholm

James Robert Spurgeon

[1870-1942]

DIPLOMAT

> The wall of segregation will crumble when the Negro
> has brought himself to a higher educational and economic
> status.
>
> —Harold Ickes, Secretary of the Interior,
> Franklin D. Roosevelt Administration

Virginia gets cold in November. Five years after the close
of the Civil War, Richmond, Virginia, was experiencing one
of the coldest Novembers in twenty years. On November 15,
1870, a young ex-slave led his mule cart through the streets
of the ex-capital of the Confederacy all day, peddling his farm
and garden produce.

James Robert Spurgeon had many deep-rooted memories
as he trudged along, shivering. It was just a few years ago
that his dad and mother, with his five brothers and sisters,
had been told by a young captain in the Union Army that
they were no longer slaves. They were then living on a small
plantation in western Tennessee. James remembered that day
well. He was just eighteen, and the good news stirred happy
expectations in him. Freedom from slavery would mean many
things for him, but, above all, it would mean that Louisa
Ann McCue could now become Mrs. James R. Spurgeon. It
would also mean that he could strike out in business for himself, since he was no longer the property of another man.

In the few years since that hopeful day, James Spurgeon had seen these dreams come true. He had been able, with the help of the Freedman's Bureau, to procure a mule and a small cart. The Freedman's Bureau was established by law in order to make possible for the ex-slave to receive help in getting food, a home, and ways to earn a living. He then purchased the farm products of his fellow ex-slaves, and sold them on the streets of the surrounding towns. The South suffered much in those early years after the close of the Civil War, and the need for food was great. James Spurgeon served that need well. His pleasant, quiet, and determined manner earned for him many customers and friends.

When he felt well enough established, he proposed to Louisa Ann. She played the part of an eighteenth-century young lady to the letter, being most careful not to react too quickly or to permit her emotions to show too plainly. James asked for Louisa Ann McCue's hand in 1866. It was not until February, 1869, that they were married. Life moved at a more leisurely pace in those days.

Shortly after they were married, James decided that, if he could move to a large city, his chances of success would be greater. He was supported in this decision by his young wife, whose advice he always sought. Slowly they made the long trek northward, with Richmond, the Pride of the South, their goal. It was spring, 1869, when the young couple, seated in the donkey cart, finally reached their destination.

All that the Spurgeons could afford was a one-room apartment over a grocery store in the old part of the city. It was from here that, each morning before dawn, James drove to the market to buy his produce. All day he cried out his wares for the housewives of Richmond.

That November 15, 1870, was not a good day for business, nor was it good as far as the weather was concerned. Cold and forlorn, James finally returned to the one-room apartment, expecting to find Louisa Ann waiting for him with a cup of hot broth. Instead, he was met by the landlady who informed him that his wife, who had been expecting their first child, had been taken to the local hospital. In the early hours of the morning of November 16th, a son was born to James and Louisa Ann Spurgeon. He was named after his father—James Robert Spurgeon, Junior.

Young James grew up in a home that was filled with love and religion. His early childhood was crammed with happy memories. It was not long before it became apparent that this boy was gifted with a keen intellect. In elementary school he led his class year after year. In many respects he was too far advanced for the type of education he was receiving.

James's father was determined that his son would get the education that he had never had the opportunity to receive himself. As a businessman, the elder Spurgeon had prospered to the point where he had many people in his employ. However, he could barely write his name, and, in most written contracts, it was James Junior who read the fine print to him.

James was now known to his friends and family as "Jim." He was popular with the boys and girls of the neighborhood, while still leading them in the academic area. In high school, Jim played baseball, ran on the track team, and debated like a professional. At graduation he was the valedictorian. In that memorable speech he said in part, "America has come a long way since 1865. Men are no longer slaves, but are free to seek their own destiny. Much can be done for us—much we can do for ourselves. Life will not be easy. Many will shun us because we are black. Show them that we have confidence and hope, and that with God's help we will succeed." This was James Spurgeon's creed in the years that would follow.

Jim Spurgeon left Richmond in September, 1888, for Hampton Institute. He was approaching eighteen years of age. This was the same age that his father was when he was freed. Hampton Institute was founded by the Freedman's Bureau in 1868. It is one of the few educational institutions set up during that period that has continued down to this day.

For two years young Spurgeon worked hard at Hampton. He could give his entire time to study because his family paid all his expenses. Shortly after he arrived at the Institute, he made up his mind to become a lawyer, so his main courses were in political science, history, and public speaking.

September, 1890, found Jim on board a train bound for New Haven, Connecticut. The president of Hampton Institute had suggested that the young black scholar seek admittance to Yale University Law School, and his family had agreed.

Jim Spurgeon spent two happy years at Yale. While there, he was most active both socially and academically. As a Negro, he found that his color was no barrier to fulfilling his most precious dreams. His interest in sports was limited to membership on the tug-of-war team. However, to have been chosen for membership on this team was in many ways comparable to being a halfback on the Yale football squad.

His constant interest in public speaking won him the honor of being the Townsend Prize orator at commencement. Before graduation, he was elected to the exclusive academic Kent Club. By June, 1892, James Spurgeon had made his mark at Yale. He earned his LL.B. from an Ivy League college just twenty-seven years after his mother and father had become freedmen.

From the beginning, James Spurgeon was determined to return to the South and work for his people there. He decided to seek his fortune and future career in Kentucky. He prepared to take his bar examination in Mayesville, Kentucky. The Yale Law School had done its job well, so Spurgeon had no difficulty in answering the questions which earned him his license to practice law. For six years he remained in this community as a lawyer and educator. His work as an attorney was given over almost completely to aiding his people in their continuous struggle to seek their civil rights. He won the praise and approval of his fellow attorneys because of his honesty, fairness, and ability.

Spurgeon was a dedicated scholar. While his interest was law, his dedication was to education. Education for the black child was most precious to him. In the 1890's, a young Negro in a southern state was not getting the best teachers, the best school facilities, or the best textbooks. When the leading Negroes of Mayesville asked Spurgeon to become the principal of Mayesville High School, he immediately accepted. From 1893 until 1898, he served in that capacity. As principal, his school was known far and wide for its fine curriculum, and for the number of its students that went on to college. During his principalship he continued his practice of the law.

The duties of a high-school principal in a Negro school in the 1890's were not easy to carry out. Spurgeon had the task of convincing his own people that education, for them, was a must. He would quote his father to the parents who wanted to take their children out of class and put them to work. He remembered his dad saying so often, "An education is something that no man can ever take from you." It is no wonder that there are successful black people in Mayesville today who still remember Jim Spurgeon as the man who was responsible for their strong interest in education.

Never a man to rest on his laurels, he kept himself busy in many areas. In the last year of his work at Mayesville High School he became counselor-at-bar of the Court of Appeals, at Frankfort, Kentucky. This again is the type of work that Jim Spurgeon found most rewarding. As a counselor at the bar, his duties were not unlike those of the present-day public defender. He defended those who could not afford to spend money for a defense attorney. His fees were paid by the community.

Following the Civil War, many Negroes flocked to support the Republican cause. The party of Abraham Lincoln had given the slaves their freedom. In return, the freedmen were determined to keep that party in power. Jim Spurgeon was active in behalf of the Republicans in Kentucky. During the presidential campaign of 1896, he worked for the election of William McKinley. The Republican victory of that year opened an entirely new career for this young attorney.

Liberia, in West Africa, was established in 1822, when a settlement was made at Monrovia, later the capital of the new country, by Negro freedmen from the United States. These founders had the assistance of various American colonization societies. Liberia was declared a republic on July 26, 1847. It was to this country that James Robert Spurgeon received, from President William McKinley, his commission as first secretary at the American Legation.

The trip to Liberia was Jim Spurgeon's first venture outside his native United States. Spurgeon was the only black holding an important assignment with the American Legation. The minister did hire blacks to work for the United States, but they were natives. Four years before he received his assignment, he had married Rosetta Cuffey. Rosetta had attended Hampton Institute with Jim, remaining on to graduate in 1892. On June 27, 1894, the young lawyer went to Norfolk, Virginia, his bride's home town, to be married by her father, the Reverend Jeremiah Cuffey. The young diplomat left New York for his new post, accompanied by Rosetta and their two children, Charlotte Louise and James Robert III.

Monrovia was a small city in those days, but the Spurgeons soon found suitable living quarters near the Legation. There were no communication difficulties, for English was the official language. The government of the republic was not unfamiliar because the constitution of Liberia was modeled on that of the United States.

James Spurgeon had always made friends easily. His pleasing personality did much to ease the way for the Legation staff in their diplomatic dealings with the Liberian officials. Shortly after settling down in this country so far from home, Jim was offered the opportunity to teach a course at the College of West Africa. Here he lectured to young Liberians who were preparing to teach in their country's schools. His course was on the methods and practice of teaching. This is again indicative of James Spurgeon's determination to see to it that people of his race realized the advantages of an education. He later became a regent examiner of logic at Liberia College. The duties of first secretary of a legation place the person holding that office in the most important position after that of the minister. He is second in command, and handles most of the correspondence between the legation and the government to which he is assigned, as well as that with the home government. Spurgeon, assigned to a small country, was able to find time for his teaching assignments.

For five years, James Spurgeon served in various capacities at the American Legation in Monrovia. He was acting minister, resident consul general, and chargé d'affaires. Finally, Mrs. Spurgeon pleaded with him to take the family back to the United States. By 1903, the couple had two more children, Julia and John, who had never set foot on their homeland. Mrs. Spurgeon had not seen her father or mother since coming to Liberia. Jim Spurgeon had been home just once, in 1899, when Wilberforce College had awarded him an honorary LL.D. degree. It was about time to return home, she insisted.

Before leaving Liberia, James Spurgeon was summoned to the home of the president of the country, where he was awarded the insignia and diploma of Knight Commander of the Order of African Redemption. The people of this young republic would not soon forget the genuine interest, hard work, and unselfish dedication that James Robert Spurgeon had given to their hopes and problems.

Arriving in New York in late 1903, the Spurgeons immediately set up a home in Brooklyn. Jim went on down to Washington to make his report to the proper State Department officials and to receive the thanks and congratulations of the American people from Secretary of State John Hay for an assignment well handled. His reports on all-important educational affairs and on the commercial relations between Liberia and the United States were published by the Department of State.

It was inevitable that James Spurgeon would return to his first love—the law. In 1904, he became a member of the firm of Atkins, Collins and Spurgeon, where he remained until 1911. During these years he devoted most of his efforts to protecting the civil rights of his people. The Negro population of New York City had been growing steadily since the turn of the century. Large numbers of black people constantly moved up from the South, full of hope and with a strong belief that New York would offer them a fair chance. They ran into all types of city residents whose prime purpose was to defraud them. It was against this exploitation that James Robert Spurgeon devoted his greatest efforts.

The youth of America were always close to Jim's heart. He associated himself with the Boy Scouts of America shortly after they were organized in 1911. His own sons were active merit badge seekers in their earlier years. This interest in Boy Scouts remained strong throughout James Spurgeon's lifetime. He volunteered, through the Division of Scout Masters, for service in the Armed Forces when the United States entered World War I. During that conflict he was promoted to first lieutenant in the Medical Corps. He served in France in 1918, as part of the 369th Infantry Division, under Colonel Charles Feldmore. The colonel remembered the friendly lieutenant many years later, "A man who found no job too small, nor any man too unimportant to deserve his complete attention."

Jim Spurgeon's home life was ideal. His wife was devoted

to him and to their children. The loss of their oldest girl, Charlotte Louise, in 1906, indeed left a void. However, the family was blessed with one more child, whom they named Blyden. Religion played a most active part in the lives of the Spurgeon family. The parishioners of St. Philip's Episcopal Church in Brooklyn would see them in their pew each Sunday morning. Jim held many important positions in St. Philip's right up to the time of his death. He was clerk, vestryman, lay leader, and Sunday School superintendent—all clear proof of his strong attachment to a belief in religion as an integral part of every man's life.

With the end of World War I, James Spurgeon returned to New York to resume the practice of law. This time he opened his own office, and simultaneously accepted the assignment as a special deputy attorney-general of the New York Supreme Court.

His family was growing up and he was in need of more income, so that his ambitions for them might be achieved. Like all public-minded men, he had devoted so much of his time to the problems of others that his own had suffered. For the next few years, James Spurgeon worked hard and developed a fine law practice. However, he still gave of himself for public welfare causes without stint. He accepted a place on the executive council of the Boy Scouts of America. This was the highest honor that could be conferred by the Scouts. His interest in the American Negro Library Association won him the presidency of the organization for two terms. As a Mason, he gave much of his time to this international fraternal organization. His varied interests won him membership in the American Academy of Political and Social Science, as well as the African Society of London, England.

In 1940, James Spurgeon was seventy years of age. Life was moving on at a different pace for this man of many talents. In 1926 he had lost his devoted Rosetta, and existence was not as calm or satisfying without her. His outside interests continued, but his participation in the legal field had diminished. Most people wanted younger men to handle their cases, and Jim could understand their desire. But when war came again to the United States, James Spurgeon was not too old or too tired to help his country. At seventy-two, there was one special area in which he could help the war effort—his Boy Scouts. He organized a special troop of Boy Scouts to do defense work for their country. The need for scrap iron to be used for defense purposes was great. These boys took their wagons and bicycles and toured Brooklyn, collecting the metal wherever it was available. They prepared vegetable gardens in the public parks and in vacant lots, to help provide the needed food supply. Those "victory" gardens did much to aid the war effort both materially and psychologically.

Diplomat James Spurgeon was not to have the joy of knowing that the Allies would triumph over the dictators. Early in November, 1942, he was taken with a case of pneumonia. The doctor was sure that he would pull through because of his strong desire to live. However, in the morning hours of November 17th, the once strong heart could bear the burden no longer, and James Robert Spurgeon died.

The Brooklyn Daily Eagle summarized this man of the people with the comment: "James Robert Spurgeon, son of slave parents, represents that character and dignity that has helped make America great. Teacher, author, diplomat, lawyer and father, he has excelled in all his callings. He was indeed a man of his people—a man for all Americans."

The New York Times saw James Spurgeon as the living proof that, regardless of any obstacles he must face, a man can be a success if he sees the need for an education, seizes the opportunity, and uses it. Harold Ickes echoed the belief of James Robert Spurgeon perfectly when he saw education as the Negro's prime weapon in his fight for his God-given rights.

Medgar Wiley Evers

[1925-1963]

CIVIL RIGHTS LEADER

> From the beginning we accepted the possibility that any
> of us might be killed. But he loved the work and I loved
> him, and whatever made him happy pleased me.
>
> —Myrlie Evers

James and Jessie Evers lived and, to a degree, prospered in
Decatur, Mississippi, where James was a funeral director.
There was nothing that particularly set him apart from his
fellow black neighbors. The family was a closely knit group.

When Medgar was born, on July 2, 1925, he was the second
child of Jessie and James Evers. His brother Charles, three
years older, became his constant companion during his entire
life. The two boys grew up in a home where there was no
drinking, smoking, or gambling. They had to be in the house
before sundown each evening. All the Evers family attended
the Church of God and Christ three times each week, to
pray to God that, as blacks, they might hope for some relief
in this "vale of tears."

In their early days, Charles and Medgar never held any
resentment toward the white population. In fact, Medgar
played happily with a white boy until this youth called him
"nigger." It was then that Medgar realized, ". . . that I came
from nothing, was myself nobody, that my children could
expect nothing more than I had."

Things did not improve. When Medgar Evers was four-teen, he watched a lynch mob murder a close friend of his father's who was charged with having insulted a white woman. When Medgar pleaded with his dad to get his gun, he was told that if he did, they all would be murdered.

Evers was eighteen in 1943, and since the United States was at war, he was drafted into the Army. He was soon ap-palled to discover that the prejudice he knew at home was still with him in the service. Even after two years of close conflict in foreign lands for a common cause, there was as yet a great deal of segregation. He wrote his brother Charles, who was also in the service, "When we get out of the army, we're going to straighten this out."

As a black, it was routine that Medgar was assigned to a stevedore battalion. He was part of a transportation corps whose job it was to move the materials of war from Normandy to the fighting front. His group brought food, guns, and other necessities of battle on the "Red Ball" highway, from the supply depot in Cherbourg to the men on the firing line. Medgar Evers won two combat stars for his service in the Normandy invasion.

His years in the Army convinced Medgar that a college education was an absolute necessity. When he was discharged, he entered Alcorn A. & M. College in 1946. Alcorn, a black institution, is located in southwest Mississippi. His brother Charles joined him, and they roomed together. Both won places on the football team. Charles became the center, and Medgar played first-string halfback. The latter was also on the track team during his junior and senior years.

Medgar Evers was a sincere and dedicated student. In his first two years at Alcorn, he was considered a loner. How-ever, during his last two years he became involved in campus activities to the extent that he was chosen editor of the Alcorn *Herald*. In his junior year he was elected class president and vice-president of the student forum. He had matured to the point where he was now considered a leader. He was, nevertheless, a humble young man whose word was his bond.

Alcorn is a coeducational college. During his sophomore year, Medgar met Myrlie Beasley, only eighteen years old and a nursing student. Medgar first noticed her when she entered the library one day as he was coming out. Struck by her beauty, he managed an introduction, which was followed by many dates. He was eight years older than Myrlie, but was determined to make her his wife. On Christmas Eve of 1951, they were married.

From the very beginning Myrlie knew that her life with Medgar would not be easy. This man of hers would be in constant danger as he fought the cause of civil rights. Even before she married him, he had embarked on a project that could have cost him his life. While still in high school, he had worked with the NAACP in setting up chapters. Three years before he was married, with a number of his fellow students, including his brother, he traveled to Decatur to attempt to vote fairly in Mississippi.

The Decatur incident could have proven to be a most serious affair. The spunk, determination, and stamina of these black Americans brought them almost to the brink of disaster. Decatur was waiting for them when they drove in from Alcorn. Medgar and his friends faced armed whites who were determined that these intruders would not vote. The blacks were also armed, but they were outnumbered ten to one. Only the pleas of a white woman eased the tension, and bloodshed was avoided.

Medgar, commenting on this incident later, declared, "You know any man with an ounce of pride who works in the Delta wants to do something for the poor black man."

Following his graduation from Alcorn in 1952, Medgar took a position with the Magnolia Mutual Life Insurance Company. He had received a bachelor of business administration degree at Alcorn. He found a small house for Myrlie and himself in Mount Bayou, a tiny village in northwestern Mississippi. Even while he was engaged in the insurance business, he was involved in a great many civil rights projects.

His first objective was to organize a boycott against gas stations that refused blacks permission to use their rest rooms. He worked to bring inactive NAACP chapters back to life. Always a strong supporter of the NAACP, he opened a chapter in Mount Bayou. This grew by leaps and bounds. He was always pressing for the neighboring Negroes to register and vote.

During 1954, when the Supreme Court ruled in favor of desegregation in the famous case of *Brown v. The School Board of Topeka,* Evers decided to go to the all-white University of Mississippi Law School. It might well be that the average black believed that 1954 was his year of liberation. It certainly was not so for Medgar. After much questioning and stalling, he was told he did not qualify for entrance because he had failed to get recommendations from two people in the community.

The work that Evers had done for the NAACP had not gone unnoticed by the national office. He was offered a position as the first paid field secretary in Mississippi. He needed this boost for two reasons—first, he was doing little that was profitable in the insurance business, and with the birth of his first child, a son named Darrell Kenyetta, he needed more money; second, he was cast down mentally because of the law school experience.

In December, 1954, Evers went to work full time for the NAACP. With that move, his entire way of life changed. To the whites he was no longer a part-time volunteer in the cause of civil rights. He now became a constant, actively engaged problem for them.

Medgar Evers was a dedicated fighter for the rights of the blacks in Mississippi. He was forced to fight not only the whites, but also the blacks, whose major problem was their understandable inferiority complex. As Myrlie expresses it, "He hated to see blacks cherish their good relations with the white man more than they did their own freedom."

Evers set up his headquarters in Jackson, Mississippi. It was logical to be where the center of action was, and that was, naturally, in the state capital. The office was manned by Medgar and Myrlie.

The first task that the field secretary faced was to get the story of crimes against blacks in Mississippi published. It was impossible to have these stories printed in the white-controlled newspapers of the state. Medgar Evers investigated personally all stories of crimes against blacks, and sent his findings to the New York office of the NAACP. It was his persistent searching and investigating that brought the terrible tragedy of Emmet Till to the attention of the nation's press. Young Till had come from Chicago to visit his aunt in Sumner, Mississippi. During his stay, he was accused of insulting a white woman. While the investigation was going on, he was shot to death. Emmet Till was fourteen years old.

Evers soon discovered that his ability to awaken national interest in the plight of the Mississippi blacks did not sit well with the "professionals" of his own race. In the early days of his crusade, the Mississippi Negro Teachers Association was unwilling to permit him to address them. The black press was equally uncooperative. It was from the black rank-and-file people that Medgar Evers received his real support.

Evers' intention was never merely to stir up other people to action. He made the moves himself. At one time he entered a Trailways bus and took a front seat reserved for white passengers only. He refused to move until he was seized by the police and taken to the station house. When he was released, he went right back to the same bus and the same seat. A white cab driver who saw him, entered the bus and punched him in the face. Evers did nothing in retaliation, for, had he fought back, it would have ended his career.

Because of his desire to show actively his feelings of sympathy for a group of sit-in demonstrators, he was beaten over the head and charged with disorderly conduct. At another time, he described what he thought of a judge's decision in a civil rights case for the national wire services. When his comments were printed, he was fined $100 and sentenced to thirty days in jail for contempt. This verdict was later reversed by the Mississippi Supreme Court.

By 1963, Medgar Evers had, for nine years, faced daily the possibility of death. The strain was beginning to tell on him, and he was at the point of exhaustion. All during the spring months, he worked to organize the blacks to demand their rights. He asked the Mayor of Jackson to appoint a biracial committee to consider the problem, as had been suggested by President Kennedy. He got nowhere. He demanded that the schools of Jackson be integrated, as the Supreme Court had determined, but the officials laughed at him.

The climax came on May 28th, when a sit-in at Woolworth's lunch counter erupted into a wild riot. Evers addressed a rally of 2,000 blacks that night, and urged them to take to the streets to protest. The local police used all the restraining methods in their book, finally arresting some 600 Negro children and placing them in a stockade on the outskirts of the city.

When deeply discouraged Medgar Evers was convinced that all his work had been for naught, and that he had failed completely, he was cheered by the appearance in Jackson of Roy Wilkins, the Executive Secretary of the NAACP. He had come to give Evers moral support and assistance. Evers and Wilkins picketed in front of Woolworth's and were arrested. They were charged with committing a felony and were held in $1,000 bail.

Myrlie Evers worried each time her husband left their home. Recently, while he was out, a car had passed the house and the driver had tossed a Molotov cocktail into the carport.

Her fears were also for their three children. (By now, Darrell had a sister, Denise, and a brother, James.)

June 7, 1963, was a Friday. That evening Myrlie and Medgar Evers attended a NAACP rally. At this gathering he spoke of his wife and children with great affection. This he had never done previously. For several days after that, he remained home, just to be with his family. During these times Myrlie and her husband spoke of death.

The morning of June 11th was a special one for Medgar. Before he left for work, he kissed the children tenderly, and held his wife close for many minutes. During that day he called home several times, something he never did. It was on this day that President Kennedy asked Congress to correct the imbalance in civil rights. Evers listened to the President, then went off to a rally at a church, where he told the black audience the good news. The meeting lasted past midnight. Evers was tired when he set out for the drive home.

The church was only a ten-minute ride from his house. When Medgar drove into his driveway, the moon was shining brightly. As he opened the door of his car, a figure moved in the brush across the street. A sharp crack of an Enfield rifle was heard. Evers took the bullet in his back. He fell forward as his wife ran out to him. It took a while before he was moved to University Hospital in a neighbor's station wagon. By 1:14 A.M., less than an hour after the attack in the dark, Medgar Evers was dead.

The sacrifice was now complete. This man of spirit, man of love, man of devotion, had given his life so that his fellowmen might someday know justice.

The days of Medgar Evers' wake (in Jackson, Mississippi) were times of tension. The blacks were angry. Even those who had turned their backs on Evers' efforts in their behalf were now demanding that something be done to apprehend the killer. Leading Negroes from all over the United States came to pay tribute to this brave man. Among those who attended the church services in Jackson were Ralph Bunche, Roy Wilkins, and Martin Luther King, Jr. Roy Wilkins gave the funeral oration. He said in part: "The killer must have felt that he had, if not an immunity, then certainly a provocation for whatever he chose to do, no matter how dastardly it might be. . . . The bullet that tore away Medgar Evers' life four days ago tore away at the system and helped to signal it in. . . ."

Following the church services, the city almost found itself in the throes of an all-out riot. The blacks had endured all they could tolerate. Several youngsters ran toward the center of town. They were followed by hundreds of others. Before they came to a showdown with the police, a Federal Justice Department member brought sanity out of chaos. He was able to restore order by telling the group, "Medgar Evers wouldn't want it this way."

President Kennedy, only months away from his own assassination, ordered Medgar Evers' burial to be in Arlington National Cemetery. The service at the graveside was conducted with great solemnity. The telling last words, before the casket was lowered into the grave, were spoken by Roy Wilkins: "Medgar Evers believed in his country; it now remains to be seen whether his country believes in him."

> Had there been any conscience or sense of decency among the white citizens of Jackson, they would have flocked to the funeral service for Medgar Evers as a mild expression of their shame over the outrage for what they and Jackson must bear the responsibility. One must conclude that white Jackson of today has the morality of the jungle.
>
> —Ralph Bunche, following Evers' funeral

Mary McLeod Bethune

[1875-1955]

> Mary McLeod Bethune rose by no golden stair or silver
> spoon, but by sheer courage, faith and perseverance.
>
> —Edward R. Embree, *13 Against the Odds*

Mayesville, South Carolina, is not a large community today. In 1875, it was a typical struggling southern reconstruction town. In a four-room cabin, some three miles from Mayesville, on July 10th, Mary McLeod was born. She was to be *the 15th.* one of seventeen children.

Mary's parents had been slaves, and when the Civil War ended, continued to work as freedmen on their former master's plantation. After a few years, the McLeods received five acres of land to cultivate as their own.

The cotton obtained from five acres was not sufficient to supply the family with the basic necessities of life. Mary added her bit by picking cotton on neighboring lands, and helping her mother do washing and ironing for white families who lived in town.

An experience she endured when she was ten, she never forgot. She had gone to one of the homes in town to deliver the laundry. While there, she picked up a book, and the little girl of the house took it away from her saying, "You can't read." From then on, Mary was determined to learn how to read and write.

Within a year, she was given the opportunity to go to school. The Missionary Board of the Presbyterian Church set up a school for Negroes close to Mayesville. The teacher, Miss Emma Wilson, asked the McLeods if they would permit Mary to be one of her pupils. Mary's parents consented because she seemed to be the only child of their seventeen who really wanted to acquire any learning.

Mary walked five miles to and from school each day. She soon learned how to read, write, and use numbers. Her family benefited from her studying, for she attempted to instruct her brothers and sisters in the lessons she had covered. Her neighbors relied on her to help them with their financial transactions as they prepared to sell their cotton in the market.

Her graduation from the Mayesville school was one of the most gratifying events of Mary's life. Her parents watched with pride as she received her diploma. Unfortunately, however, it appeared that while Mary had done well with her lessons, there would be no opportunity for her to continue her education.

As if by a miracle, the door was opened that permitted Mary McLeod to go further with her schooling. Miss Mary Crissman, who resided in Denver, Colorado, offered to provide a scholarship for one of the students of the Mayesville Mission School. Miss Wilson recommended Mary for the grant. The school that she would attend was Scotia Seminary, in Concord, North Carolina.

It was at Scotia that this young girl learned what was meant by the word *brotherhood*. Here she met white people who proved that they believed in practicing the Christian principles they preached. Her training convinced her that she wanted to go to Africa as a missionary. When she finished at Scotia, there were no openings in the African missions, so Miss Crissman gave her another scholarship, this time to Moody Bible Institute in Chicago, Illinois. At Moody, Mary met black and white people from all over the world. This cosmopolitan experience proved to be a distinct asset in the years to come. Her ability to get along with all types of people was the result of her experiences at Moody.

For two years, Mary McLeod toured throughout the South, helping the institute set up new missions. She traveled with her Bible team, serving as chief vocalist; occasionally she preached on these missions. When the time came for her to graduate from Moody Bible Institute, there were still no openings in the African missions. She knew how to teach and she was determined to do so. If there were no African missions to go to, then she would teach her own people down South.

Mary wrote to Miss Lucy Laney, who was at the Harris Institute in Augusta, Georgia. She told Miss Laney, a great Negro educator, that she was ready and willing to help her. Mary McLeod soon became known far and wide throughout the South as a teacher and a benefactor of her race. She received invitations to work from almost every black community. She answered one of these invitations by going to Sumter, South Carolina.

It was while she was in Sumter that Mary McLeod met and married Albertus Bethune. The young couple decided to leave Sumter for Savannah, Georgia. In their new home, Albertus opened a tailor shop. Business was poor in Savannah, and Albertus did not have much energy, so they moved on to Palatha, Florida. In the meantime, Mary had given birth to a son, Albert. It was necessary for her to teach if her family was to have enough of the necessities of life.

The opportunities for a decent livelihood were not too much better for the Bethunes in Florida than they had been in Georgia. For five years they struggled, and at the end of that time Mary was struck a cruel blow in the death of Albertus.

The young widow, left to support a five-year-old son, was

resolutely determined to make a go of it, however. She had always wanted to open a school for impoverished Negro girls. She hoped to be able to teach them those subjects to which she had been exposed at their age. A friend told her that Daytona Beach was the place where she should go.

Daytona Beach was becoming a well-known resort spot for the wealthy; consequently, many Negroes were also moving to eastern Florida to obtain work, so this appeared to Mary to be the ideal place for her to begin her pet project. However, she found the poverty among the black population in Daytona even worse than any she had left in Palatha. Her greatest sorrow came, though, when she discovered that the Negroes opposed her desire to build a school for them.

In spite of this setback, Mary Bethune decided to stay in Daytona and open a school. She rented a shanty near the railroad tracks. The rent was eleven dollars a month. She could only offer the landlord one dollar and fifty cents and promised to pay him the rest when she had it.

The school opened on October 4, 1904. It was named the Daytona Educational and Industrial Training School for Negro Girls. The student body consisted of five little girls and Mary's son. Tuition was to be fifty cents a week.

Mary Bethune was a practical woman. She taught her charges how to cook and sew. They also received some instruction in reading, writing, and arithmetic. She believed, with Booker T. Washington, that students should be taught to earn a living.

Mary Bethune had a tremendous interest in choral work. She organized a choir, and before long, the group was performing for some of the most prominent people in America. John D. Rockefeller had a home in Daytona Beach, and he often had Mary and the choir sing at his social gatherings. He always aided her educational project with a sizeable check. Henry J. Kaiser, the World War II industrial wizard,

no

had her choral group sing before many of the wealthy people who vacationed in Florida.

By 1906, the school had grown to 250 pupils and four teachers. However, things were still touch and go financially. It was not until James M. Gamble, of Procter and Gamble, the large soap manufacturing company, came to Daytona and decided to help Mary Bethune, that things really began to change for the better.

Within a few years, Mrs. Bethune had raised a sum of money that permitted her to build a substantial school structure on lots that formerly had been the city dump. She was able to convince Thomas H. White, a sewing machine manufacturer, to help. When Mr. White died, he left a trust fund of $67,000, which made possible the erection of a main assembly hall in 1918. At the dedication of the building, the Governor of Florida and the Vice-President of the United States were both present to praise the achievements of this fine woman.

In 1923, Mary Bethune's school was chartered as a junior college. It was merged with the Cookman Institute for Boys, and the school was renamed the Bethune-Cookman College. It had grown to be an educational project with 794 students and forty-two faculty members.

Not satisfied with giving her people an education, Mary Bethune began to work for the establishment of a hospital for Negroes in Daytona. She was made acutely aware of the need for such a health facility when a young black girl almost died with acute appendicitis because there was no local hospital that would admit her. It was only when Mary Bethune convinced a white doctor he should operate that the life of the desperately ill girl was saved.

Mrs. Bethune raised $5,000 to purchase a frame cottage in back of the college grounds. The money, in part, was obtained from Andrew Carnegie, the steel magnate. This simple building was turned into a hospital which was named after its founder's family, "The McLeod Hospital." It grew steadily and received Negro patients from all over the South.

Never willing to rest on her laurels, Mary Bethune attended many conferences at Tuskegee Institute, which was under the direction of Booker T. Washington. It was after one of these conferences that she developed the idea of a county fair for Negroes. She planned all types of exhibits, a baby show, and food judging contests. Women displayed their jams, jellies, and pies, while the men showed their cattle and produce. Proud mothers presented their babies to demonstrate how well cared for they were. The friendly competitive spirit that these county fairs produced made the black participants more aware of the necessity of improving their lives.

Mary McLeod Bethune was considered one of the leading educators in the United States. She became the friend and advisor of Presidents. In 1930, she was invited by President Hoover to take part in the White House Conference on Child Health and Protection. The next year, she attended the President's Conference on Home Building and Home Ownership.

With the coming of the New Deal under President Franklin D. Roosevelt, one of the main worries held by the Administration was the right guidance of the youth of the country. For millions of young people there were no jobs, nor was there the money for them to continue in school. The United States Government organized the National Youth Administration Program. President Roosevelt invited Mary Bethune to come to Washington to present her thoughts on the problem. She pleaded that the young Negroes must not be forgotten in these trying times. She was so successful that she was selected by President Roosevelt to become a member of the Advisory Committee of the National Youth Administration.

For more than twenty years Mary Bethune served as a

special advisor on minority affairs to both President Roosevelt and President Truman. She was, indeed, because of her honesty, clarity, and determination, a binding link between the black and white communities.

Like all famous people, honors were bestowed on Mary McLeod Bethune by the dozens. The two that she cherished most were the Spingarn Gold Medal and the honorary degree of Doctor of Humanities from Rollins College. The Spingarn Medal represented the highest honor her own people could offer her, while the honorary degree came from one of the oldest colleges for whites in the South.

For many years, Mary Bethune had suffered from severe asthmatic attacks. It was decided to operate, and she entered Johns Hopkins Hospital in Baltimore. She soon discovered what it meant to be very ill—and black. She could not get a room in either the surgical or the medical divisions. She was forced to go to another department. There were no Negro nurses or doctors on the staff. However, after she left—and ever since—Johns Hopkins Hospital has had Negro nurses and doctors. Once more, Mary Bethune had taught her lessons on race relations well.

On May 18, 1955, Mary McLeod Bethune died at the age of seventy-nine. Her life had not been easy—but it certainly had been rewarding. Thousands of people, both black and white, were better off—and better human beings—as a result of knowing her.

> I leave you love; I leave you hope; I leave you the challenge of developing confidence in one another; I leave you a thirst for education; I leave you a respect for the use of power; I leave you faith; I leave you racial dignity; I leave you a desire to live harmoniously with your fellow men; I leave you a responsibility to our young people.

> —Mary McLeod Bethune, Last Will and Testament

Asa Philip Randolph

[1889-   ]

LABOR LEADER

> Philip Randolph . . . holds his tall figure with such
> dignity, wears so serene a look and talks in such rumbling
> basso-robusto accents that he brings to mind the image
> of "De Laud" in the play *Green Pastures*—patient oval
> face, grizzly gray hair and all.
>
> —Lester Velie, *Labor U.S.A.*

A. Philip Randolph is now over eighty years of age. When he
was born in Crescent City, Florida, April 15, 1889, the labor
movement was just beginning to stir in the United States.
The American Federation of Labor (AFL) had been founded
just three years before Philip saw the light of day. The old
Knights of Labor, that had been established shortly after the
Civil War, was dying as an effective voice of the American
laboring man. While young Randolph grew to manhood, the
labor movement was also growing and developing into a
significant factor in the economy of his country.

The African Methodist Church in Crescent City was filled
to capacity. It was Good Friday night, in the year 1889, and
the preacher, the Reverend James William Randolph, was
seated, waiting patiently to enter the pulpit while the choir
finished its second hymn. As he glanced at the pages of his
sermon, he felt a tug at his right arm. Looking up, he saw an
old parishioner, who whispered that Mrs. Randolph had just

given birth to a baby boy. The minister smiled, rose, and entered the pulpit. Looking earnestly at his parishioners, he declared, "Tonight we are here to solemnly remember the death of Our Lord while down the street that same Lord has just given life to my new son."

James Randolph had married Elizabeth Robinson, one of his parishioners, in 1886. Randolph, who could never have lived on his income as a minister, was, by trade, a tailor. His flock were mainly sharecroppers, and hence his salary as their preacher was paid in kind—a shoulder of pig, a bag of sweet potatoes, a cabbage or two. Cash was so scarce that the Randolph boys, Philip and an older brother, James, sometimes remained home from school because they lacked shoes.

The Randolphs lived in a shack—two rooms upstairs, two below, with the "living room" largely taken over by the father's mending work. Six days a week a tailor, on Sunday a minister, he had his own inspired way of dealing with the problem of rearing children in the difficult world in which they lived.

From the very beginning, Philip was an inquisitive boy. He discovered early that he was not permitted to browse in the public library, or unrestrainedly borrow books there. He was limited to the meager "colored section." Sometimes he went into nearby Jacksonville with his brother, James, to pick up newspapers to sell. On these occasions the white boys pushed them to the end of the line unless they battled their way to the front. He remembers clinging to his mother's skirts when he was ten, as this fine-featured mulatto, with her long, flowing hair, stood just inside the door of their shack with a shotgun. It was a long night of vigil, and Philip was terror-stricken. His father had rounded up a number of his black neighbors and they had gone off to the county jail to stop a lynching. Mrs. Randolph was prepared to defend her home and family if there was an unfavorable reaction to her husband's humanitarian move.

Their father taught the two boys that color has nothing to do with intellectual capacity, or with character. What they would be in the world depended solely on themselves. Whenever he took his sons into the white section of Crescent City to deliver clothes, he would say to the customer, "Aren't these fine boys? They'll be great men someday."

Instead of fine clothes—as a morale builder—the minister clothed his sons in fine English speech. Although he had no formal education, Philip Randolph's father had read widely and, endowed with a sensitive ear, he had picked up from visiting troupes of Shakespearian actors a clear diction and a South-of-England accent. To this day, Philip professes a strong attachment to Shakespeare and George Bernard Shaw, as far as his reading preferences are concerned.

Philip Randolph never liked his first name. From the time he could understand, he refused to answer when he was called Asa by his family or friends. His mother, who was not too fond of it, either, began calling him Philip. However, as a courtesy to his father, who liked the name, he never dropped it completely, so that he is widely known as A. Philip Randolph.

Once he and his brother were old enough to attend school, they found whatever jobs they could to help their impoverished family. Philip sold newspapers, worked in a grocery store, and did other odd chores around the town.

It was a book taken from the local library that helped direct Philip on the road he would pursue as a man. *Souls of Black Folks,* by W. E. B. DuBois, stressed the idea of the "Talented Tenth," which is that one of every ten blacks must be educated for leadership. Booker T. Washington had taught that blacks were best off in manual training and manual work. DuBois taught that blacks, like other races, have among them persons of superior intellect who should supply the necessary leaders to help their fellow blacks rise to secure those jobs for which their talents and education fitted them. Philip determined to prepare himself to be one of the "Talented Tenth"—a leader of his people.

Young Randolph had the good fortune to live in a community where the American Missionary Association had established, during the days after the Civil War, a high school for blacks with a faculty of whites. All of the faculty came from New England. The Cookman Institute, with its dedicated New England faculty—called Marms—taught more than just what was in the text books. They expounded on the thesis that their students must have faith in themselves so that they might serve as examples to other blacks. They also stressed that, as blacks, they must fight for equal economic opportunity.

When Philip graduated from Cookman Institute, he was asked to give the class oration. His brother, James, who graduated on the same day, was the valedictorian. In the audience that day was an insurance man who was so taken with Philip's oratory that he hired him to sell insurance. Young Randolph took the job for a short time, but he was too restless and ambitious to stick with it. He was dreaming of college and the "Talented Tenth." At nights, after a hard day trying to sell insurance, he would pore over the catalogs of Harvard, Princeton, Oberlin, and other such schools, hoping to find the opportunity to register in some college. To the struggling Randolphs, college was but a distant dream, however.

The South had nothing more to offer Philip. What he wanted was enough money to get North, where he felt that his dreams might have some possibility of coming true. He got a job as a section hand on a railroad, loading cars with sand and laying crossties and rails. This provided him with the needed cash to go to New York City.

After renting a furnished room in Harlem, he set out to look for a job. His first position was that of an elevator operator in one of the new skyscrapers in downtown Manhattan. As soon as he could manage a few free hours, he applied at the College of the City of New York for admission to their evening session. Here he studied political science, economics, and philosophy, and polished up his English. He made a lifelong friend, the late philosopher Morris R. Cohen, who gave Philip scientific papers which showed that, while individual people differ greatly, the black is just another member of the human family, neither inferior nor superior to other races. Later, Randolph also attended Howard University.

In 1917, Philip Randolph and a close friend, Chandler Owen, founded *The Messenger*, a "revolutionary and militant magazine." Earlier, both had been employed as editors of the *Hotel Messenger*, published by the Headwaiters and Sidewaiters Society of New York, but they had left that magazine in a dispute over its policy. Randolph had become involved with the waiters when he was working in that capacity on the coastal Fall River Line. The new *Messenger* was committed to "economic radicalism" and pledged that it would be an organ of labor unionism and socialism among blacks, although the socialism was of non-Marxian variety. In June, 1918, Randolph was arrested in Cleveland, Ohio, by the Department of Justice because of his strong opposition to World War I. Within a few days, he was released without any further attempts being made to detain him.

A. Philip Randolph had been a very busy person since leaving Florida. However, he had not been too busy to find time to court Lucille Campbell, whom he had met at a friend's home in Harlem. Lucille was a graduate of Howard University and was employed as a social worker. She had much in common with Philip in that she loved to read, enjoyed sports, and, above all, passionately believed that blacks must have their rightful place in human society. It was a whirlwind courtship, for, after knowing each other for only two months, they were married. No children blessed the union, but their mutual interests and their sincere affection for one another have made the marriage a completely satisfactory one.

With the war's end, Randolph began to contribute articles to the magazines *Opportunity* and *Survey Graphic*. Both these publications were Socialistic and pro-labor. He also became an instructor at the Rand School of Social Science, which was dedicated to the principles of Socialism. In 1921, Randolph became the Socialist candidate for Secretary of State in New York.

Up until 1925, A. Philip Randolph considered himself primarily a writer and editor. However, he had always shown an interest in the labor movement. While he was working as a waiter on the Fall River Line, he had been discharged for attempting to organize his fellow waiters. He had been successful in organizing a small union of elevator workers in New York City. He was also involved in campaigns to organize the motion picture operators and garment trade workers.

Philip Randolph was now one of the educated "Talented Tenth," the goal to which he had long aspired. In order to give himself a spot from which to operate and to prove the stamina of the black man, he took up one of the toughest organizing jobs in union annals—the twelve-year fight to form the Brotherhood of Sleeping Car Porters.

In 1925, the Pullman porter worked about seventy hours a week at an eighteen-dollar wage—or twenty-five cents an hour. Tips brought his gross monthly income to around one hundred dollars. Out of this money, he had to purchase his uniforms, shoe polish, etc. He was also forced to pay for his meals that were purchased from the dining car. He was never sure he would get an assignment, and at times he would wait all day in the Pullman office and not be called. All these points were considered and agreed upon in a "contract" worked out between the Pullman Company and a company union that was formed and financed by the employer.

In spite of all the problems connected with the job, there were more applicants than positions. The porters were constantly haunted by the thought of idleness and consequent hunger, so they were afraid to organize.

Eventually, Randolph was able to stir up public opinion against the Pullman Company—but he aroused everybody except the porters themselves. Their wives would not permit them to join in the movement for fear they would lose their jobs.

The fight to organize the sleeping car porters was more difficult for the black workers than it was for the Pullman Company. The latter employed inspectors to ride the cars to get information on the union activities of the porters—especially the new men. They were fired at any hint of cooperation. At the same time, the black press refused to print any news of Randolph's organizing progress, and even, at times, attacked him. This usually went along with threats by the Pullman Company to cut their advertisements in the black press.

Those porters who joined Randolph in many cases failed to pay their dollar-a-month dues. This left him and his aides without any salaries or operating funds. They had no lights or telephones in their headquarters. Randolph and his wife were dispossessed from their Harlem flat. Often he did not even have a nickel to pay for the subway ride to the office.

As the general organizer of the Brotherhood of Sleeping Car Porters, Philip Randolph was forced to visit the porters secretly in their homes. He met trains and held meetings at railroad yards when the railroad police weren't watching. After three long years of undaunted effort, he had organized locals with a membership of three thousand.

The real problem for Randolph now was that while he had organized a majority of the porters and had been granted the right to bargain for them by the Railway Labor Board, it was impossible to do so. The company union, organized by the Pullman Company, was the only union with which the latter would bargain. The Railway Labor Board explained to Randolph that they could do nothing, because his union's dispute with the Pullman Company did not represent a "substantial interruption of commerce."

By 1928, Randolph was ready to threaten a strike if the Pullman Company refused to draw up a contract with his union. However, the strike was cancelled when the other railway unions of engineers, trainmen, etc., did not give their support. Randolph was back where he had started! He had a union that was unable to talk to the bosses because the other unions that could have helped refused to cooperate.

The depression hit in 1929. Nine years had gone by since Philip Randolph had assumed the position of general organizer for the porters. Five years later, with the depression lingering on, they still had no contract and no improved working conditions. The organization treasury was empty. Lucille Randolph had lost her social worker's job. There was literally nothing with which she and her husband could buy food or pay their rent.

New York City had as its mayor a reformer who won the spot from Tammany Hall. Fiorello N. LaGuardia had been a good friend of labor when he served in the House of Representatives. As mayor of the then largest city in the world, he told Randolph that he would never succeed in his drive to make his porters' union a recognized group. LaGuardia offered Randolph a twelve-thousand-dollar-a-year job on the city payroll. Humanitarian though he was, the mayor failed to understand what Philip was attempting to do. To him, it was just another union drive. To Randolph, it was a test of stamina for the blacks. If they, led by Philip Randolph, could only hold out a little longer, they could achieve their goal under the most difficult conditions. This was a challenge for the entire black community. Randolph borrowed the five-cent fare to ride down to City Hall and tell Mayor LaGuardia he would not take the proffered job.

Franklin D. Roosevelt had moved rapidly to aid labor after becoming President in 1933. He pushed for a labor law that would permit the working man to join a union without fear of his employer. The National Labor Relations Act made that possible. It was the National Labor Relations Board that held an election among the Pullman porters in 1937 and declared Randolph's union the victor. The contract that Philip won for his members gave them a forty-hour work week and a monthly minimum salary of $250. The contract also gave Randolph and his fellow officers machinery for settling future grievances.

The Brotherhood of Sleeping Car Porters had but eighteen thousand members, yet it was more significant than the 400,000 members of the United Automobile Workers. Randolph had won a fight that gave the black man faith and pride in himself. As a black labor leader, Philip Randolph became a champion of the rights of his people everywhere. Now he had a firm base from which to operate. His union became a launching platform for other black-equality drives.

Philip Randolph had used what he called "the propaganda of the *word*" in order to alert the white people to the problems of their black brothers. It was an attempt to stir the whites into cooperation by complaining to them. Once the Brotherhood was strong enough to act as the rallying point, however, Randolph urged "the propaganda of the *deed*."

His first move using the "deed" was a drive to open war plants to black workers. With the attack on Pearl Harbor, in 1941, Randolph was once again critical of the drafting of men to fight. His opposition was not on principle, as had been his stand on World War I. He saw the war as "the graveyard of our civil liberties." He was a strong advocate of the theory that, "we do everything short of war to help Britain."

To Randolph it appeared that it would be necessary to stop pleading with white officials for equal employment in the war plants. He believed that conferences with whites concerning the rights of blacks was the wrong approach. He told the vice-president of the Sleeping Car Porters, Milton Webster, "We don't impress the government until we impress the Negro himself. . . . We're talking a lot about being the Arsenal of Democracy. Suppose we dramatize the fact that in this Arsenal of Democracy of ours there is no democracy for the Negro citizen. Suppose we put the Negro in motion, get him to march 100,000 strong in protest on Washington."

The March on Washington Movement was born out of that talk Randolph had with Webster. In New York, Randolph and his aides walked from one end of Harlem to the other, recruiting marchers. When some whites heard of his plans, they offered to help swell the ranks. But this, Philip decided, was to be an exclusively black affair. Only blacks would be permitted to organize, give money, and march. He put it this way: "You take ten thousand dollars from a white man; you have his ten thousand dollars, but he's got your movement. You take ten cents from a Negro; you've got his ten cents, and you also have the Negro."

The idea of a large demonstration was accepted by all, and in many cities such as Boston, Chicago and San Francisco, blacks began to organize marchers and arrange transportation to Washington. Philip Randolph and Walter White, then director of NAACP, made it clear that, unless the Government did something to eliminate prejudice in war plants, thousands of blacks would march on Washington. What they specifically protested was the opposition of the Southern Railroads and others to the establishment of a Fair Employment Practice Committee by Congress.

President Roosevelt became alarmed and decided to send Mrs. Roosevelt to talk Randolph out of the proposed march. She was an old friend of A. Philip Randolph. Eleanor Roosevelt attempted to point out that a lack of housing, insufficient police protection, and such large crowds could lead to rioting and injury to many innocent people. Randolph answered, "No earthly price can stop us." Even Mayor LaGuardia spoke to Randolph, hoping to convince him to give up the idea. When he failed, Mrs. Roosevelt told her husband, "Ask Mr. Randolph to come to the White House." The President agreed and the meeting was arranged.

President Roosevelt put on a real production for the meeting. He had his Cabinet and members of the War Production Board present to impress Randolph as to the seriousness of the problem. Franklin Roosevelt turned on all his personal charm. Finally, Philip Randolph responded, briefly and firmly, "The plants must be opened to Negroes, Mr. President, or I must let my people march."

The President yielded and issued an executive order that told war producers to drop the color barrier. In order to police the order, on the suggestion of Randolph, a committee was formed and named the Fair Employment Practices Committee.

In late 1947, Philip Randolph, with a man named Grant Reynolds, a former minister, organized the League for Nonviolent Civil Disobedience Against Military Segregation. In 1948, the league made very clear that it would mount a campaign of mass civil disobedience and nonviolent resistance unless race segregation in the Armed Forces was ended.

This was Randolph's second move using the "propaganda of the deed." He told President Truman, "I haven't found one Negro interested in serving his country if Jim Crow continues." The President, who had a quick temper, was angry with this statement. Randolph went on to make the President even angrier when he declared, "I may break the law by urging my people to refuse to move, but, Mr. President, I'll be serving a higher moral law by opposing discrimination." The result was an executive order that ended segregation in the Armed Forces.

Successful as Randolph was in the area of desegregation in war plants and the Armed Forces, he was only partially successful in the area of the unions. This is the area which controls jobs.

Philip Randolph's first fight, in behalf of his Sleeping Car Porters, was a contest against an employer. When he attempted to come to the aid of black railroad workers in other areas, his chief enemies were the white unions. These organizations not only prevented blacks from joining their ranks, but they demanded that blacks already employed be fired. When the blacks went to court, the white unions used their vast treasuries to fight back.

Randolph's first move to help black workers outside of his own unions was to save the jobs of black locomotive firemen. This move meant only trouble with the all-white Brotherhood of Locomotive Firemen.

To keep a steam locomotive running was a hot, nasty job if you were the fireman, shoveling coal into a blazing oven. On most southern railroads, particularly, this task was given readily to blacks. However, when automatic devices for putting coal on were used, or where electric and diesel engines were substituted, the white unions wanted the jobs exclusively. There was much hatred stirred up as a result of the attempts to drive the blacks from their work as firemen. Strikes, murders, and firings were the order of the day.

Randolph could not organize the black locomotive firemen into a union of their own because the white unions had the jurisdiction. Once again he called on the "propaganda of the deed." He formed a "Committee of Negro Firemen," who proceeded to sue the white union for damages. The charges were that the white union members had caused the black firemen to lose pay by taking their jobs. Suit after suit was being won regularly and the union's treasury was being depleted. In 1944, as a result of the Supreme Court's decision and the loss of money by the union, war against black firemen was finally given up.

In 1955, the American Federation of Labor merged with the Congress of Industrial Organizations to form one big union in the United States (AFL-CIO). The CIO had been a separate group since the 1930's, when certain labor leaders broke with the old trade union practice of the AFL. As a result of that merger, A. Philip Randolph became a member of the Executive Board of the AFL-CIO. One of his first moves, after being selected for the board, was to urge reforms in hiring practices by the craft unions. The steelworkers' union and other craft organizations maintained time-honored racial practices.

All Randolph got for his trouble was to have George Meaney, the President of AFL-CIO, shout at him, "Who the hell gave you the right to speak for Negroes?" Meaney then had the executive board censure Randolph for "anti-union activities." Philip Randolph's fight was far from won if men like Walter Reuther and David Dubinsky would vote to censure him for merely attempting to get fair play for black workers in the trades.

Randolph discovered early that, regardless of who occupied the White House, the black man always seemed to be pushed around. His experiences with Presidents Roosevelt and Truman were repeated with Dwight Eisenhower. In 1956, President Eisenhower refused to see Randolph. One writer explains Eisenhower's position by stating, ". . . the President's Committee on Appointments decided it would not be wise at this time to see A. Philip Randolph . . . because it would license Southern Governors and other persons who had wanted to talk to the President about the race situation and have been denied."

President Kennedy gave the October 28th "March on Washington" his blessing and simply asked Randolph in what "unofficial" way the Government could help keep the march peaceful and under responsible control, and where they should deliver the box lunches and portable rest rooms.

A. Philip Randolph has been active in many areas other than labor. Mayor LaGuardia of New York City, in 1935, appointed him a member of the Commission on Race. In 1942, he served as a member of the New York City Housing Authority. He attended the second world congress of the International Confederation of Free Trade Unions in 1951, at Milan, Italy. His task was to present the views of the North American delegation on ways in which the confederation could organize free trade unions in the underdeveloped areas of the world.

Randolph has received the honorary degree of Doctor of Laws from Howard University, and the third annual David L. Clendenin award of the Workers' Defense League. This last award was for his distinguished service for labor's rights.

In addition to his writing, Randolph has gained wide acclaim with his oratory. His speeches reflect the influence of the frequent reading and rereading of Shakespeare and other prose masters. Still the President of the Brotherhood of Sleeping Car Porters, Randolph often shakes the entire house of labor with his determined demands that blacks be allowed a full share of the fruits of labor and of the American economy.

> For nearly forty years Randolph, whose union was never very big and grows smaller each year, has been the symbol of the Negro fighting for recognition within the trade unions.
>
> —Ray Marshall, *The Negro and Organized Labor*

Marian Anderson

[1908-   ]

CONCERT SINGER

"What I heard today, one is privileged to hear only once
in a hundred years."

—Arturo Toscanini, after hearing Miss Anderson sing

The parents of Marian Anderson were poor. They lived in
the southern section of the city of Philadelphia, where many
impoverished Negroes resided. However, the Andersons had a
richness that stood them in good stead—church was their
most precious possession.

Marian was only six years of age when she first appeared
as a member of the Union Baptist Church Choir. The congregation was impressed with this small girl's potential, and
started a trust fund, "Marian Anderson's Future," for the
purpose of securing adequate musical training for her.

The Anderson family did everything to encourage Marian
in her desire to follow a musical career. They bought her a
second-hand piano, but could not afford to have her take
lessons. She learned how to work out simple accompaniments
for herself.

By the time she was ten years old, she was singing in
concerts that were sponsored by local lodges, churches, and
clubs. Her reputation was beginning to be noted in Negro
areas.

When this promising young artist was twelve, her father

died. Her mother was forced to move into Grandmother Anderson's house. Grandmother acted as a babysitter while the mothers in her house went out to work. It was a crowded residence, but Grandma did all she could to keep up Marian's interest in singing.

High school opened up the real opportunity for Marian to study music. Upon entering the William Penn High School, she received the opportunity to sing at an assembly. The principal recommended that she enroll in another high school, South Philadelphia High School, which offered courses in music.

Aided by Mary Saunders Patterson, a teacher at South Philadelphia High School, Marian began to develop her full potential. However, she realized that what was needed was more advanced training. Her mother agreed to enroll her in a well-known music school in downtown Philadelphia. After waiting in line for several hours to register, she was told, "We don't take colored." Marian Anderson now knew the heartbreaking meaning of discrimination.

Graduation from high school opened up the chance she had been waiting for, however. During her last two years in school, she had continued to sing in churches. She had also made several trips to the South to give concerts on the campuses of Negro colleges. Dr. Lucy Wilson, the principal of South Philadelphia High School, arranged an audition for Marian with the famous teacher, Giuseppe Boghetti. If Boghetti accepted her as a student, the money from the church fund would pay for one year's lessons.

When Marian appeared before the great Boghetti for her audition, she realized fully that this was the one great chance for which she had waited so long. Nevertheless, she was calm and composed as she began to sing:

> Deep River; deep river
> Lord, I want to cross over
> Into camp ground. . . .

Boghetti realized immediately that this young girl indeed was as talented as her loyal supporters had stated. While the money provided by the church fund lasted for only one year of lessons, the great maestro gave Marian an additional year without cost.

Following her work with Boghetti, she resumed her southern tours. In 1925, she felt that she was ready for a private concert at Town Hall in New York City. The concert was a failure. Marian Anderson was convinced that her chances of being a concert singer were over. In 1926, she was invited to sing at the Spingarn Award dinner for Roland Hayes, who was universally recognized as one of the outstanding singers in the nation. Marian took on new hope when Hayes encouraged her to continue with her singing.

In the meanwhile, Boghetti had never lost confidence in Marian Anderson's vocal ability. In 1926, he entered her in a contest which was sponsored by the Lewisohn Stadium Concerts of New York. About three hundred other soloists were competing. After hours of waiting, Marian's name was finally called.

She was determined that what had happened at Town Hall would not happen again. When she finished singing, she was told she was one of the sixteen semi-finalists. After the competition had narrowed down to these final few, they were told to go home, and that they would be notified about the results within a few hours. Marian waited at Boghetti's studio. When the telephone rang, Boghetti answered it. After a brief pause, he turned to her and exclaimed, "We have won!"

At Lewisohn Stadium on August 26, 1926, Marian Anderson sang spirituals and operatic selections with great ability and feeling. This time the critics praised her performance.

The demand for her appearances grew steadily after this concert. She could have toured the country, had she so desired. However, tours were expensive, and it was not easy to find suitable accommodations in most cities if you were black.

A desire to go to London, where she could take lessons from Professor Raimund Von Zur Muhlen, had been uppermost in Marian Anderson's mind for a long time. After discussing the possibility with her family, she came to the conclusion that she should go.

All her ambitious planning was frustrated by the fact that, after two lessons with Von Zur Muhlen, he fell sick. She took unsuccessful lessons with several other teachers and then came home at the end of the year, for her money had just about run out.

Back in the United States, Marian Anderson toured the country until she raised enough money to return to Europe. She was anxious to go to Germany to learn the language and get more training.

In a Berlin school, Marian gave a program of Negro spirituals. In the audience were a Norwegian agent and a Finnish pianist. They were looking for new talent, and invited Miss Anderson to tour the Scandinavian countries. She accepted with high hopes.

During this tour, Marian worked with Kosti Vehanen, the Finnish pianist whom she had met in Berlin, and from then on he became her regular accompanist. That tour was one of her most successful because it helped to give her the confidence she needed.

A great event for this American Negro singer was an invitation to visit the Finnish composer, Jean Sibelius. She went to the Sibelius villa with Vehanen and was welcomed cordially by her host and hostess.

Marian sang two of Sibelius' songs. The great composer praised her singing but suggested that she should give her audience, "More Marian Anderson and less Sibelius." Later he wrote a song and dedicated it to Marian Anderson.

During the summer of 1935, in Salzburg, Austria, Arturo Toscanini heard Miss Anderson sing. He was tremendously impressed with the talent of this Negro woman. She now realized that she had developed her voice to its fullest extent.

One of the best-known producers is Sol Hurok. He handles talent from all over the world. In 1935, he booked Marian Anderson for a concert tour of Russia. Her first recital in Leningrad was sold out. Before each number, an interpreter translated the words into Russian.

Marian Anderson went on to Moscow, where she had the opportunity to meet the great composer Shostakovitch. She also met the theatrical director Stanislavsky, whose acting techniques are world-famous. When Stanislavsky visited the United States some years later, the first person he asked for was Marian Anderson.

Late in 1935, Marian Anderson returned to America after her triumphs in Europe. She was booked for her second appearance at Town Hall. During the voyage, her ship encountered rough seas, and she fell down several steps. As a result, she gave her recital standing on one foot and leaning against the piano. This appearance was very different from that first concert at Town Hall. The critics were most gracious. One wrote, "She has returned to her native land one of the greatest singers of our time."

In 1939, the national capital was alerted to the fact that Marian Anderson was to give a concert in Constitution Hall. The nation was shocked to learn that the Daughters of the American Revolution, who controlled the leasing of Constitution Hall, would not permit Miss Anderson to use it. Deems Taylor, Walter Damrosch, and other important musical leaders condemned the D.A.R. Mrs. Eleanor Roosevelt, the President's wife, resigned from the organization.

Marian Anderson did not appear in Washington, D.C., until four years later—1943. No one was more startled than the Capital police when some 75,000 people gathered to hear her sing the Easter Sunday sunrise service at the Lincoln Memorial. They were attempting to tell this fine Negro singer that what the D.A.R. had done to her did not represent the thinking of a great many Washingtonians.

The highest honor that the black community can bestow is the Spingarn Medal. This medal was awarded to Marian Anderson in 1939. She also received in that same year the $10,000 Bok Award, which is granted annually to a distinguished citizen of Philadelphia. With this money Marian established the Marian Anderson Award, a fund to help talented young American singers develop a career in voice without regard to their race, creed, or color.

It was not until 1955 that Miss Anderson reached what she considered to be the pinnacle of her career. She was the first Negro to sing a leading role at the Metropolitan Opera House in New York City.

The United Nations, always aware of the advantage of having good public relations, asked Miss Anderson to tour the Far East in 1957. She went to India, where she spoke in front of the statue of Mahatma Gandhi. It was the first time a foreigner had been invited to do so.

Marian Anderson made her last concert tour in 1964. When she completed this triumphant tour, she retired. There is no question that this great woman, through her superb singing and her ladylike demeanor, has contributed greatly to the current success of other Negroes in and out of show business.

> Marian Anderson has been endowed with such a voice as lifts any individual above his fellows, and is a matter of exultant pride to any race. And so it is fitting that Marian Anderson should raise her voice in tribute to the noble Lincoln whom mankind will ever honor.
>
> —Harold Ickes, Secretary of the Interior

Louis "Satchmo" Armstrong

[1900-   ]

MUSICIAN AND "AMBASSADOR OF GOOD WILL"

More than any other musician, it was the trumpeter and vocalist Louis (Satchmo) Armstrong who took jazz out of the Negro quarter of New Orleans where it was born, made it a socially accepted part of American culture, and introduced it around the world.

—*Ebony*, November, 1964

New Orleans had been experiencing a hot, dry two weeks. The horse-drawn wagons were stirring up the dust until it stuck in the throats of the populace like glue. Independence Day, 1900, dawned very warm and humid. It was going to be another day of intense heat. In James Alley, in a fifty-cents-a-month, two-room shack, Mary-Ann Armstrong gave birth to a son. Here, in the heart of the black ghetto, this granddaughter of slaves presented to the world a son who would truly emulate the words of "Yankee Doodle Dandy," "A real live son of my Uncle Sam."

Willie Armstrong had married Mary-Ann filled with the hope that some day things would be better. When their first child, a little girl, came along, they decided to name her Beatrice. As soon as she was able, Mary-Ann returned to her job as a domestic because her husband, a turpentine worker, was unable to bring home enough money to keep his family in the mere necessities for living.

While he was still very young, Louis, named for his pater-
nal grandfather, was toddling through James Alley. He was
not a handsome child, but he was a lovable and friendly little
fellow. He never seemed to tire watching the older boys and
girls dancing and singing in the alley. When Beatrice would
attempt to get him to come home, he would run and hide so
that he could remain in the alley and listen to the music
some more.

When Louis was just five years old he moved with his family to the Third Ward in New Orleans. Their little apartment was located at Liberty and Perdido Streets. Living with
the Armstrongs was Mary-Ann's mother, who remembered
when blacks were "sold on the hoof like dumb cattle."

Louis ran the streets with his schoolmates and did the
things all young boys do. He swam in the Mississippi River,
and was part of the usual short-lived fights that boys engage
in all over the world. However, it was to music that Louis
turned most frequently. The youngsters of the neighborhood
discovered early that, if you could put on a good street show,
the audience would pelt you with coins. Singing for pennies
was a daily routine for Louis Armstrong. He became a member of a strolling quartet in which he played a cigar-box
guitar.

It was inevitable that a boy who found himself on his own
for a great deal of his early life would get into trouble. Louis
was attracted to any place where there was music. One area
in New Orleans where there was always music was in the
Storyville section of the city. Louis spent his nights in this
entertainment center, at Dago Tony Tonk's. Here he could
listen to the jazz combos of New Orleans.

It was on New Year's Eve, 1913, that Louis got into trouble
with the law. Overexcited by the music, singing, shouting,
and general confusion, the thirteen-year-old boy discharged a
gun. Following his arrest, he was sent to the Negro Waifs'
Home for one year. This was not a prison, but a shelter for

youngsters who had run afoul of the law. The year he spent
there was most fruitful. The Home had a drill instructor and
bandmaster named Peter David. This young man presented
Louis with a bugle and taught him how to play it. It was the
boy's first horn—in fact, his first musical instrument—and he
fell in love with it. Before he left the Negro Waifs' Home he
had learned how to read music and also to play the cornet.
He became the leader of the Home's band—and just the hap-
piest youngster in New Orleans.

When Armstrong was released from the Negro Waifs'
Home in 1914, he was not yet old enough to work in a band.
Until he could stand proudly on a bandstand and blow his
horn, he had to live. For three years he found any type of
work that he could get in order to help out at home. He
delivered coal, sold bananas, peddled newspapers, delivered
milk. He even went as far as picking through garbage cans
to find food for his family.

The cornet was never far from Louis Armstrong's side
during these three years of struggle and waiting. He realized
that what he had learned in the Negro Waifs' Home would
never make him a great cornet player. However, he had the
good fortune to run errands for Joe "King" Oliver, who was
the leading exponent of the new music craze called jazz.
Oliver offered to give Louis lessons in Dixieland jazz. This
up-and-coming music form is a combination of Negro music,
whose rhythms came from Africa, with instrumentation from
the French culture of New Orleans, enhanced by the excitement of the blues, and the shouts and general glee of a people
who had only recently been in slavery.

World War I came to the United States in 1917. New Orleans, as was to be expected, became a Navy town. The authorities demanded that the Storyville section of the city be
closed down. With that decision, "King" Oliver left New
Orleans for an engagement in Chicago. This opened up a

place for Louis to become a "regular" in Kid Ory's band. It was in this band that Oliver had made his reputation.

It must be stated that, when the opportunity came to play in Ory's band, he had already prepared himself well. When he was seventeen, Armstrong had formed his own band and, as was to be expected, he modeled it directly after Kid Ory's. This provided valuable experience in preparing him for the major assignment with Ory's band, which he secured on Oliver's recommendation.

Louis Armstrong married young. It was not a happy marriage, so he decided to leave New Orleans when he was given the opportunity by another well-known jazz artist, Fate Marable, to play on the Mississippi excursion boat *Dixie Belle*. These excursion boats traveled as far north as St. Louis during the summer months. In the winter, they moved about in the vicinity of New Orleans. Some of the best ragtime music in the country was heard on the decks of these boats. For nearly two years Louis blew his cornet on the *Dixie Belle,* while traveling almost five thousand miles. He considered this a great experience, stating it in this way: "I could read music very well by now and was getting hotter and hotter on my cornet. My chest had filled out deeper and my lips and jaws had got stronger, so I could blow much harder and longer than before without getting tired. I had made a special point of the high register, and was beginning to make my high-C, and more often."

In 1922, "King" Oliver was playing at the Royal Palm Gardens in Chicago. He had never forgotten Louis. Moreover, he had been hearing about the young musician's success on the Mississippi River, so he telegraphed Louis to join him. Armstrong became the second cornettist with Joe "King" Oliver. When Louis Armstrong came to Chicago it was already well on its way toward being the capital of jazz, not only because it had absorbed many of the greatest of New Orlean's ragtime artists, but also because its musicians were capable of creating a school of their own.

Before Louis left for Chicago he had already written several songs. One of his tunes was published under the title, "I Wish I Could Shimmy Like My Sister Kate." This song was one of the most popular during the 1920's and 30's. It was typical of the period in which Armstrong worked that, like many another talented young musician, he never was given credit for being the composer—nor did he receive the fifty dollars he had been promised by the publishers.

Oliver's group was known as the Original Creole Jazz Band. It was one of the most successful combos then playing in the Windy City. Armstrong was now performing with the best. In Chicago, he made his first recording and began to develop as a mature musician. He was beginning to experiment with new ways of presenting his music.

In 1924, Armstrong married for the second time. His new wife was a brilliant jazz pianist, Lillian Hardin. It was she who induced him to leave Oliver and go out on his own. Louis went to New York and joined another popular band led by Fletcher Henderson, which was then playing at Roseland. The latter is still a famous dance spot. Armstrong did not last long with Henderson because his band was the first black ensemble that played only what was on the page. Louis could not be handicapped by the notes on the sheet. He wanted to play the way he felt.

It was not long before Armstrong returned to Chicago to become a member of a band organized by his wife. They were playing in a place called the Dreamland Cafe. Once more in the jazz spot of the United States, Louis felt he was truly back home. During the next few years he became the toast of the city. He performed at the Vendome Theater and the Savoy.

The return from New York brought other innovations for Louis Armstrong. He changed his instrument from the cornet to the trumpet. He also began to do some singing. It was Louis who introduced what became known as Scat singing, which means using no words but improvising voice melodies. He did this type of singing first while he was in a recording session for the Okeh label. It started because of an accident. His music fell to the floor, and, not knowing the words, he had to make up the sounds until he was handed back his sheets. From that time on, his gravel type voice became almost as famous as his trumpet. One merely has to remember the success of his record "San Francisco."

It was during this period that he acquired his business manager, Joseph G. Glaser. The owner of the Dreamland Cafe saw the potential in this fine musician. For over forty years Glaser has managed "Satchmo's" career under the title of the Associated Booking Corporation.

In 1926, Louis formed his own band and named it "Louis Armstrong and His Hot Five." With this group he continued to make recordings on the Okek label, but he also appeared with small combos where he had the opportunity to experiment with his own sounds. Rudi Blesh, the well-known jazz critic of *Jazz Trumpets,* feels that it was during this period that Armstrong reached his greatest heights. It was the time when "cool" jazz came into its own. Armstrong gets the credit for giving the music world this "cool" jazz. It is that method which permits each member of the combo to come up with any sounds he sees fit to use. As one leading jazz man put it, "You can't play anything on a horn that Louis hasn't played."

In the 1930's, Louis Armstrong's career took another original turn when he began to perform in front of big bands. In these performances he would use popular songs for his material, rather than Dixieland, blues, or original instrumental numbers. It was Armstrong who paved the way for the swing band era that developed during the late 1930's. He was forced to face the criticism of the jazz buffs for giving up pure jazz. He was now a swing performer in vaudeville. Some blacks have declared that Armstrong was an "Uncle Tom" because of his performances before white audiences. However, this man of good humor has built up a strong and loyal following of all races and creeds who respect his humanity and his integrity.

Even in his wildest youthful dreams, Louis Armstrong never believed that he would travel abroad professionally. In 1932, he made his first trip to Europe. The audiences took to this lively, lovable, inexhaustible performer like one of their own. He toured France, Italy, Switzerland, Norway, Holland, and England. During most of his European stay, this former New Orleans street urchin made his home on le rue de l'Auvergne, in Paris.

It was during this European tour that Louis Armstrong acquired the nickname of "Satchmo." When he was in England in 1934, he was asked to appear before King George V at the Palladium, one of the most famous theaters in Europe. On that great night, Louis turned and bowed to the royal box, in which sat the King and his party. With a twinkle in his eyes, he looked up at the King and declared, "This one's for you, Rex." In writing of this incident, the editor of the London *Melody Maker* incorrectly wrote "Satchmo" for Louis' original nickname "Satchelmouth." The name "Satchelmouth" had been given to Armstrong because of his large lips and gleaming white teeth, and the way his cheeks bulge when he blows the trumpet.

During this time that Armstrong was in Europe his second marriage ended in divorce. The years he was married to Lillian Hardin were the years of his greatest professional growth. There is no doubt that she was greatly responsible for the image that Louis "Satchmo" Armstrong developed then and the progress that he made. However, the great amount of time during which they were separated, because of the demands of their individual professional careers, made the divorce inevitable. For ten years Louis remained a bachelor. In 1942, he married Lucille Wilson, who accompanies him on tour. She cooks the dishes that he loves so well and which cannot be obtained in most hotels. Louis has never lost his early taste for red beans and rice.

Armstrong was starred in a New York play entitled, "Hot Chocolates." This proved to be a musical hit. It was in this lively show that he introduced the well-known song "Ain't Misbehavin."

There seemed to be no way for Louis Armstrong to go but up. His star was certainly on the ascendant when he moved to Los Angeles to appear in his first motion picture. He took the hard work of Hollywood in stride and was well received in "Pennies from Heaven," but he never pretended to be another Sidney Poitier. He continued to receive parts in movies, appearing in "Everyday's a Holiday," "Going Places," and "Cabin in the Sky." Armstrong will play bit parts in the movies as long as he can blow his trumpet and his gravel voice can sing a tune.

Until war came to the world in 1939, "Satchmo" made several more trips to Europe. His tours brought him into contact with two future kings of England—the Prince of Wales and the Duke of York. After the war, he played the Palladium in the presence of Princess Margaret, sister of Queen Elizabeth. She enjoyed Armstrong's uninhibited remark as he prepared to play the New Orleans jazz classic "Mahogany Hall Stomp": "We really goin' to lay this one on the Princess."

During World War II, Louis spent his time—between movies with Bing Crosby and Jack Benny—entertaining the troops in posts all over the United States. He continued to perform in theaters and night clubs, and to make records. One of the most important jobs that the government had to carry on during the war was to keep the civilian morale high. Entertainment was a major means of doing the job. Louis "Satchmo" Armstrong was one of America's "secret weapons" as he moved across the screen in "Jam Session," played his trumpet on stages all over this broad land, and sang and frolicked in camps and hospitals for American men in uniform.

Ever since Louis had cut his first record in the mid-twenties, he has always enjoyed the long sessions in the recording studios. In those early years, he recorded numbers that brought him worldwide fame. These records were done with the jazz luminaries, Earl (Fatha) Hines, Kid Ory, Zutty Singleton, and Baby Dodds. For anyone who knows and enjoys jazz, these records are collectors' items. It was not long before the record business recognized the potential of Louis as a singer, and he was teamed with the great Ella Fitzgerald. His strange and unique manner of putting over a song placed his records of "Mack the Knife" and "Blueberry Hill" on the top of the hit parade. In 1964, Louis cut a record that he considered would be "just another number." The song, "Hello, Dolly," was a catchy, lively tune from the show of the same name. Armstrong was more than surprised when it sold 2,000,000 copies and took the Beatles right off the top of the best seller list!

Armstrong traveled more than 200,000 miles, to all the states in the Union and to most countries in Europe, but he was never considered an envoy of his nation. At the end of World War II, thanks to the American GI, the whole world knew jazz and its counterpart, big-band swing. When, in 1956, Louis made his first trip to Africa, he was received as a conquering hero. In Ghana, when he picked up his trumpet, 100,000 natives went into a wild demonstration. Coming back to Africa in 1960, on a cultural mission for the State Department, Armstrong was carried on a canvas throne into Leopoldville Stadium, in the Congo. Moscow was quite shaken by the success that the Armstrong mission had in Africa, calling it a "capitalistic distraction." The proof of his success in Africa was the invitation he received, in the spring of 1965, to visit Central and Eastern Europe. In one of the most strenuous four weeks of his career, Louis moved through Prague, Leipzig, East Berlin, West Berlin, Frankfurt, Belgrade and Magdeburg. Shortly after his return to the United States, he was asked to go back to Eastern Europe. In Budapest, 91,000 persons jammed the NEP Stadium to hear him play.

Television has opened up another avenue for the talents of Louis "Satchmo" Armstrong. Most of the first-rank TV variety shows have Louis appearing on them several times each season. In 1965, he was making one of his many appearances on "Hollywood Palace" when he received a telegram from President Lyndon B. Johnson, congratulating him on his fiftieth anniversary in show business. When the networks announce "Satchmo's" appearance on Ed Sullivan's, Dean Martin's, or the Smothers Brothers' shows, the ratings of these shows hit the top. Another entertainment field has fallen under the spell of Louis "Satchmo" Armstrong.

Esquire magazine conducts an annual poll to discover the leading musical talent. In 1944, Louis won the poll. Since that time, "Satchmo's" name appears regularly on polls conducted by periodicals such as *Down Beat, Melody Maker, Jazz Hot* (France), *Jazz Echo* (Germany) and *Muziek* (Holland).

December, 1965, saw Carnegie Hall in New York City crowded to the rafters as Louis "Satchmo" Armstrong's admirers came to salute him on his fifty years in show business. The one reason why Louis was willing to permit this gathering was that the money made from it would go to the AGVA youth fund. The American Guild of Variety Artists (AGVA) presented Louis with a plaque which states he is "a passionate American who makes the United States strong." Louis Armstrong finds it difficult to take this popular acclaim. He told a *New York Times* writer: "Long as I'm playin', I'm not lookin' to be on no high pedestal."

Louis Armstrong has never taken a public position on the matter of civil rights. However, he is, indeed, vitally aware of his people's problems. He often contributes generously to black organizations. He made his feelings on the civil rights question very clear when he told a reporter for *Ebony* magazine, following the attack on freedom marchers in Selma, Alabama: "They would beat Jesus if he was black and marched." Armstrong, following the passage of the Civil Rights Act of 1964, returned to New Orleans in triumph and played a benefit with an integrated band. The money made by this performance was used to maintain the city's jazz museum, which is located on the site of the house where Louis was born.

Louis Armstrong is five feet eight inches tall and finds it difficult to keep his weight at 200 pounds. He has rarely attended church in his adult life, although he never sits down to a meal without saying grace. Born a Baptist, he wears a Star of David around his neck. "Satchmo" loves the comfort of his little house in Corona, New York City. His wife, Lucille, plans and cooks his meals, and attempts to make his periods of rest significant. More and more, Louis has felt the pressure of his work, and the rest periods at home have become more necessary. Talking to a reporter recently, he stated that he felt he was in a rut and had become "a prisoner of this grind" in which he found himself enmeshed.

Impractical Armstrong is not an easy man to handle. His manager, Joe Glaser, has the full responsibility of booking Louis and the people who work with him. This man of music, like many in the entertainment field, is an easy prey for those who attempt to get money from him. As a result, Glaser has put Louis on a monthly allowance, even though he is considered a millionaire.

Louis "Satchmo" Armstrong has, by his virtuosity on the trumpet and his influence on early jazz, earned a secure place in the annals of popular music. He has played for kings, but when he puts his trumpet to his lips and lets his musical imagination wander, he speaks to royalty as an equal, for he, too, is a king.

> Concerning the selection of Louis Armstrong as trumpeter on the "first team" of the All-American Band there can be . . . no dispute. He made jazz and is the true king of jazz. Anyone who knows anything about the subject will concede this.

> —"Esquire All-American Band," *Esquire,* February, 1944

Select Bibliography

Aptheker, Herbert. *The Negro in the Civil War*. New York: International Publishers, 1938.

Armstrong, Louis. *My Life in New Orleans*. Englewood Cliffs, N.J.: Prentice-Hall, Inc., 1954.

Baker, Augusta. *Books About Negro Life for Children*. New York: New York Public Library, 1963.

Bontemps, Arna. *One Hundred Years of Negro Freedom*. New York: Dodd, Mead & Co., 1961.

Brazeal, Brailsford. *The Brotherhood of Sleeping Car Porters*. New York: Harper Bros., 1946.

Chambers, Lucille. *America's Tenth Man*. New York: Twayne Publishers, 1967.

Cuney-Hare, Maud. *Negro Musicians and Their Music*. Washington, D.C.: The Associated Publishers, 1936.

DuBois, W. E. B. *Souls of Black Folk*. Chicago: A. C. McClurg Co., 1903.

Ebony Magazine Editors. *The Negro Handbook*. Chicago: Johnson Publishing Co., 1966.

Ewen, David. *Men of Popular Music*. Chicago, New York: Ziff-Davis Co., 1944.

Franklin, John Hope. *From Slavery to Freedom: A History of American Negroes*, 3rd ed. New York: A. A. Knopf, 1961.

Goffin, Robert. *Horn of Plenty: The Story of Louis Armstrong*. New York: Allen, Towne, Heath, Inc., 1947.

Harris, Abram. *The Negro as Capitalist*. Philadelphia: American Academy of Political and Social Science, 1936.

Hughes, Langston. *Famous Negro Music Makers*. New York: Dodd, Mead & Co., 1955.

King, Martin Luther, Jr. *Stride Toward Freedom: The Montgomery Story*. New York: Ballantine Books, 1960.

Kugelmass, J. Alvin. *Ralph J. Bunche: Fighter for Peace*. New York: Julian Messner, Inc., 1962.

Metcalf, George R. *Black Profile*. New York: McGraw-Hill, Inc., 1968.

Myrdal, Gunnar. *An American Dilemma*. New York: Harper Bros., 1944.

Northrup, Herbert. *Organized Labor and the Negro*. New York: Harper Bros., 1944.

Oak, Vishnu V. *The Negro's Adventure in General Business*. Yellow Springs, Ohio: The Antioch Press, 1949.

Pierce, Joseph. *Negro Business and Business Education*. New York: Harper & Bros., 1947.

Reddick, Lawrence. *Crusader Without Violence: A Biography of Martin Luther King, Jr*. New York: Harper & Row Inc., 1959.

Robinson, Jackie. *Jackie Robinson My Own Story*. New York: Greenberg Co., 1948.

Rowan, Carl T. *Wait Till Next Year*. New York: Random House, Inc., 1960.

Taylor, Julius, ed. *The Negro in Science*. Baltimore: Morgan State College Press, 1955.

Velie, Lester. *Labor U.S.A*. New York: Harper Bros., 1958.

——, ed. *A Documentary History of the Negro People in the United States*. New York: Citadel Press, 1951.

——. *Fight For Freedom: The Story of the NAACP*. New York: Berkley Publishing Co., 1962.

Index

James Joseph Flynn

was born in Brooklyn and is still a resident of the "Borough of Churches."

Following his graduation from Fordham College, with a B.A. degree in history, he began his teaching at Bishop Loughlin Diocesan High School, in Brooklyn. After several years of high-school teaching, he went to the faculty of Fordham University. For twenty years he taught history and political science in the School of Business, and was an associate professor and chairman of department. In 1961, he went to St. Francis College, in Brooklyn, as Chairman of the Division of Social Studies, where he is now teaching.

After serving in the Office of Naval History during World War II, he came back to New York and received his Ph.D. in history from Fordham University. He has written the following books: *Medieval History, American Government, Comparative Government, Famous Justices of the Supreme Court,* and *Negroes of Achievement in Modern America.* He reviews for *The Annals* of the American Academy of Political and Social Science.

James Flynn has a keen desire to travel, and does so at every opportunity he gets. Relaxation is found in golf, reading and playing bridge. As a member of Phi Alpha Theta, the history honor fraternity, he works constantly to get his students interested in this worthwhile project, especially American history.